D1200729

Milestones
of the First Century of Flight

Also by F. Clifton Berry, Jr.

Air Cav

Chargers

Gadget Warfare

Inside the CIA

Inventing the Future

Sky Soldiers

Strike Aircraft

Co-author

CNN: War in the Gulf (with Thomas B. Allen and Norman Polmar)

Flights (with C.V. Glines and Harry M. Zubkoff)

Milestones
of the First Century of Flight

F. Clifton Berry, Jr.

Presented by the
Aerospace Industries Association of America, Inc.

Howell Press, Inc.
Charlottesville, Virginia

Design by Spot Color Incorporated, www.spotcolor.com

Howell Press, Inc.
1713-2D Allied Lane
Charlottesville, VA 22903-5335 USA
www.howellpress.com

Library of Congress Cataloging-in-Publication Data

Berry, F. Clifton.
Milestones of the first century of flight / F. Clifton Berry, Jr.--
1st ed.
p. cm.
"Presented by the Aerospace Industries Association of America, Inc."
Includes bibliographical references and index.
ISBN 1-57427-076-1 (hardcover: alk. paper)
1. Aeronautics—History. I. Title.
TL515 .B4245 2002
629.13'009—dc21

2002009399

Printed in Singapore.

10 9 8 7 6 5 4 3 2 1

To the men and women who have made humankind's age-old dream of flight a reality not just for the few, but the many.

Contents

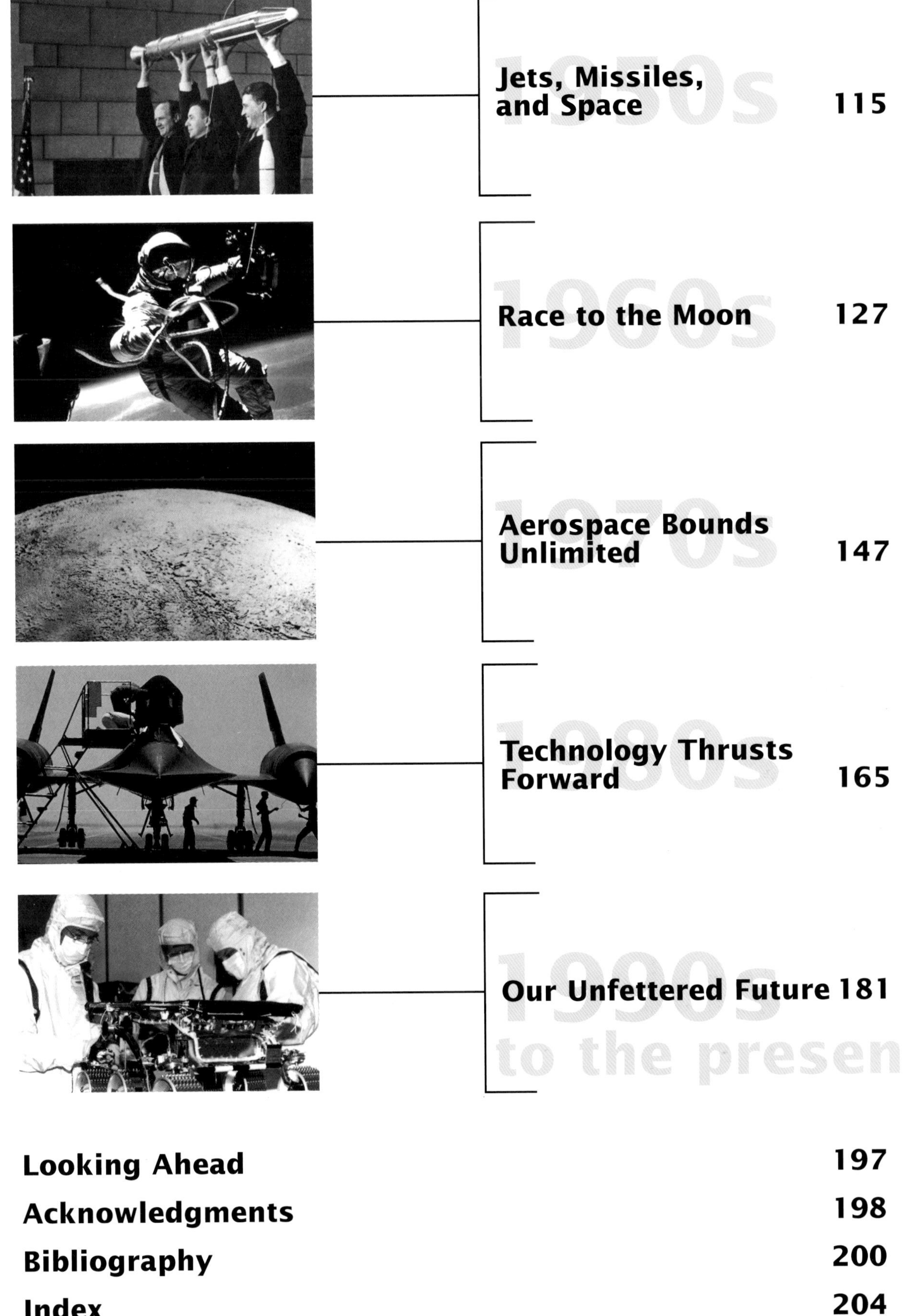

Foreword

In *Milestones of the First Century of Flight*, the people, and the machines they invented, have been singled out for recognition because their achievements advanced the art of aerospace. They believed they could accomplish things that everyone else said could not be done. The risks they took often seemed reckless—and perhaps some were, but most were inspired by a unique blend of courage, inspiration, and solid engineering.

Powered, controlled flight was only 16 years old when the Aerospace Industries Association (AIA) was initially organized in 1919 as a trade association charged with educating the public about aviation. Orville Wright and Glenn Curtiss became charter members of this organization because they believed, along with other aviation pioneers, that the industry would not survive unless air transportation was part of the average American's life.

The post–World War I American aircraft industry reeled from a sharp drop in orders, and aviation was struggling for acceptance as a new factor in commerce. At peak production during the war, U.S. aircraft manufacturers produced 21,000 planes per year. Lacking a commercial business base, aircraft manufacturing fell to ten percent of its wartime size, a situation that caused alarm in the industry and government. There were concerns that without intervention, aviation would become a lost art in peacetime and the nation would lose an indispensable element in national defense.

Our country needed a national policy to promote a healthy, viable civil aircraft industry, so that technology and production facilities would be available in the event of future wars. In those early years, AIA worked closely with government and industry for federal regulations to examine and license pilots and navigators, inspect aircraft and engines, coordinate weather forecasts, and develop landing fields.

In the decades that followed, AIA, industry, and the government were involved in the genesis of space exploration. Once again, visionaries took "a giant step for mankind" when they designed and built satellites and unmanned spacecraft, and later, manned spacecraft.

Thanks to their vision, the designers and engineers, the financial backers, and of course, the pilots and their navigators, created an entirely new field of science and technology that has had an unprecedented impact on the world's population.

In the 1919 edition of the *Aircraft Yearbook*, the editor wrote that they were ". . . compelled to take a stand against the prejudice that dared not present itself during the war, the same old prejudice that has tried in vain to check the progress of each new idea necessary to the advance of civilization."

We owe a great deal to the efforts of the men and women who stood against the prejudice that impeded new ideas. As we embark on the second century of flight, it is fitting for us to renew the spirit of adventure that began in 1903. The second century of flight promises the potential to carry mankind to the planets and beyond. Like the first century, we are likely to be limited only by our courage, our inspiration, and our engineering.

John W. Douglass
President and CEO
Aerospace Industries Association
of America, Inc.

Preface

The history of human flight, in Earth's atmosphere and outside it, is rich with remarkable achievements. Some achievements, such as the Wright Brothers' four flights at Kitty Hawk, North Carolina, on December 17, 1903, are well known. Others are less well known, but some have had such importance in the story of aerospace progress they qualify as milestones on our path up from ground level and into space.

This book documents 100 such milestones. A special panel convened by the Aerospace Industries Association (AIA) was hand picked for the purpose of choosing each milestone. The panel (including the author) was directed to select, among the thousands of aerospace achievements, 100 that met the standards for milestone status. The process was cordial and instructive thanks to the goodwill of the panelists and the AIA's sound guidance and preparation.

The milestones in this collection fit into several categories. The first category includes clear-cut, obvious choices, such as the first flight and the first lunar landing. Record-setting feats, including around-the-world flights, constitute another category. The advances in space flight fit into another category that can rightly be called "engineering marvels." The panel also gave milestone recognition to trends such as the advent and growth of business jets and regional airlines. Finally, legislative developments such as the Kelly Act and airline deregulation made our list because they acted as catalysts for profound social and economic changes.

Readers who are knowledgeable about aerospace history will doubtless have identified their own milestones. It is certain that some will not be among those chosen for inclusion in the pages that follow. For the larger purpose of stimulating thought and discussion about all aspects of aerospace history, that is all to the good.

Whether flying an airplane or recounting achievements in flight, one must exercise care in the details. I have been mindful of that requirement. If errors have crept in, they are my sole responsibility.

F. Clifton Berry, Jr.
Northern Virginia

September 1908. Orville Wright demonstrates the Wright Flyer to the U.S. Army over the parade ground at Fort Myer, Virginia. (National Archives)

The Early Years 1903–1910s

The airplane is an instrument of transformation. In the early years of the 20th century, it wrought transformation rapidly, not just by its actual use, but by its very existence. Though only 16 years had passed from the Wright Brothers' first successful powered flight on December 17, 1903, to the close of the second decade of the century, aviation had changed people's lives all over the world.

The magnitude of the changes already wrought and still in progress by aviation in every sphere of human activity was not widely perceived. Most of those who did understand how fundamentally aviation was transforming human life, unsurprisingly, were people in aviation itself—the pilots, mechanics, engineers, and visionaries who had, collectively, done the work of turning the possible into the real in flight after Kitty Hawk.

Especially in the United States, these were the kinds of people whose beliefs and passions the Manufacturers Aircraft Association reflected on when, in its annual yearbook for 1919, it declared that:

> The airplane came at the time when the world urgently needed it. The physical need was great and the mind of man was ready to accept it. So it came with liberty riding upon its wings.

The aviation developments in the first 16 years of the first century of flight are sketched in the milestones presented on the next several pages. These are the stories of pioneers, of the men and women whose achievements changed the world, by making—in the words of the Association—what had been "romance" into "reality."

First Successful, Powered, Sustained, and Controlled Flight

The wind blew at more than 21 miles per hour from the Northeast across the hills near Kitty Hawk on North Carolina's Outer Banks at 10:35 A.M. on Thursday, December 17, 1903. Orville Wright of Dayton, Ohio, took off into the wind in the airplane he and his brother Wilbur invented and built. When the airplane settled back onto the cold sands, it had flown for 12 seconds and covered 120 feet over the ground. Orville Wright had made the first successful manned, powered, controlled, and sustained flight in history.

Wilbur Wright, Orville's older brother, took the controls for the second flight. Then Orville flew again. After that, Wilbur took his second turn to make the fourth flight. It was the longest and final flight of the day. The *Flyer* stayed up for 59 seconds and covered 852 feet over the ground on that flight. After the fourth flight they took the *Flyer* back to their camp nearby, where a severe wind gust overturned and damaged the *Flyer*. The brothers secured the airplane and ate a quick lunch. Then they walked four miles to the village of Kitty Hawk to send a telegram notifying their father of the success. Bishop Milton Wright received the telegram at home in Dayton, Ohio, on the evening of December 17.

Tom D. Crouch quoted the telegram in his biography of Orville and Wilbur Wright, *The Bishop's Boys* (New York, W.W. Norton & Company, 1989):

> Success four flights Thursday morning all against twenty one mile wind started from Level with engine power alone average speed through air thirty one miles longest 57 (sic) seconds inform Press home ##### Christmas.
> Orevelle Wright.

Although the telegraphist got the duration of flight wrong by two seconds and Orville's name was misspelled in the communication process, the message was clear. He and Wilbur had succeeded.

Although they were born four years apart (Wilbur in 1867, Orville in 1871), the brothers were as inseparable as twins. They shared an intense intellectual curiosity, perseverance, devotion to principles, mechanical aptitude, and the dream of flight. However, before turning to development of the first successful flying machine, they built businesses in printing and bicycles. They repaired bicycles, then began to manufacture bicycles in 1895.

By the late 1890s the brothers had concluded that it was reasonable to believe that man might fly, and decided to turn their belief into action. At that time, Wilbur and Orville were far from alone in the quest for manned flight. Others pursued the dream, in the United States and elsewhere. For example, Samuel P. Langley, Secretary of the Smithsonian Institution, was working hard on a flying machine he called an "aerodrome." The Wrights had read of Langley's work and the glider experiments of Otto Lilienthal in Germany, as well as the experiments by Octave Chanute in Illinois.

The Wrights wrote to the Smithsonian for suggestions on the best books on the subject. The prompt response from the Smithsonian recommended books by Langley and Chanute and aeronautical annuals reporting on efforts to fly. The return reply included several pamphlets on the subject. With those materials in hand, they began their quest for flight, which succeeded where so many others had failed.

Why did Wilbur and Orville Wright succeed? They undertook original research on airfoils, building their own wind tunnel and designing and testing airfoils. The results of their research enabled them to create more efficient wings and, later, efficient propellers. They observed how birds controlled their flight and adapted the knowledge to a system for controlling their own flying machines.

The brothers designed and built gliders to test and prove their theoretical findings. To find a location with strong and reliable winds, they wrote to the Weather Bureau and determined that Kitty Hawk, on the Outer Banks of North Carolina met their needs. They went there in 1900 to test the glider they had invented. After the tests they refined the designs, making more than a thousand glider flights at Kitty Hawk in 1901 and again in 1902.

Following their exhaustive unpowered-flight research, they were ready to add power and really fly instead of simply gliding. Internal-combustion engines of the time were unsatisfactory for flight. The "power-to-weight" ratio was inadequate. The Wrights, with assistance of their shop foreman Charles Taylor, built their own engine from scratch. It weighed 170 pounds, produced 12

Alberto Santos-Dumont flies his design number 19, the graceful Demoiselle *monoplane, which flew farther and faster than his ungainly 14-bis. (National Air and Space Museum, Smithsonian Institution SI Neg. No. 93-626)*

horsepower, and performed admirably. After the successful flights of December 17, 1903, the brothers returned to Dayton. In 1904, they leased the use of land at Huffman Prairie east of the city. They continued to improve the design of the Wright *Flyer* as well as their ability to control it. They made flights lasting as long as five minutes and flew complete circles with the airplane.

Amos Ives Root, editor of the journal *Gleanings in Bee Culture,* was present at Huffman Prairie on September 20, 1904, when the Wrights flew the world's first complete circle. So impressed was Root that he wrote, "When Columbus discovered America he did not know what the outcome would be, and no one at the time knew. In a like manner these two brothers have probably not even a faint glimpse of what their discovery is going to bring to the children of men."

Wilbur Wright died of typhoid fever in 1912, when it was still unclear how powerfully his and Orville's "discovery" of a means by which humans could fly would transform the world. Orville died 36 years later, after a continued long and distinguished career in the aviation world he helped create. By then, Orville Wright certainly had more than a "glimpse" of what he and his brother Wilbur had brought to all people with their achievement at Kitty Hawk on a windy December day in 1903.

First Flight in Europe

News of the Wright Brothers' gliding experiments had reached Europe in 1902. Stimulated by the Americans' work, British and European inventors raced to pioneer powered flight. The Wrights won the race, and it was almost three years after the Kitty Hawk flights, on November 12, 1906, at Bagatelle, near Paris, that Alberto Santos-Dumont finally achieved the first powered flight in Europe.

One of the most intriguing of a generation of colorful aviation pioneers, Santos-Dumont was born in Brazil on July 20, 1873. His father sent him to France in his late teens to advance his technical education. He became interested in lighter-than-air flying. By 1898 he designed and built his first steerable airship, the *Santos-Dumont Dirigible No. 1.*

His activities and personality excited public and professional interest, and led to formation of the Aero Club of France. A member of the club, Deutsch de La Meurt, established the Deutsch Prize of 100,000 francs. The prize would be won by the first balloonist to take off from the Parisian suburb of Saint-Cloud, fly around the Eiffel Tower, and return to the starting point in less than 30 minutes. Santos-Dumont won the prize on October 19, 1901, flying his *Dirigible No. 6.* He followed that success by designing and flying dirigibles 7, 8, and 9 between 1901 and 1903. Then he turned his talents and energies to the challenges of powered heavier-than-air flight.

Santos-Dumont designed and built his own airplane and designated it No. 14-bis. The flight on November 12, 1906, at Bagatelle lasted for 21.2 seconds and covered a distance of 220 meters. Santos-Dumont won the Aero Club of France prize of 1,500 francs, given for the first powered flight in Europe of at least 100 meters.

The boxy and ungainly Santos-Dumont 14-bis biplane was the first airplane with wheeled undercarriage. (The undercarriages of the Wright *Flyers* consisted of wooden skids mounted beneath their fuselages.) Although the Santos-Dumont 14-bis was underpowered and lacked adequate controls, its success encouraged Santos-Dumont himself and many others in Europe to continue their explorations in powered flight. His later airplane designs evolved to the graceful monoplane No. 19, nicknamed *Demoiselle*, for dragonfly.

Henri Farman made the first flight in Europe with duration longer than one minute on November 9, 1907. Farman flew from a field at Issy, south of Paris, in a Voisin-Farman I biplane. That flight covered 1,030 meters in one minute, 14 seconds. Two months later on January 13, 1908, Farman flew the first official circle in Europe also in the Voisin-Farman I, covering a distance of one kilometer.

Also in France at that time, Leon Delagrange advanced the times and distances flown. On April 11, 1908, Delagrange flew a Voisin-Delagrange II biplane at Issy for six minutes, 30 seconds. He exceeded that record two months later in Milan, Italy when he flew the Voisin-Delagrange III biplane for 18 minutes, 30 seconds over a distance of 14.27 kilometers.

Meanwhile, another Frenchman, Louis Blériot, also made progress with his own designs. On July 6, 1908, at Issy, he flew his monoplane the Blériot VIII-bis for eight minutes, 25 seconds.

3

Glenn Curtiss Wins Scientific American Trophy

Alexander Graham Bell, inventor of the telephone, formed the Aerial Experiment Association (AEA) in 1907 to advance the science of aviation. Original members of the AEA included Bell and two young Canadian engineers, John A. D. McCurdy and Frederick Baldwin. Bell invited Glenn H. Curtiss of Hammondsport, New York, to join. Curtiss was a motorcycle builder and racer and expert on gasoline engines. The U.S. Army detailed Lieutenant Thomas E. Selfridge as an official observer of the AEA's activities. Selfridge graduated from the U.S. Military Academy at West Point in 1903 and was interested in aviation.

On March 12, 1908, at Curtiss's base of Hammondsport, New York, the AEA's first airplane, the *Red Wing*, flew 319 feet, piloted by Frederick Baldwin. Two months later Glenn Curtiss flew the second AEA airplane, the *White Wing*, on May 21, covering 1,017 feet.

By July 4 of that year the AEA was ready to fly its third airplane, the *June Bug*, to strive for the

Glenn Curtiss flies June Bug *to win the Scientific American Trophy on July 4, 1908. (National Archives)*

Glenn Curtiss flies Silver Dart, *the successor to* June Bug. *(Library of Congress)*

Scientific American Trophy. The trophy was to be awarded to the first airplane to fly at least one kilometer (3,281 feet) in a straight line. Charles Manly represented the Aero Club's contest committee at the scene. Manly had been Samuel P. Langley's assistant and pilot of Langley's failed "Aerodrome" machine.

Glenn Curtiss piloted *June Bug* on the record-making flight. At 6:00 P.M. when the afternoon thunderstorms had abated and the weather cleared, Curtiss made his first attempt, which fell short by 1,000 feet. On his second effort, made at 7:00 P.M., Curtiss flew the course at an altitude of 20 feet for one-minute, 42 and 2/5 seconds, covering a distance of 5,090 feet. Curtiss won the Scientific American prize.

June Bug was a pusher biplane with wheeled undercarriage. Its propeller, with a diameter of six feet two inches, mounted directly on the engine crankshaft. The engine delivered 25 horsepower at 1,200 revolutions per minute.

Bell recounted the flight in the July 18, 1908, issue of *Scientific American*. He concluded the article by writing, "We congratulate him (Curtiss) on his success in winning our trophy for the first time, and we hope that progress in aviation will be so rapid, that he will stand an excellent chance of winning it again in the future and much more difficult contests to be held."

After *June Bug*, the Aerial Experiment Association built an improved airplane, the *Silver Dart*. Curtiss flew it at Hammondsport for the first time on December 6, 1908. Soon after that, on February 23, 1909, John McCurdy flew the *Silver Dart* off the ice at Baddeck Bay, Nova Scotia (site of Alexander Graham Bell's estate), recording the first controlled, powered airplane flight in Canada.

Glenn Curtiss created the first successful "hydro-aeroplane," as it was called then. It was a floatplane derived from the *June Bug*. He flew it for the first time on January 26, 1911, at San Diego, California. Twenty years later the U.S. Navy dedicated a plaque to Curtiss at the spot. Curtiss also developed and flew the first successful flying boat. He received the Aero Club of America Trophy (later the Robert J. Collier Trophy) in two consecutive years. It was awarded to him in 1911 for development of the hydro-aeroplane and in 1912 for the flying boat.

Plaque commemorating the 20th anniversary of Glenn H. Curtiss's first seaplane flight at San Diego, California, on January 26, 1911. (National Archives)

Aerial Experiment Association members, July 24, 1907. From left: F. M. Baldwin, Thomas E. Selfridge, Glenn H. Curtiss, Alexander Graham Bell, and J. A. D. McCurdy. Louis Post of the Aero Club of America is at far right. (Library of Congress)

4

Blériot Flies the English Channel

As heavier-than-air flight became more popular in the first decade of the 20th century, the *Daily Mail* newspaper of London offered a prize of 1,000 pounds sterling for the first powered airplane flight across the English Channel.

On July 25, 1909, Louis Blériot won the prize, flying an airplane of his own design and construction, the Blériot XI monoplane. His feat put an end to England's apparent safety behind the "moat" of the Channel and further stimulated interest in aviation in Europe and around the world.

Blériot was born in Cambrai, France, on July 1, 1872. At the turn of the century he was a successful manufacturer of acetylene headlamps for automobiles. Becoming fascinated with heavier-than-air flight, he began to build and fly airplanes. He flew his first airplane in 1907, teaching himself to fly in the process. By mid-1908, in his Blériot VIII-bis, he stayed aloft for more than eight minutes. On October 31, 1908, he flew an improved version of his Blériot VIII for 11 minutes. The Blériot VIII was the world's first successful monoplane aircraft.

In January 1909, Louis Blériot flew his Blériot XI monoplane for the first time. It was an improvement over the Model VIII, and radical by contrast with the pusher biplanes being flown by the Wright Brothers and Glenn Curtiss and Henri Farman, among others. The contrasts were apparent. The Blériot XI was a tractor airplane, with the engine and propeller pulling instead of pushing. The elevators were not sticking out in front, but instead were mounted on the tail of the structure along with the vertical rudder. The undercarriage consisted of two main wheels in front and a tail wheel aft. The wheels of the main gear were castered so the airplane could handle a crosswind. The pilot sat in a cockpit behind the engine.

Blériot's flight across the English Channel began at Les Barraques, near Calais on the Normandy coast. He took off at 4:41 A.M. on July 25, and flew nearly 23 miles across the Channel's choppy water and turbulent weather, landing almost 40 minutes later in a meadow near Dover Castle in Kent, England.

Blériot received universal acclaim upon his return to France. Orders for his airplane kept his factory busy. A Blériot XI became the first airplane to see combat during the war between Italy and Turkey in 1911. When World War I began, eight squadrons of the French Air Force were equipped with Blériots, and a few served in the Royal Flying Corps and Italian Air Force.

Louis Blériot remained active in the aircraft industry until his death. He died on August 2, 1936.

Louis Blériot, the first aviator to fly across the English Channel. (Musée de l'Air et de l'Espace/Le Bourget)

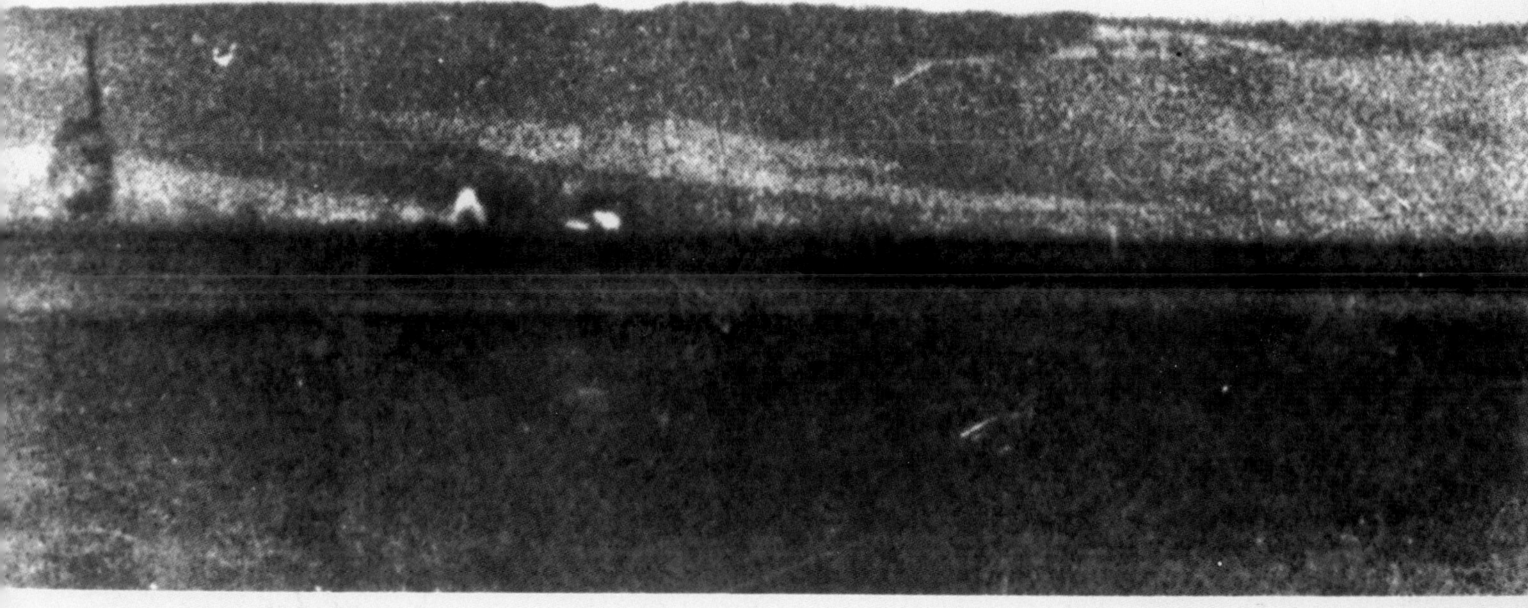

Louis Blériot in his Blériot XI aircraft before takeoff on July 25, 1909. Above: Blériot in the air off the Channel coast. (Musée de l'Air et de l'Espace/Le Bourget)

5 August 1909: the "Grand Week of Aviation"

Excitement about aviation intensified in 1908 and 1909 in the United States and Europe. The enthusiasm reached a peak in August 1909 during the "Grand Week of Aviation" at Reims, France.

A few officers of the U.S. Army saw some potential in aircraft, and in September 1908, invited Orville Wright to make several demonstration flights at Fort Myer, Virginia, across the Potomac River overlooking Washington. Orville flew on September 17 with Lieutenant Thomas E. Selfridge as passenger. A propeller malfunction caused the airplane to crash from a height of 75 feet. Lieutenant Selfridge was killed, becoming the first person to die in an airplane accident. Orville Wright was seriously injured. Eleven months later and after recovering from his injuries, Orville completed the demonstrations at Fort Myer, and the Army bought its first airplane.

Meanwhile, Wilbur Wright had sailed to Europe to demonstrate and sell the Wright *Flyer*. He made a series of successful flights near Le Mans, France, from August 8 until December 31. On the last day of the year Wilbur established a world record for distance, flying 77 miles in two hours and 20 minutes. He won the Michelin prize of 20,000 francs for the feat.

Early in 1909, Wilbur shifted his flying to Pau in the south of France. Orville and their sister Katharine joined him. The kings of England and Spain came to watch the flights, along with throngs that included many celebrities. The Wrights moved their operations to Italy in the spring of 1909. Wilbur flew from Centocelle Field near Rome, his flights as spectacularly successful as elsewhere, and further spread aviation enthusiasm.

Milestones of aviation came fast in Europe in 1908 and 1909. Leon Delagrange made the first powered flight in Italy in May 1908 in an airplane

Wright Flyer *in Italy, 1909. (National Air and Space Museum, Smithsonian Institution SI Neg. No. 86-14845)*

built by the Voisin brothers, Gabriel and Charles. Also in May 1908 Henri Farman, an Englishman residing in France, made the first airplane flight in Belgium. The Danish aviator J. C. H. Ellehammer made the first airplane flight in Germany in June 1908. Samuel F. Cody, an American resident in England, designed British Army "Aeroplane No. 1" and flew it at Farnborough, southwest of London, on October 16, 1908. The first Englishman to fly in England was J. T. C. Moore-Brabazon, who flew a Voisin biplane on April 30, 1909.

The time was ripe for an international aviation meeting. The Champagne industry of France promoted and financed the "Grande Semaine d'Aviation." It was held at Reims, capital of the Champagne region, from August 22 through 29, 1909.

The Champagne companies offered 200,000 francs for prizes in speed, altitude, distance, and endurance. Flying an Antoinette airplane, Hubert Latham flew highest, to 508 feet. Henri Farman set world records in distance and duration. He flew a closed circuit of 111.8 miles in three hours and five minutes.

The speed contest for the Gordon Bennett Cup highlighted the weeklong meet. James Gordon Bennett, publisher of the New York *Herald* newspaper and its Paris counterpart offered the cup and a cash prize of 25,000 francs for the first time. The rules were worked out with the Fédération Aéronautique International (FAI). The aero clubs of the nations that were members of the FAI would make entries for the race. Each entry in the race would fly individually, making two timed laps around a 10-kilometer course, for a total of 20 kilometers.

The aero club of the winning nation would receive the cup and host the next competition for the prize. Three nations entered competitors for the race: France, with three pilots and three alternates; Great Britain, with one pilot; and the United States with one. The Wright Brothers declined to enter the race.

George Cockburn of Great Britain was eliminated by a mishap on the first lap.

Glenn Curtiss represented the Aero Club of America. He flew his new biplane, the *Reims Flyer*, for the first time. He covered the 20-kilometer course in 15 minutes, 50 and 3/5 seconds, for an average speed of 47.65 miles per hour (75 km/hr).

Two of the French aviators flew the course at significantly slower speeds than Curtiss. Hubert Latham took 17 minutes, 32 seconds. Eugene Lefebvre took 20 minutes, 47 and 3/5 seconds. That left Louis Blériot to beat Curtiss if he could.

Blériot was the current hero of France, fresh from his flight across the English Channel in the previous month. He was the sentimental and technical favorite, flying his Blériot XII monoplane. He knew Curtiss's speed and set out to beat it. However, Blériot's flight took 15 minutes, 56 and 1/5 seconds. That was almost six seconds longer than Curtiss. Thus victory in the first Gordon Bennett race went to Glenn Curtiss.

In all, six Gordon Bennett races were held; one each year after the Reims debut in 1909, until 1914, when World War I interrupted the sequence. The postwar race in 1920 was the sixth and last. French entries won the final three competitions. Thereafter the Gordon Bennett Cup was retired and remains in permanent custody of the Aero Club of France.

Spectators paid an admission fee of 10 francs to the first international air meet held at Reims, France, in August 1909. (Photo courtesy of Goodrich Corporation)

First Female Pilots

6

Elise de Laroche, also known under the name of Baronne Raymonde de Laroche, became the first licensed female pilot in the world. She was an artist and auto driver who learned to fly with Gabriel Voisin on a Voisin biplane in October 1909. She was killed in an airplane crash in 1919.

Harriet Quimby was the first licensed female pilot in the United States. From 1903 to 1912 she achieved fame as a noted photojournalist and as drama critic for *Leslie's Illustrated Weekly*, in New York. During the summer of 1911, Quimby took flying lessons at the Moisant Aviation School on Long Island and earned FAI License No. 37 on August 2. She immediately flew at aviation exhibitions in the United States and Mexico.

While touring in Mexico during November 1911, Quimby was inspired to be the first woman to pilot her own airplane across the English Channel from England to France. She ordered a 70 hp, two-seat monoplane from Louis Blériot's Paris factory. However, when she arrived to take delivery, the airplane was not ready in time for her planned 22-mile flight between Dover and Calais.

Blériot loaned her a single-seat, 50-hp monoplane. On April 16, 1912, at 5:30 A.M., following hasty instructions on the use of a borrowed

Elise de Laroche of France, first licensed female pilot. (National Air and Space Museum, Smithsonian Institution SI Neg. No. 82-11929)

Harriet Quimby, first American female pilot.
(National Air and Space Museum, Smithsonian Institution SI Neg. No. A-44401-C)

compass, Quimby took off over Dover Castle. She flew through dense fog at 2,000 feet, then descended and emerged over the coast of France. Although off-course, almost 30 miles south of Calais, she made a smooth landing on the beach at Hardelot, then celebrated with a cup of tea. She later wrote that she took the train to Paris that evening, "a very tired but a very happy woman."

On July 1, 1912, Quimby and William Willard, manager of the Third Annual Boston Air Meet, flew around the Boston Lighthouse for a promotional flight. On the return approach her new Blériot suddenly pitched forward, tossing them both to their deaths in the shallow waters of Dorchester Bay. She was 37 years old.

For further information on Harriet Quimby, write to The Harriet Quimby Research Conference at P.O. Box 46, Woodland Hills, California 91365.

7 Naval Aviation Begins

Orville Wright demonstrated the Wright *Flyer* for the U. S. Army in 1908, and the Army bought its first airplane from the Wright Brothers in 1909. The U.S. Navy also developed an interest in airplanes. Two Navy representatives observed Orville Wright's Army demonstration flights at Fort Myer, Virginia, in September 1908. One of them, Lieutenant George C. Sweet, recommended acquisition of airplanes for naval uses.

Eugene Ely landing on USS Pennsylvania, *January 18, 1911. (National Archives)*

Ely on the deck of USS Pennsylvania *before takeoff. (National Archives)*

Ely takes off from USS Pennsylvania *on his return flight to shore. (National Archives)*

Glenn H. Curtiss flies the Navy's first seaplane, designated A-1, at Lake Keuka, Hammondsport, New York. In 1914 the Navy changed its designation to AH-1 for heavier-than-air (A), hydroaeroplane (H) number 1. (National Air and Space Museum, Smithsonian Institution SI Neg. No. A-43389-C)

Commander Frederick L. Chapin, the U.S. Naval Attaché in Paris, attended the August 1909 Grande Semaine d'Aviation in Reims. He reported his observations to Washington on September 1. He concluded that the airplane would be useful in warfare and suggested two means by which airplanes could operate from ships at sea. The first method he proposed was a catapult for launching airplanes from battleships. The second was to construct a flight deck on auxiliary ships for takeoff and landing.

In 1910, the Secretary of the Navy designated Captain Washington Irving Chambers as the officer to receive all correspondence to the Navy on aviation. He became the focal point and key person for Naval interest in airplanes.

In the summer of 1910 Glenn Curtiss used buoys to designate a target shaped like a battleship and of the same size in Keuka Lake near his base in Hammondsport, New York. Flying over the target, he dropped 22 simulated bombs, 15 of which fell into the target's outline.

Captain Chambers and two other officers went to an aviation meet at Halethorpe, Maryland, in October 1910. They met Glenn Curtiss and Eugene Ely, whom Curtiss had trained to fly. At that time there were rumors of French intentions to build an aircraft carrier and German plans to fly an airplane off a ship to speed up mail service. If the U.S. Navy was not to be left behind, it must test the feasibility of operating airplanes from its ships. Captain Chambers got permission to try to launch an airplane from the deck of the cruiser USS *Birmingham*. Eugene Ely agreed to make the attempt.

Glenn L. Martin also built seaplanes. He made a record-setting 34-mile, 37-minute flight from Newport Bay to Catalina, California, in his Pusher Seaplane on May 10, 1912. (Lockheed Martin Corporation)

The Navy constructed a wooden platform above the foredeck of the USS *Birmingham* at the Navy yard in Norfolk, Virginia. Ely embarked with his Curtiss biplane and on November 14 the ship took up a stationary position in Hampton Roads at the entrance to the Chesapeake Bay. At about 3:00 P.M., Ely took off. His plane dipped after leaving the ship and touched the water briefly, damaging his propellers. However, he maintained control and landed on Willoughby Spit near the Army's Fortress Monroe, 2.5 miles away.

Glenn Curtiss made an offer to the Navy at the end of November 1910 to teach a naval officer to fly at no charge to the government. The Navy took him up on the offer and soon sent Lieutenant Theodore G. Ellyson to join Curtiss at San Diego, California, to learn to fly.

Captain Chambers moved to the next test, a demonstration that an airplane could land on a ship. The armored cruiser USS *Pennsylvania* was designated for the test. Another platform was constructed and mounted aboard the ship at San Francisco. A set of 22 weighted lines was stretched across the platform perpendicular to the line of flight. Hooks to snag the lines were fitted to Ely's airplane. All was ready on the morning of January 18, 1911.

Eugene Ely took off from a shore base at 11:01 A.M. and soon made a successful landing aboard the USS *Pennsylvania* anchored in San Francisco Bay. After less than an hour on board, Ely took off at 11:50 A.M. and landed at Selfridge Field, San Francisco.

On January 26, 1911, Glenn Curtiss made the first successful hydroaeroplane (seaplane) flight from his camp at North Island, San Diego. Lieutenant Ellyson was present for the flight. Three weeks later, on February 17, Curtiss taxied his seaplane from North Island to the USS *Pennsylvania*. It was hoisted aboard and then put back on the water to taxi back to North Island.

These experiments opened the way for naval aviation in the United States and in Europe. Captain Chambers ordered two Curtiss biplane seaplanes on May 8, 1911. Glenn Curtiss made the first flight of the A-1 on July 1. He took off and landed from Keuka Lake, New York, and flew for five minutes. Curtiss promptly made one more flight of the A-1 carrying Lieutenant Ellyson as a passenger, then Ellyson made two solo flights in the A-1. The Navy had its first airplane. Curtiss and Ellyson each made flights with the second airplane, the A-2, on July 13.

8 First Parachute Jump from an Airplane

Jefferson Barracks, St. Louis, Missouri, March 1, 1912. Before first parachute jump from an airplane. Left to right, Captain Albert Berry, USA, the jumper; Anthony Jannus, the pilot; Thomas Benoist, the airplane builder. (Courtesy St. Petersburg Museum of History)

A Frenchman, Andre Jacques Garnerin, made the first successful parachute descent from a balloon tethered over Paris at about 3,000 feet. The date was October 22, 1797.

Nearly 115 years later, on March 1, 1912, Captain Albert Berry of the U.S. Army made the first successful parachute descent from an airplane. The airplane was a Benoist biplane piloted by Anthony Jannus, flying at about 1,500 feet over Jefferson Barracks near St. Louis, Missouri. Eighteen months later, on June 21, 1913, Georgia Broadwick, nicknamed "Tiny," became the first woman to make a descent by parachute from an airplane. Glenn L. Martin flew her to about 1,000 feet above Los Angeles, California, in his Model T airplane. Broadwick subsequently became a renowned performer at air shows.

Even with Berry's successful demonstration, the U.S. Army did not adopt the parachute for its aircrews. During World War I, many German balloonists and airplane pilots were equipped with parachutes, but Allied aviators were not. However, the benefits of parachutes for aircrews were so obvious that in the years after World War I, parachutes became standard equipment for military aviators, either worn on the body or immediately accessible in case of in-flight emergency.

Parachutes demonstrated obvious utility in saving aircrew lives. Beyond that function, military theorists toyed with the prospect of "vertical envelopment," dropping large formations of combat troops deep in enemy territory. Several nations, notably the Soviet Union and Germany, began experimenting with the concept of forming airborne assault forces to be dropped by parachute. Awareness of Soviet developments in the 1930s and German airborne operations in Norway, the Low Countries, and Crete in 1940 stimulated the British and American armed forces to form their own airborne assault units during World War II.

Albert Berry's parachute is tested before starting. (National Air and Space Museum, Smithsonian Institution SI Neg. No. 2000-3650)

Georgia "Tiny" Broadwick boards Glenn L. Martin's Model T airplane for free-fall parachute jump. (Lockheed Martin Corporation)

9

The Grand, World's First Four-Engine Airplane, Flies

Igor Sikorsky designed, built, and in 1913 flew the world's first four-engine airplane. Designated the S-21, for his 21st design, the airplane was nicknamed *The Grand* for its size and dominance. With a wingspan of nearly 89 feet and gross weight greater than 9,000 pounds, the airplane was the largest in the world and a magnificent engineering achievement for Igor Sikorsky.

Sikorsky built the airplane during the winter of 1912–1913 at the St. Petersburg aviation factory of the Russo-Baltic Wagon Company (R-BVZ). He was already established as a successful aircraft designer and builder.

Born in 1889 in Kiev, Sikorsky's fascination with aviation began early in life. He studied at the Russian Naval Academy for three years, then in Paris and after that at the Polytechnic Institute of Kiev. He learned about the Wright Brothers' flights and visited France in 1909 where he met many of the pioneering aviators and saw their aircraft. He was initially impressed with the potential for vertical flight via a helicopter, but his first efforts at constructing a vertical lift aircraft were not successful.

Sikorsky turned to designing fixed-wing airplanes. Beginning in 1910, he created a series of successful single-engine "S" designs. In the summer of 1911 he received pilot's license number 64 from the Imperial All-Russian Aero Club.

By late 1912, Sikorsky was ready to create a multi-engine airplane. *The Grand* was the result. Four 100-horsepower Argus engines mounted on the lower wing powered tractor propellers.

When the airplane was ready to fly in early May 1913, Igor Sikorsky made taxi tests on the ground and lifted briefly into the air. He made the first flight of *The Grand* on the evening of May 26, 1913. The flight was made from the Komendatskiy airfield near St. Petersburg. During the 10-minute flight Sikorsky flew a complete circle before descending to land before a large crowd.

Sikorsky made improvements to the airplane and demonstrated its capabilities throughout the summer of 1913. Tsar Nicholas II of Russia was among those treated to a close-up inspection of the airplane. They saw many innovations for control and comfort, including an enclosed cabin with dual controls for pilot and copilot and an observation balcony forward of the control cabin. An enclosed cabin with capacity for eight passengers was behind the control cabin.

The flights of *The Grand* rebutted skeptics who feared that multi-engine airplanes would be unsafe. News of its accomplishments in the hands of its young designer inspired others throughout Europe to take the steps toward multi-engine flight.

Sikorsky improved upon *The Grand* with his next airplane, dubbed the *Il'ya Muromets*. Its wingspan was 105 feet and fuselage length 70 feet. Sikorsky's demonstration flights with the *Il'ya Muromets* included carrying 16 passengers and his dog on a flight over St. Petersburg in February 1914. He made a round-trip flight over the 1,200-mile distance between St. Petersburg and Kiev, his

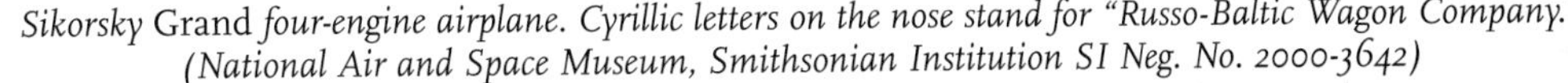

Sikorsky Grand *four-engine airplane. Cyrillic letters on the nose stand for "Russo-Baltic Wagon Company." (National Air and Space Museum, Smithsonian Institution SI Neg. No. 2000-3642)*

birthplace, at the end of June and beginning of July 1914.

World War I began one month after that flight. The Imperial Russian Air Force acquired 70 of the *Il'ya Muromets* type for long-range bombing and reconnaissance missions. Following the Russian Revolution and installation of the Bolshevik regime in 1917, Sikorsky decided to leave Russia. He left in February 1918 and made his way to Britain and then France. He saw greater postwar opportunities across the Atlantic and arrived in the United States on March 30, 1919.

Anthony Jannus (left) cranks the Roberts engine for first flight of the St. Petersburg–Tampa Airboat Line, January 1, 1914. Percival Fansler, the organizer, stands at right. (Courtesy St. Petersburg Museum of History)

10 First Scheduled Airline Begins Service

Abraham C. Pheil, a former mayor of St. Petersburg, Florida, made the high bid of $400 for the privilege of being the first passenger on a scheduled airline. The airline was named the St. Petersburg–Tampa Airboat Line and it flew the Benoist XIV seaplane.

In December 1913, entrepreneur Percival Fansler put together the deal between the St. Petersburg officials and Thomas Benoist, designer and builder of the Benoist line of aircraft.

Scheduled service began on New Year's Day, January 1, 1914. A crowd estimated at 3,000 people, about one-third of the city's winter population, crowded the St. Petersburg waterfront to watch the debut. Many among the spectators knew that the trip to Tampa took an average of two hours by boat, while the rail trip around the bay took eight and one-half hours.

A few minutes before 10:00 A.M. Pheil sat next to pilot Anthony H. Jannus in the open cockpit of the Benoist XIV, a pusher biplane. Jannus started the engine and took off from the water for the 18-mile flight across Tampa Bay.

St. Petersburg, Florida, January 1, 1914. (Left to right) Percival Fansler, Abraham C. Pheil, and Anthony Jannus, with Benoist XIV seaplane. (Courtesy St. Petersburg Museum of History)

Anthony Jannus pilots a Benoist XIV seaplane for the first flight of the St. Petersburg–Tampa Airboat Line, January 1, 1914. (Florida State Archives)

After a brief stop halfway across to adjust the engine, Jannus landed the Benoist at Tampa 23 minutes later. Another crowd waited to celebrate the arrival. Jannus and Pheil flew back to St. Petersburg in 20 minutes. The round-trip flight inaugurated the age of scheduled air transportation.

The airline contracted with the city of St. Petersburg to make two round-trip flights per day, six days a week, for a period of three months. The flights left St. Petersburg at 10:00 A.M. and 2:00 P.M. and departed from Tampa for the return flights at 11:00 A.M. and 3:00 P.M. Passenger fare was $5.00 for a one-way trip and $10.00 for the round-trip.

Each passenger was allowed up to 200 pounds, including the passenger's own weight. The airline also carried freight for $5.00 per hundred pounds, with a minimum freight charge of 25 cents. The enterprise offered special charter flights to nearby cities such as Clearwater and Sarasota at a minimum charge of $15. In its three months of service the St. Petersburg–Tampa Airboat Line operated two of the Benoist XIV aircraft and carried 1,205 passengers. Its contract ended on March 31, 1914, coinciding with the end of the winter tourist season.

Anthony H. Jannus, the chief pilot, was born in Washington, D.C., in 1889. He flew as test pilot for the Benoist Aeroplane Company in St. Louis, founded by Thomas Benoist. As a Benoist test pilot, Jannus accomplished many aviation feats.

The Florida Aviation Historical Society constructed and flew a replica of the Benoist XIV in 1984 to celebrate the 70th anniversary of the first scheduled airline flight. The replica is on display at the St. Petersburg Museum of History.

The Air Transport Association cited the operations of the St. Petersburg–Tampa Airboat Line as part of its 1995 celebrations to mark the 10 billionth passenger carried in U.S. scheduled airline service.

11 Air-to-Ground Radio Communication Established

As the 20th century began, Guglielmo Marconi's invention of telegraphic radio added a new dimension to communication. Wireless radio had obvious potential for communication via Morse code between an airplane in flight and ground stations.

John A. D. McCurdy, one of Alexander Graham Bell's colleagues in the Aerial Experiment Association, is credited with making two-way wireless contact with a ground station in August 1910 while flying over Sheepshead Bay, Long Island.

Lieutenant John H. Towers of the U.S. Navy conducted experiments with airborne wireless on December 20, 1911, at Annapolis, Maryland. He flew a Curtiss A-1 and after takeoff, unreeled a long wire antenna. Results were unsatisfactory.

Three months later, Navy experimenters at Mare Island, California, were more successful.

Transmissions from a dummy airplane hoisted to 85 feet were received at a station 20 miles away.

Additional tests at Annapolis on July 26, 1912, continued the string of successes. Ensign Charles H. Maddox, flying with Lieutenant John Rodgers in a Navy Wright B-1 airplane, transmitted wireless Morse code messages to the torpedo boat USS *Stringham.*

Meanwhile, the U.S. Army was doing its own experiments between aircraft in flight and between aircraft and ground stations. On October 16, 1917, some six months after the United States entered World War I, Army pilots and technicians achieved a range of 25 miles for radio communication between aircraft, and 45 miles between a ground station and an aircraft at tests held at Langley Field, Virginia.

Despite these early successes, and although the usefulness of sending and receiving radio messages between ground stations and aircraft in flight seemed clear to the visionaries, airborne radio telegraphy was not adopted widely until the 1920s.

12 Sperry Develops the Gyroscopic Compass

Magnetic compasses served as primary directional aids for nautical navigation at the beginning of the 20th century. However, because the mass of steel in modern ships distorted magnetic fields, magnetic compasses often proved unreliable. Elmer A. Sperry solved the problem by applying the principle of the gyroscope to produce an accurate sensing of direction.

A gyroscope spins about its base and remains in a fixed position no matter how the base moves. Elmer Sperry used the principle to invent the electrically driven gyrocompass. He received Patent 1,242,065 in 1908 for his gyrocompass. It was unaffected by the steel in a modern ship and functioned smoothly as a ship rolled and pitched on the sea. The U.S. Navy soon embraced Sperry's gyroscopic compass, and began installing the device on its ships in 1911.

The Navy also used Sperry's gyroscopic stabilizer, or autopilot steering system, in its ships. In 1913 the Navy tested Sperry's gyroscopic equipment in airplanes. Lieutenant (Junior Grade) Patrick N. L. Bellinger and Lawrence Sperry, Elmer's son, flight-tested the installation in a Curtiss C-2 flying boat on August 30, 1913, at the Curtiss base at Hammondsport, New York.

In 1916, the Navy decided to expand development of gyroscopic capabilities for instruments and equipment in its airplanes, including compasses, bombsights, and the "baseline," a forerunner of the turn-and-bank indicator. The Navy allocated funds on May 20, 1916, for the Sperry Company to develop a gyroscopically operated bombsight.

The Aero Club of America awarded Elmer Sperry the Collier Trophy in 1914 for gyroscopic control. He received the Collier Trophy again in 1916 for the Sperry drift indicator.

Elmer Ambrose Sperry. (Northrop Grumman Corporation)

National Advisory Committee for Aeronautics Established

A rider to the Naval Appropriations Act of 1916 created the Advisory Committee for Aeronautics. President Woodrow Wilson signed the Act into law on April 12, 1915, as Public Law 63-271. The language of the committee's charter directed it ". . . to supervise and direct the scientific study of the problems of flight, with a view to their practical solution." Its name later became the National Advisory Committee for Aeronautics, or NACA.

Twelve persons were designated to serve on the committee. Two members each came from the War Department and Navy Department. The Smithsonian Institution, the Weather Bureau, and the Bureau of Standards each contributed one member. Five aeronautics-minded persons from outside government rounded out the membership. Members of the advisory committee served without compensation. An executive secretary was hired to run the office in Washington.

As an advisory group, NACA identified problems in aeronautics, with the study and solution performed by government agencies or university laboratories. However, the need for an independent NACA laboratory quickly became apparent.

Seal of the National Advisory Committee for Aeronautics. (NASA)

National Advisory Committee for Aeronautics' first wind tunnel, April 21, 1921. The first wind tunnel at the Langley laboratory was approved in April 1918 and became operational in June 1920. An advanced variable density wind tunnel began operations in 1922. (NASA)

Members of the National Advisory Committee for Aeronautics gathered at Langley Field on May 23, 1934. Seated from left to right: Charles A. Lindbergh; Vice Admiral Arthur B. Cook, USN; Charles G. Abbot, Secretary of the Smithsonian Institution; Dr. Joseph S. Ames, NACA committee chairman; Orville Wright; Edward F. Warner; Rear Admiral Ernest J. King, USN; and Eugene L. Vidal, Director, Bureau of Air Commerce. Standing, left to right: Dr. George W. Lewis, Director, NACA; Dr. Henry J. E. Reid, Director, Langley Aeronautical Laboratory; and John F. Victory, Executive Secretary, NACA. (NASA)

Funds were appropriated in 1916 for construction of a NACA laboratory. A site was selected adjacent to the new Langley Field military aircraft proving ground near Hampton, Virginia. This became the Langley Memorial Aeronautical Laboratory, named in honor of Samuel Pierpont Langley. It was dedicated on June 11, 1920. The laboratory had an initial staff of 11 people. For research it had a wind tunnel and dynamometer laboratory.

Young engineers gravitated to Langley, stimulated by its informal atmosphere and opportunities for challenging research. Flight-testing began in 1922, at first using wartime aircraft to validate theoretical work and to solve practical problems. The test fleet comprised 19 aircraft by 1925, when the laboratory staff had grown to 100 persons.

In addition to its activities in the technical arena, NACA had an influence on national aviation policy. It recommended federal actions to enhance civil aviation and establishment of weather service and a system of airways for the success and safety of air navigation. The recommendations bore fruit when a Bureau of Aviation was established within the Department of Commerce in 1926.

NACA's achievements show the value of an agency that can work independently over long periods of time in pursuit of engineering solutions to basic problems. Others can then apply the solutions. This happened throughout NACA's existence. An early example is provided by NACA's development of the low-drag cowling for radial air-cooled aircraft engines, achieved under leadership of Fred E. Weick. The streamlined cowling reduced drag and improved cooling of radial engines, enabling aircraft to fly faster and farther on less fuel. NACA received the Collier Trophy for 1929 in recognition of that valuable contribution to flight.

14 First across the Atlantic

In August 1917, Rear Admiral David W. Taylor of the United States Navy established a requirement for the Navy's development of flying boats that could span the Atlantic Ocean. The new aircraft were intended to combat enemy submarines and make deliveries across the ocean easier.

Glenn Curtiss took on the job of designing and assembling the NC flying boats (N for Navy, C for Curtiss), working closely with the Navy. The NC-1 was the first airplane completed under the Navy contract. It flew for the first time on October 13, 1918, lifting off the water of Rockaway Bay, Long Island.

In Washington, D.C., Commander John Towers at the Aviation Section of the Navy Department soon recommended that the Navy make the effort to be the first to fly across the Atlantic. Secretary of the Navy Josephus Daniels approved the project in early February 1919. The approved route was to be from the United States to Newfoundland and from there to the Azores, arriving in Europe at Lisbon, Portugal.

Eventually, four NC flying boats were constructed. However, the NC-2 was cannibalized to replace damaged wings on the NC-1. Thus three NC flying boats comprised the Navy's Seaplane Division One. Commander Towers commanded the division. He also commanded the NC-3 airplane. LCDR Patrick N. L. Bellinger commanded the NC-1 aircraft. LCDR Albert C. Read was in command of NC-4.

Commander Albert C. Read graduated from the Naval Academy at Annapolis in the class of 1907. (National Archives)

NC-4 taxiing in the Tagus River at Lisbon upon completion of the first transatlantic crossing by air. (National Archives)

NC-4 in flight. NC-4's wingspan of 126 feet exceeded the length of Orville Wright's first powered flight by six feet. Four Liberty 12A engines lifted NC-4's gross weight of more than 26,000 pounds. (National Archives)

John Alcock (later Sir John) stows provisions (perhaps a vacuum bottle of hot tea?) aboard the Vickers Vimy he and Arthur W. Brown flew nonstop across the Atlantic. (National Air and Space Museum, Smithsonian Institution SI Neg. No. 88-17782)

The three aircraft of Seaplane Division One flew from the naval air station at Rockaway, Long Island, on May 8, 1919, and headed for Newfoundland on the first leg of the transatlantic adventure. In Newfoundland, they made final preparations for the transatlantic flight from an improvised base at Trepassey Bay on the south coast.

By May 16 the three NC aircraft were tuned up and provisioned for the transatlantic attempt. The Navy deployed a picket line of destroyers at intervals along the route to provide assistance to the flying boats if necessary. Radios in the NC aircraft enabled them to communicate with the ships via Morse code.

All three flying boats took off from Trepassey Bay soon after 6:00 P.M. local time on May 16. Read and his crew in NC-4, after flying for more than 15 hours, landed at Horta in the Azores at 11:23 A.M. local time on May 17.

NC-4 arrived alone. The NC-1 and NC-3 aircraft lost their way in thick fog more than halfway across the Atlantic. Both aircraft were damaged while landing at sea to establish their positions. The NC-1 sustained further damage from heavy seas and was abandoned. Commander Towers taxied NC-3 for two days. He and his crew arrived at Ponta Delgada on the next island east of Horta on May 19.

Read and his crew spent 10 days at Horta. They departed on May 27 and flew directly to Lisbon, Portugal, the same day. Although the flight spanned 11 days, an airplane had flown across the Atlantic Ocean.

After festivities and honors in Lisbon, Read and his crew flew northward over the Bay of Biscay and across the western mouth of the English Channel to land in the harbor at Plymouth, England, on May 31.

Two weeks after the NC-4 completed its journey, two British aviators captured the honor of flying the Atlantic nonstop. Captain John W. Alcock and Lieutenant Arthur Whitten Brown had flown with the Royal Air Force in World War I. Their aircraft was a Vickers Vimy bomber modified for the long distance flight. They took off from St. John's, Newfoundland, on June 14, 1919, taking a more northerly route than the U.S. Navy. They flew 1,890 miles in 15 hours and 57 minutes before landing in a peat bog near Clifden, Ireland. The aircraft ended the trip nose-down in the soft bog, but the record-setting aviators were uninjured. A statue at London's Heathrow International Airport honors the memory of Alcock and Brown's feat.

15 Beginnings of International Air Travel

The first attempts at international air passenger travel took place within a few months after the Armistice of November 11, 1918. Beginning in 1919, British and French entrepreneurs converted wartime bombers into crude passenger airplanes and offered service between major cities such as London, Paris, and Brussels. Similar ventures in Germany offered passenger flights within the country.

Weekly air service between Paris and Brussels began in March 1919. A British company called Aircraft Transport and Travel began offering daily service between London and Paris on August 25, 1919. Other fledgling airlines started up in western Europe, where plenty of demobilized pilots and surplus aircraft existed. But the business was not profitable and most of the early ventures soon went out of business.

However, KLM Royal Dutch Airlines survived. It has the distinction of operating continuously under that name since its founding on October 7, 1919. KLM flew its first flight on May 17, 1920, between London and Amsterdam.

Robert H. Goddard at Auburn, Massachusetts, before the 2.5-second flight of the first successful liquid-propellant rocket on March 16, 1926. (NASA, courtesy Mrs. Esther C. Goddard)

Aviation Comes of Age 1920–1929

Aviation development accelerated during World War I. Airplanes flew faster, higher, and farther with larger loads. Rapid advances in aviation continued in the decade of the Roaring Twenties. Surplus aircraft and plenty of war-trained pilots provided ready-made solutions for postwar civilian endeavors. At war's end, the U.S. Army Air Service possessed 8,403 airplanes while the Navy and Marine Corps owned 2,107 airplanes, including 1,172 flying boats.

Progress in aviation in the 1920s led to airmail, commercial passenger travel, transoceanic flights, global flights, polar exploration, aerial refueling, and "blind" flight, among others. Aircraft speeds tripled from 100 miles per hour to 300 miles per hour. Aviation truly came of age in this decade.

The National Advisory Committee for Aeronautics alerted the nation to the need for continued development. NACA said in its annual report of 1923: "Progress in aeronautics is being made at so rapid a rate that the only way to keep abreast of other nations is actually to keep abreast, year by year, never falling behind."

16

The U.S. Navy Commissions Its First Aircraft Carrier

Although the United States led in aircraft development at the beginning of the first century of flight, other nations soon overtook and surpassed it in development and application of airplanes.

This was especially true for the U.S. military forces. Farsighted officers in the Army and Navy saw the potential of airplanes for military missions and pressed for their infusion in the forces. However, resistance and ignorance throughout the government resulted in almost glacial progress in military aviation.

When World War I began in August 1914, the Royal Navy already possessed an aircraft carrier. HMS *Hermes* was a former cruiser modified to launch seaplanes. Seaplanes operated from four other ships of the Royal Navy in World War I. A Sopwith Pup land plane made the first landing aboard a British ship, HMS *Furious,* on August 2, 1917. British and American interest in aircraft carriers was not shared at this time by the major European powers, however. Italians saw no need for an aircraft carrier. The Germans gave more focus to the use of airships over airplanes for naval missions. The French lost interest after early unsatisfactory experiments.

The U.S. Navy finally got its first aircraft carrier nearly four years after World War I ended. The Navy converted the USS *Jupiter,* a collier (coal-hauling ship), for the purpose. Renamed USS *Langley* (CV-1), the ship was commissioned on March 20, 1922, at Norfolk, Virginia. *Langley* was slow and ungainly, steaming at only 14 knots. But she had the advantage of length, permitting construction of a flight deck 534 feet long. (The flight deck of the Royal Navy's *Argus,* its first postwar aircraft carrier, was 558 feet long.) Other advantages of the former collier included high headroom and capacious cargo holds with large hatches that made it easier to stow and move airplanes around the ship.

October 17, 1922. LCDR Virgil C. Griffin, flying a Chance Vought VE-7 Bluebird makes first takeoff from USS Langley. *LCDR Godfrey Chevalier made the first landing on USS* Langley *four days later in an Aeromarine aircraft. (Vought Aircraft Industries, Inc.)*

LCDR Virgil C. Griffin, the naval aviator who made the first takeoff from the U.S. Navy's first aircraft carrier, USS Langley*, stands before a Chance Vought VE-7 Bluebird. (Vought Aircraft Industries, Inc.)*

To LCDR Virgil C. Griffin went the honor of making the first takeoff from USS *Langley*. He flew a Chance Vought VE-7 Bluebird biplane off the flight deck on October 17, 1922. The aircraft was a product of the company founded by Chance M. Vought, a pioneer aircraft designer and builder. In succeeding years, several types of Vought aircraft flew in U.S. Navy service, including the UO-1 and O2U "Corsair."

USS *Langley* served as a seaborne proving ground for naval aviation for more than 14 years before becoming a seaplane tender in September 1936.

Two more aircraft carriers joined the U.S. fleet in 1927. Converted from battle cruisers, the USS *Saratoga* (CV-3) was commissioned on November 16 and the USS *Lexington* (CV-2) was commissioned on December 14. *Lexington* and *Saratoga* were the first U.S. aircraft carriers to have the "island" superstructure located on the starboard side of the ship. Fast ships, they could steam at top speed of 33 knots and were capable of launching aircraft scouting and striking forces to extend the reach of their power.

USS Langley *at Pearl Harbor, 1928, with a flight deck full of airplanes, mainly Vought UO-1, Vought O2U Corsair, and Boeing F2B types. (Naval Historical Foundation)*

17 Aerial Refueling Becomes Reality

Aviation pioneers of the 1920s invented or developed systems that enabled airplanes to fly faster, higher, and farther. U.S. Army aviators achieved many of the innovations along the path of aviation progress. Army Lieutenant John Macready set a new altitude record in 1921, climbing to 35,409 feet. In May 1923, Macready and Lieutenant Oakley Kelly made the first nonstop transcontinental flight. They flew a Fokker T-2 single-engine monoplane a distance of 2,520 miles from Long Island, New York, to San Diego in 26 hours and 50 minutes and three seconds. A Liberty 12-cylinder in-line liquid-cooled engine powered the Fokker T-2.

Tanker crew: U.S. Army 1st Lieutenant Frank Seifert (left) and 1st Lieutenant Virgil Hine. June 27, 1923. (USAF photo via Air Force History Support Office)

Receiver crew: Captain Lowell H. Smith (left) and 1st Lieutenant John P. Richter. June 27, 1923. (USAF photo via Air Force History Support Office)

During the first plane-to-plane aerial refueling, a hose from the deHavilland DH-4B tanker dangles over the DH-4B receiver. June 27, 1923. (USAF photo via Air Force History Support Office)

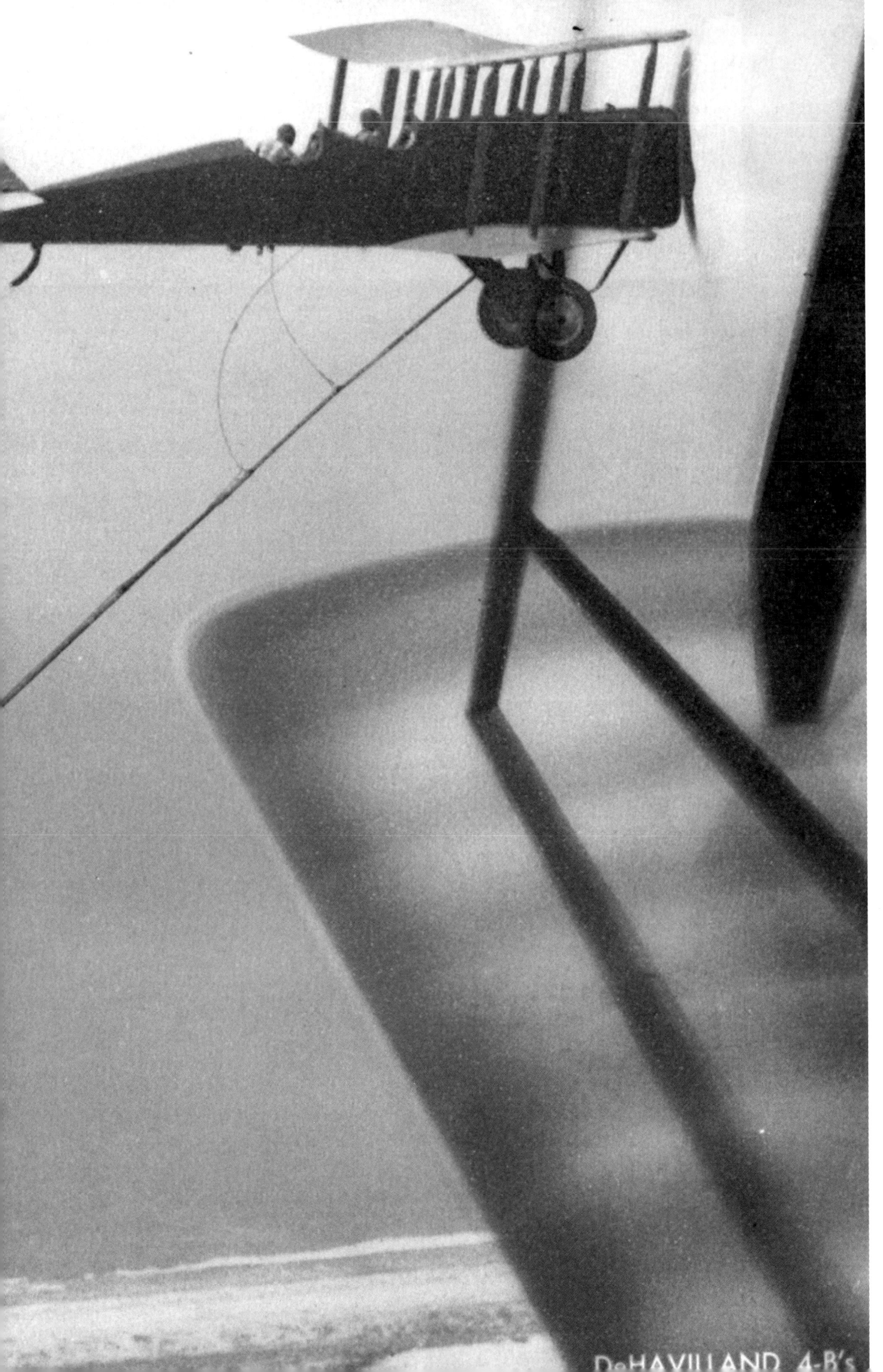
DeHAVILLAND 4-B's

Record-setting crew of Question Mark*: Major Carl Spatz (left, white shirt), Captain Ira Eaker, 1st Lieutenant Harry Halverson, 1st Lieutenant Elwood Quesada, Staff Sergeant Roy Hooe. January 7, 1929. (USAF photo via Air Force History Support Office)*

Army aviators reasoned that flights of even longer duration could be achieved if fuel could be transferred in flight. Army crews flying two single-engine deHavilland DH-4B airplanes achieved the first successful aerial refueling on June 27, 1923, flying over North Island at San Diego.

Lieutenant Frank Seifert in the aft cockpit of the DH-4B tanker dangled a 50-foot rubber fueling hose within reach of Lieutenant John Richter in the receiving DH-4B. In the front cockpits of the two airplanes, Captain Lowell Smith piloted the receiving craft while Lieutenant Virgil Hine flew the tanker. The mission lasted for six hours and 38 minutes.

Two months later, on August 27 and 28, 1923, the Army aviators established a world record for endurance. Smith and Richter in the DH-4B receiver orbited over San Diego for 37 hours and 25 minutes while two DH-4B tankers made 14 deliveries of gasoline, oil, and food.

Six years passed before the Army demonstrated aerial refueling again. Meanwhile, the Belgian Air Force had surpassed the Smith-Richter endurance record in June 1928, by staying aloft for 60 hours and seven minutes. News of the Belgian feat spurred the Army Air Corps to surpass the Belgians and establish a new record.

Lieutenant Elwood R. Quesada developed the plan with the encouragement of Captain Ira Eaker. Major Carl Spatz (who later changed his surname to Spaatz) flew in command of the receiver airplane, a Fokker C-2 trimotor nicknamed *Question*

The large white question mark identified the Fokker C-2A receiver airplane and referred to speculation about the length of its record-setting refueling mission. Answer: 150 hours, 40 minutes. January 1–7, 1929. (USAF photo via Air Force History Support Office)

Mark. Two Douglas C-1 transports flew as tankers. One operated from Rockwell Field at San Diego. The other flew from Metropolitan Airport at Van Nuys, California.

Major Spatz and his crew took off from Metropolitan Airport on January 1, 1929. They flew back and forth nonstop between Van Nuys and San Diego for more than six days. The tankers made 43 deliveries to *Question Mark* during the operation, including 12 at night. After 150 hours and 40 minutes Spatz and his crew landed on January 7, having set a new world record for time aloft.

At the time, neither the United States nor other nations' air forces adopted aerial refueling. Advances in aeronautics technologies gave aircraft greater range and speed, and the demands of World War II took priority.

Aerial refueling languished until the demands of the Cold War led the Air Force (especially its Strategic Air Command) to adapt British developments and support research for refueling techniques suitable for long-range bombers in the dawning jet age.

On February 26, 1949, a Boeing B-50 bomber named *Lucky Lady II* took off from Carswell AFB, New Mexico, to fly the first nonstop flight around the world. The flight took 94 hours and one minute, and included four aerial refuelings using a system developed by Britain's Flight Refuelling Limited.

A general overview of aerial refueling appears in Richard K. Smith's Seventy-Five Years of Inflight Refueling: Highlights, 1923–1998 *(Washington: Air Force History and Museums Program, 1998).*

18 First around the World

Leaders of the Army Air Service wanted Army airmen to be the first to fly around the world. They turned to the Douglas Company to build the aircraft to perform the feat. Donald W. Douglas incorporated his airplane company in Santa Monica, California, in 1921. His first military contract was with the Navy, for the DT-1 and DT-2 bombers (Douglas, Torpedo, 1 and 2).

Douglas upgraded the DT-2 to create the aircraft for the Army's round-the-world flight. He called them Douglas World Cruisers (DWCs). After testing the prototype World Cruiser, the Army ordered four more aircraft for the globe-girdling project. Those four aircraft left the

Army 1924 round-the-world pilots in the cockpits of their Douglas World Cruiser airplanes. Clockwise from upper left: Major Frederick L. Martin (Seattle)*; Captain Lowell H. Smith* (Chicago)*; 1st Lieutenant Erik H. Nelson* (New Orleans)*; and 1st Lieutenant Leigh Wade* (Boston)*. (National Air and Space Museum, Smithsonian Institution SI Neg. No. 90-10633)*

A festive crowd surrounds Douglas World Cruiser biplane Seattle. *(Copyright The Boeing Company)*

Douglas plant in Santa Monica, California, on March 17, 1924, for Seattle, the point of origin for the global circumnavigation. They were named *Seattle* (No. 1), *Chicago* (No. 2), *Boston* (No. 3), and *New Orleans* (No. 4).

A single 420-horsepower Liberty V-12 engine powered the Douglas World Cruiser biplanes. Their wings spanned 50 feet. The aircraft cruised at 103 miles per hour. Two persons, a pilot and a skilled mechanic, comprised each crew.

Mindful of the 8,000-foot ceiling of the World Cruisers, the project planners kept the flight route away from mountain ranges. They also called for the Army to set up improvised bases along the route stocked with spare engines, floats, and airframe parts. Arrangements were made with local suppliers to provide fuel and other consumables.

The aircraft took off from Seattle on April 6, 1924, and flew via the Alaska coastline and the Aleutian Island chain around the North Pacific Ocean. *Seattle* was lost off the Aleutians, but the crew survived. The three other airplanes continued across Asia, the Middle East, and Europe. Lieutenant Leigh Wade made a forced landing with *Boston* in the North Atlantic near the Faeroes. The crew was rescued but the airplane had to be abandoned. The prototype airplane, christened *Boston II* to honor the lost aircraft, was activated. Lieutenant Wade and Sergeant Henry Ogden flew it to join up with the two surviving airplanes for the end of the journey.

Captain Lowell Smith and Lieutenant Leslie Arnold in *Chicago*, and Lieutenants Erik Nelson and John Harding in *New Orleans*, with Wade and Ogden in *Boston II*, completed the epic journey at Seattle on September 28 after covering more than 26,000 miles in 175 days. Lowell Smith had piloted the receiver airplane on the first successful aerial refueling flights in 1923.

In recognition of the epic globe-girdling flight, the U.S. Army Air Service received the Collier Trophy for 1924. The Douglas Aircraft Company

A poster promotes airmail service from San Francisco to other points at 10 cents per half-ounce. When airmail service began in 1918, the rate was 24 cents per ounce. (FAA)

subsequently adopted the motto "First Around the World—First the World Around."

19

Federal Government Stimulates Aviation

The Post Office Department played a key role in aviation development in the United States. The department established experimental airmail routes in 1918. Army aviators flying Curtiss JN-4 Jennies began the service on May 15, flying between New York and Washington with a stop in Philadelphia. On August 12, 1918, the Post Office took over the operation with its own civilian pilots and new airplanes from Standard Aircraft Corporation.

Transcontinental airmail service began in segments established during 1919 and 1920. The Chicago–Cleveland portion was first, followed by New York–Cleveland. The route was extended from Chicago to Omaha in May 1920 and from Omaha to San Francisco on September 8, 1920. Intermediate stops were made between the terminal cities.

At first the airmail was flown only during daylight and transferred to trains overnight. Soon a system of rotating-light beacons about 10 miles apart marked the airway for night flight. Regular 24-hour transcontinental airmail service began in July, 1924. Eventually, the Post Office lighted 2,041 miles of the transcontinental airway.

The Post Office paid attention to pilot standards and ground support in the airmail service. Pilots were required to have a minimum of 500 flying hours. Regular medical examinations

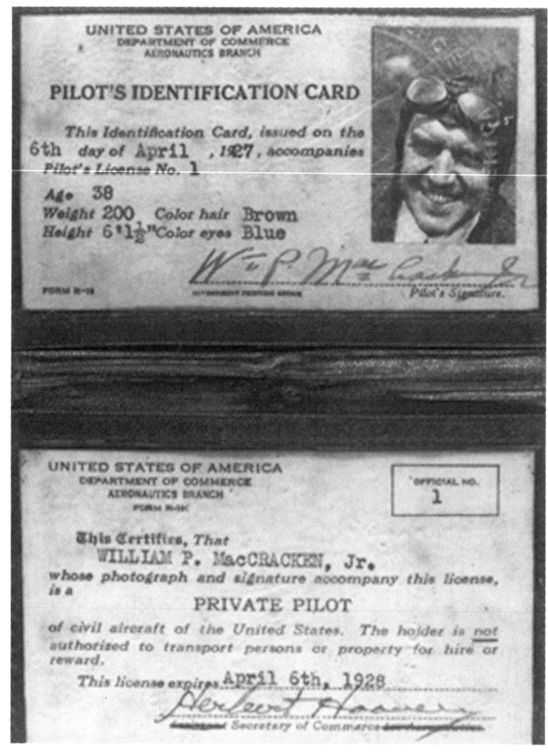
UNITED STATES OF AMERICA
DEPARTMENT OF COMMERCE
AERONAUTICS BRANCH

PILOT'S IDENTIFICATION CARD

This Identification Card, issued on the 6th day of April , 1927, accompanies Pilot's License No. 1

Age 38
Weight 200 Color hair Brown
Height 6'1½" Color eyes Blue

W. P. MacCracken Jr.
Pilot's Signature.

UNITED STATES OF AMERICA
DEPARTMENT OF COMMERCE
AERONAUTICS BRANCH

OFFICIAL NO. 1

This Certifies, That WILLIAM P. MacCRACKEN, Jr. whose photograph and signature accompany this license, is a

PRIVATE PILOT

of civil aircraft of the United States. The holder is not authorized to transport persons or property for hire or reward.

This license expires April 6th, 1928

Herbert Hoover
Secretary of Commerce

April 6, 1927. First pilot's license issued by a civilian agency of the U.S. government. Certification for aircraft, pilots, and mechanics began under the Air Commerce Act of 1926. William P. MacCracken, a World War I aviator and the first chief of the Aeronautics Branch of the Department of Commerce, offered Orville Wright the honor of receiving License No. 1. Mr. Wright declined, noting that he was no longer flying. Also, he did not need a license to prove that he was the first man to fly. (FAA)

ensured their fitness for flight. Mechanics inspected the aircraft after each flight, and engines were overhauled at 100-hour intervals.

The meticulous attention to qualifications and maintenance paid off in safe operations. The

White House, January 14, 1929. President Coolidge (left) awards the 1928 Collier Trophy to the Department of Commerce for developing the air navigation system of the United States. William P. MacCracken, Assistant Secretary of Commerce for Aeronautics, is on the right. Between them, left to right, are Clarence M. Young, Director of Aeronautics at Commerce; Senator Hiram Bingham; and an unidentified man. The five-cent airmail stamp of 1928 depicts one of the 51-foot light beacon towers erected along the airways. (FAA)

airmail service received the Collier Trophy in two successive years. The 1922 award was for a year's operation without a single fatal accident. The award for 1923 recognized development of night flying in commercial transportation.

With passage of the Federal Air Mail Act of 1925, the Post Office got out of operating the airmail service and opened the field for commercial carriers. Congressman Clyde Kelly (R-PA), chairman of the Post Office Committee of the House of Representatives, sponsored the legislation. The law became known as the "Kelly Act." It aimed to encourage commercial aviation and authorized the Postmaster General to contract for mail service. President Calvin Coolidge signed the Kelly bill into law on February 2, 1925, as Public Law 69-309.

Passage of the Kelly Act stimulated the infusion of capital into commercial aviation. Companies could bid for airmail routes and be paid for carrying the mail. The first airmail contracts were awarded in the fall of 1925. Henry Ford received two routes, one from Detroit to Cleveland and the other from Detroit to Chicago. Henry Ford's motor company had begun flying its own freight service between Detroit and Chicago in April of that year.

Other budding airlines received the early contracts for carrying airmail. Colonial Air Lines was awarded the route between New York and Boston. The route between Chicago and Dallas went to National Air Transport. Other contracts were awarded in succeeding months, including those for transcontinental service.

Besides encouraging the development of commercial air carriers, the Kelly Act set the stage for federal regulation of aviation. After the commercial carriers began operation the Post Office Department transferred its system of lights, airways, and radio stations to the Department of Commerce.

Meanwhile, Congress deliberated, debated, and passed the Air Commerce Act, which became Public Law 69-254 when President Coolidge signed it on May 20, 1926. The Air Commerce act set the cornerstone for orderly growth of civil aviation in the United States. Execution of the Air Commerce Act was given into the charge of a new Aeronautics Branch in the Department of Commerce under an assistant secretary, William P. MacCracken.

The bureau's challenge was to promote and encourage aviation while developing regulations and procedures to protect the industry and the public. Its early rules established the framework that guided commercial aviation development for decades. The regulations covered air-traffic procedures and certification of aircraft engines as well as certification, registration, and inspection of aircraft. They also set standards for licensing pilots and mechanics. Aircraft Type Certificate No. 1 was issued to the Buhl Airster C-A3 airplane on March 29, 1927. Frank Gardner of Norfolk, Virginia received the first aircraft mechanic license.

20 Ford Trimotor Leads the Way in All-Metal Passenger Airplanes

William B. Stout wanted to build all-metal airplanes at a time when most of them were built of wood and covered with fabric or plywood. Stout put his ideas into reality. He formed the Stout Metal Airplane Company and built the single-engine Stout 2-AT (for Air Transport), a high-wing monoplane with a Liberty engine as power plant.

Stout chose duralumin as the metal for building his airplane. Duralumin is an alloy formed by

William B. Stout in 1929. Stout's concepts for all-metal airplanes led to the successful Ford Trimotor series and stimulated other airplane manufacturers to step up from wood and fabric to all-metal construction. (From the Collection of Henry Ford Museum & Greenfield Village)

Ford Trimotor 5-AT-112 Tin Goose *on the ramp, 1932. Its 74-foot wingspan was the longest for a commercial landplane of its day. Franklin D. Roosevelt chartered a Ford Trimotor to fly from Albany, New York, to Chicago for the Democratic National Convention in July 1932, making him the first presidential candidate to fly in an airplane. (From the Collection of Henry Ford Museum & Greenfield Village)*

heating aluminum with copper, magnesium, and manganese. The resulting alloy is lightweight but harder and stronger than aluminum.

Auto magnate Henry Ford and his son Edsel invested in Stout's company. In 1925, they bought the company and made it a division of Ford in factory space in Dearborn, Michigan. Henry and Edsel Ford applied their automobile-production and marketing knowledge to the business of building commercial aircraft. They aimed to produce reliable airplanes that met the needs of their customers, the new airlines being formed under stimulus of the Kelly Act.

Henry Ford began scheduled airfreight service between Detroit and Chicago on April 13, 1925, using the 2-AT airplane. Orders for the 2-AT came in from airlines and the Post Office.

The company's first attempt at a three-engine airplane, the 3-AT, was unsuccessful. However, its successor, the Ford Trimotor 4-AT, proved to be a winner. The *Tin Goose* flew for the first time on June 11, 1926. It was designed for passenger carriage instead of mail or freight alone. Eight passengers could be carried in its first version. Passenger capacity grew to 12 in a later version, then to 13, and ultimately to 17 in the improved Ford Trimotor 5-AT.

Airlines quickly placed orders for the Trimotor. The airplane was safe, comfortable, and reliable. It soon became the standard for airline passenger and freight operations. Production continued until June 1933, when the last Ford Trimotor was delivered to Pan American Airways.

21 Goddard Launches First Successful Liquid-Fueled Rocket

Robert H. Goddard laid the foundations for modern rocketry. Goddard developed the theories of rocketry, and also built and tested workable rockets. He taught physics at Clark University in Worcester, Massachusetts, where he had earned his doctorate in 1911.

His early research led to the award of U.S. patents and $5,000 in financial assistance from the Smithsonian Institution. In 1919, Dr. Goddard submitted a progress report to the Smithsonian. The serious parts of the paper received little public notice. Instead, the newspapers seized upon and scoffed at Goddard's notion that a small rocket could fly from the Earth to the Moon. The negative comments convinced Goddard to remain out of the public eye while he continued his research.

In his laboratory at Clark University, Goddard built the first rocket motor fueled by liquid propellants, using a mixture of gasoline and liquid oxygen. He had to solve innumerable problems such as fuel flow, pumping, mixing propellants, and control.

Early in 1926, Goddard was ready to turn his laboratory accomplishments into flight-testing. He flew the world's first successful liquid-propellant rocket on March 16, 1926, from a snow-covered field on his Aunt Effie's farm near Auburn, Massachusetts. In a flight that lasted 2.5 seconds the rocket lifted off to a height of 41 feet and flew a distance of 184 feet.

For rocketry, Goddard's first launch was comparable to the Wright Brothers' first flight at Kitty Hawk. He continued his rocket flights until the local authorities complained that they were too noisy and frightened livestock. Goddard received research

Robert H. Goddard in his laboratory at Clark University with his complete rocket using successful double-action pumps. (NASA, courtesy Mrs. Esther C. Goddard)

Robert H. Goddard at Auburn, Massachusetts, before the 2.5-second flight of the first successful liquid-propellant rocket on March 16, 1926. (NASA, courtesy Mrs. Esther C. Goddard)

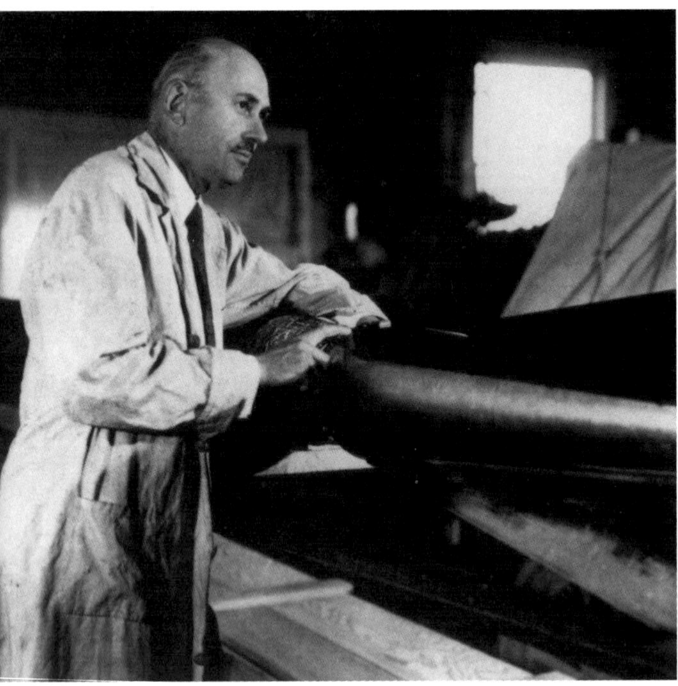

Robert H. Goddard with liquid-fueled rocket in his workshop at Roswell, New Mexico, October 1935. (NASA, courtesy Mrs. Esther C. Goddard)

grants from the Guggenheim Fund and the Smithsonian. He left Massachusetts and moved westward to establish a rocket laboratory near Roswell, New Mexico, with a team of assistants. They developed and flew larger and more complex rockets, adding gyroscopic stabilization and effective controls.

In 1935, Goddard's rockets reached an altitude of 7,500 feet and exceeded the speed of sound. His second report to the Smithsonian, titled "Liquid Propellant Rocket Development," was published in 1936.

Goddard's advances in rocketry did not excite much interest in the United States. However, rocket developers in Germany had been busy on their own lines of research. They took notice of his work and blended his findings into their own experiments. Walther Dornberger, a captain in the German Army, headed rocket research there. In 1932, Dornberger had enlisted a brilliant young man named Wernher von Braun in the liquid rocket work. By 1936, the German Army moved the research and development activities to Peenemunde, an island on the coast of the Baltic Sea. Their progress led to the creation and flight of the A4, later named the V-2, in 1942.

Robert Goddard continued his rocket research throughout the 1930s. During World War II he directed Navy research on liquid-propellant rockets and jet-assisted takeoff rockets for airplanes. He received more than 200 patents for his research.

Goddard can be considered the "father of the space age."

22 First Polar Flights

Roald Amundsen, the Norwegian Arctic explorer, was the first human to see both poles of the Earth. Amundsen led the expedition that arrived first at the South Pole, reaching it on foot on December 14, 1911. In May 1926, Amundsen was in charge of another polar expedition based at Kings Bay on Spitsbergen, a Norwegian island midway between Norway's North Cape and the North Pole.

Amundsen's team planned to fly over the North Pole and traverse the polar region to Alaska aboard the Italian-built dirigible *Norge.* Umberto Nobile, an Italian airman, designed and flew the *Norge.*

Commander Richard E. Byrd of the U.S. Navy headed another expedition at Kings Bay, with the goal of flying over the North Pole. He would make the attempt in a Fokker FVII-3m trimotor airplane fitted with skis instead of wheels. Henry Ford and his son Edsel contributed the airplane and other financial support for the expedition. Byrd named

Commander Richard E. Byrd, polar explorer. (National Archives)

Ford Trimotor 4-AT-15 piloted by Bernt Balchen of the Byrd Antarctic Expedition of 1929. Henry and Edsel Ford donated the airplane to Byrd for the South Pole expedition. Byrd named the airplane Floyd Bennett *in memory of the Navy pilot who flew him on the 1926 attempt to reach the North Pole. (From the Collection of Henry Ford Museum & Greenfield Village)*

the airplane *Josephine Ford* after Edsel Ford's daughter. Floyd Bennett, a noncommissioned naval aviator, piloted the airplane. Byrd navigated.

During a test flight before the main effort, the ski mounts on the *Josephine Ford* buckled. Amundsen permitted Bernt Balchen, one of his expedition members and an experienced Arctic aviator, to assist Byrd. Balchen fashioned sturdier skis out of long lifeboat oars taken off Byrd's expedition ship. The Balchen solution worked.

Byrd and Floyd Bennett took off from Kings Bay at 37 minutes after midnight on May 9, 1926, headed for the North Pole. They returned at seven minutes after 4:00 P.M. the same day. They had been in the air for 15 hours and 30 minutes. The distance to the Pole was 1,529.5 statute miles. Byrd claimed that he and Bennett were first to fly over the Pole and announced it to the world by radio.

Two days later, at 8:50 A.M. on May 11, 1926, Amundsen's expedition, including American explorer Lincoln Ellsworth, launched from Kings Bay aboard the dirigible *Norge*. They flew over the North Pole at 1:25 A.M. on May 12 and continued onward nonstop over the polar cap. *Norge* landed on the morning of May 14 at the village of Teller, about 60 miles south of Nome, Alaska. They had been airborne for 71 hours.

Byrd encouraged Bernt Balchen to join him in the United States, and the Norwegian did so. Balchen and Bert Acosta piloted Byrd's Fokker trimotor named *America* nonstop across the Atlantic to the French coast at the end of June 1927.

In 1928, Commander Byrd made plans for an expedition to fly over the South Pole. Henry and Edsel Ford came through with support again and donated a Ford 4-AT Trimotor airplane. The National Geographic Society also supported the effort. Byrd named the Trimotor airplane *Floyd Bennett* in memory of the loyal Naval aviator who had died of pneumonia in April 1928. Byrd recruited Balchen to fly the airplane.

The Byrd Antarctic Expedition set up base camp called Little America in January 1929. The base was perched on the Ross Ice Shelf south of New Zealand at about 165 degrees west longitude. The expedition prepared and reconnoitered during the Antarctic winter months and into the period of longer daylight in November.

On November 28, 1929, Bernt Balchen lifted the Trimotor from Little America bound for the South Pole. Richard E. Byrd and a radioman and photographer were aboard. The airplane was heavily laden with equipment and supplies. Some of the excess weight had to be jettisoned overboard for the *Floyd Bennett* to reach altitude sufficient to clear the Queen Maude Mountains barring their route to the Pole.

Balchen's navigation calculations put them over the South Pole at 1:14 A.M. on November 29. Byrd had carried an American flag weighted with a stone from Floyd Bennett's grave. He dropped it over the Pole. After circling for several minutes, Balchen flew the *Floyd Bennett* to a supply cache set up months before. They landed and refueled, then returned to Little America. Byrd radioed the news to the world and began receiving acclaim for the feat.

Many years later, doubts surfaced about whether Byrd and Floyd Bennett had actually reached the North Pole in May 1926. After that expedition, Bernt Balchen had flown the *Josephine Ford* around the United States with Floyd Bennett. He determined, and Bennett agreed, that its cruising speed was 70 miles per hour. The distance from Kings Bay to the North Pole was more than 1,500 miles. Balchen concluded that Byrd and Bennett could not have reached the Pole in their flying time of 15 hours and 30 minutes, and must have turned back when they were about 120 statute miles short of their goal.

Other experts evaluated the 1926 flight and meteorological data in the late 1990s, having new access to previously unreleased Byrd papers. They also concluded that Byrd and Bennett did not reach the North Pole in the *Josephine Ford*. The details are told completely in Carroll V. Glines's biography of Balchen titled, *Bernt Balchen, Polar Aviator* (Washington, Smithsonian Institution Press, 1999).

23 Air-cooled Engines Roar Forth

Liquid-cooled aircraft engines such as the ubiquitous 12-cylinder Liberty presented a narrow cross section to the air and created less drag than a radial air-cooled engine. However, liquid-cooled engines suffered weight penalties because of the necessary pumps, radiators, pipes, and gallons of cooling fluids. The Navy did not like liquid-cooled engines for its carrier based airplanes because the repeated pounding of carrier landings caused cracks and leaks in the cooling systems.

Air-cooled engines were free of the weight penalties imposed on their liquid-cooled counterparts. However, the radials' broad cross-section added drag and reduced aircraft performance. To be successful, an air-cooled radial had to deliver extra horsepower and be reliable over many hours of operation.

The Lawrance Corporation, led by Charles L. Lawrance, developed the J, an air-cooled radial delivering 200 horsepower, and won a Navy contract in 1921. The Wright Aeronautical Company bought the Lawrance Corporation in 1923 and began producing the more powerful J-4 and J-5 engines, nicknamed the Whirlwind. Charles Lawrance became a vice president of Wright Aeronautical.

Wright Aeronautical produced Whirlwind engines in versions of five, seven, and nine cylinders radiating outward from the central crankshaft. Power output ranged from 175 up to 450 horsepower. They soon became popular with aircraft manufacturers and the Air Corps in addition to the Navy. (The military designation for the J-5 Whirlwind was R-790, designating a radial engine of 790 cubic inches of piston displacement.) Anthony Fokker used the Whirlwind in the FVII-3m trimotor airplane. Customers buying Ford Trimotor 4-AT airplanes could choose the Whirlwind. Lockheed selected the Whirlwind to power its single-engine Vega.

Frederick B. Rentschler, president of Wright Aeronautical, differed with Lawrance on the direction of the company. He left Wright Aeronautical and formed the new Pratt & Whitney Aircraft Company in 1925. Pratt & Whitney developed its own air-cooled radial aircraft engine named the Wasp, which first ran in December 1925. After passing Navy qualification tests, the nine-cylinder Wasp engine was introduced in 1926. It produced 400 horsepower. The Army Air Corps first bought the Wasp engine in 1932.

Charles L. Lawrance received the Collier Trophy for 1927 for developing the Whirlwind engine.

24 Lindbergh Conquers the Atlantic Alone

In 1919 Raymond Orteig, a New York hotel owner, offered a prize of $25,000 to the first aviator to fly a heavier-than-air craft nonstop from New York to Paris or from Paris to New York. The National Aeronautic Association, as the United States' representative to the Fédération Aéronautique Internationale, administered the rules for the competition.

The Orteig Prize went unclaimed until 1927. Aircraft engines of the day were not reliable enough to make the distance. That changed when the Wright Whirlwind became available. Its reliable endurance made the nonstop flight of 3,610 miles a feasible proposition.

In May 1927 aviators from both France and the United States prepared to make the flight. Two French airmen, Charles Nungesser and Francois

Charles A. Lindbergh and his Spirit of St. Louis *airplane. The Parker Appliance Company (now Parker Aerospace) supplied tube couplings for the aircraft. B.F. Goodrich (now Goodrich) provided the tires. (Courtesy of ASME, via National Air and Space Museum, Smithsonian Institution. SI Neg. No. 86-13507)*

Three transatlantic aviators of 1927 with the Spirit of St. Louis. *Charles A. Lindbergh (left), Richard E. Byrd, (center), and Clarence Chamberlin. (National Air and Space Museum, Smithsonian Institution SI Neg. No. A-48626-C)*

Coli, set off from Paris on May 8. They disappeared over the Atlantic.

Meanwhile, Richard E. Byrd made preparations at Roosevelt Field, Long Island, with a new Fokker Trimotor sponsored by Rodman Wanamaker and named *America*. At nearby Curtiss Field, Clarence Chamberlin readied his airplane named *Columbia*, a Bellanca monoplane, for the crossing.

Into the bustle and excitement on Long Island flew Charles A. Lindbergh, a 25-year old experienced aviator. Lindbergh had "flown the mail" between Chicago and St. Louis and was a captain in the Missouri National Guard. He arrived at Curtiss Field from San Diego by way of St. Louis on May 12 in his Ryan-built monoplane dubbed *Spirit of St. Louis*. The name honored the nine St. Louis businessmen who joined Lindbergh to put up the money to build the airplane and finance the adventure.

Wright Whirlwind engines powered all three of the competing transatlantic airplanes.

When he laid plans for the flight, Lindbergh decided his chances would be better if he flew solo. A reliable engine was the key, mounted in an airplane that had the performance characteristics and could carry enough fuel to make the distance. After unsatisfactory tries with Fokker and Bellanca, Lindbergh established contact with the Ryan Airlines Company in San Diego. In a telegram to the company, Lindbergh asked if Ryan could construct a plane with a Whirlwind engine capable of nonstop flight from New York to Paris. After an exchange of telegrams, the company replied that they could do it within 60 days.

Lindbergh took the train to San Diego and entered into the contract with Ryan Airlines. Donald Hall, the company's engineer, recommended making modifications to the company's Ryan M-2 high-wing monoplane then in airmail service in the western states. Lindbergh and his St. Louis colleagues approved the plan. Work began on February 25, 1927. Wingspan grew by 10 feet from 36 to 46 feet, and the fuselage was extended to make room for a 200-gallon fuel tank. Added to the fuel in a nose tank and three wing tanks, total fuel capacity rose to 425 gallons.

Teamwork exemplified the design and construction activities of the *Spirit of St. Louis*. Charles Lindbergh remained at the Ryan plant, working

Charles Lindbergh addressing Edison Scholarship contestants July 31, 1929, in the courtyard of the Edison Laboratory in West Orange, New Jersey. Thomas Edison is seated to the right of Lindbergh. (National Park Service)

The U.S. Postal Service (USPS) issued this stamp honoring Charles A. Lindbergh on May 14, 1998. The stamp was one of several in the USPS series saluting the "Roaring Twenties." (U.S. Postal Service)

with Hall and company executives and workmen as the airplane took shape. On April 28, 1927, Lindbergh made the first and second test flights from Dutch Flats near the Ryan plant. In a succession of test flights, the design proved sound and Lindbergh developed flight data on the airplane's performance characteristics with varying fuel loads. He left San Diego on May 10, flying nonstop to St. Louis and setting a new speed record of 14 hours and 25 minutes for the distance. After ceremonies in St. Louis, Lindbergh departed for Long Island on May 12, flying a fast passage of seven hours and 20 minutes.

During the time the airplane was being built, Lindbergh had worked out his navigation plans. He subdivided the transatlantic route into 100-mile sections and cut out a special chart section for each. He figured the correct compass headings for each segment and marked the course on the chart for easy access in his cramped cockpit during the flight.

The forecast on the night of May 19–20 offered fair flying weather for the North Atlantic. Lindbergh was prepared and did not delay. He took off from Roosevelt Field, Long Island, at 7:52 A.M. local time on May 20, 1927. He fought fatigue and low ceilings on the crossing, with his altitude ranging from 50 feet above the water up to 10,500 feet. His superb dead-reckoning navigation put him at Dingle Bay on the Irish coast on course in the late afternoon. From that landfall he flew over Plymouth and Cherbourg on his planned course to Paris.

After 33 hours and 30 minutes in the air Lindbergh made a night landing at Le Bourget airport in the northwestern suburbs of Paris at 10:22 P.M. local time. Upon landing he still had 80 gallons of fuel remaining. A crowd of 100,000 persons broke through police lines to greet him and his airplane. People avid for souvenirs ripped fabric off the fuselage. Lindbergh had the damage repaired during his triumphal eight-day visit in Paris.

President Calvin Coolidge dispatched the cruiser USS *Memphis* to transport Lindbergh and the *Spirit of St. Louis* back to the United States. The "Lone Eagle" and his airplane joined the ship at Gosport on the English south coast on May 31 for the voyage home. The USS *Memphis* reached the Washington Navy Yard on June 11, where Lindbergh received a hero's welcome and international acclaim. Raymond Orteig wrote the $25,000 prizewinning check to Lindbergh on June 17, 1927.

Two weeks after Lindbergh's solo transatlantic flight, Clarence Chamberlin flew the Bellanca *Columbia* monoplane nonstop from New York to Eisleben, Germany. Charles A. Levine, a New York businessman, rode with Chamberlin as a passenger.

On June 29, Richard E. Byrd commanded the Fokker trimotor monoplane *America* flown by Bernt Balchen and Bert Acosta on the crossing from New York to France. After more than 42 hours in the air their flight ended in a night ditching in the surf off the village of Ver-sur-Mer near Caen in Normandy.

Lindbergh's feat sparked worldwide enthusiasm, for him in particular and for aviation in general. He used his international stature and celebrity to help advance aeronautical development not only in the United States, but throughout the world. Lindbergh also served with Orville Wright on the National Advisory Committee for Aeronautics.

25 Graf Zeppelin Flies around the World

Captain Hugo Eckener commanded *Graf Zeppelin* (LZ-127) when the giant rigid German airship lifted off from the naval air station at Lakehurst, New Jersey, on August 8, 1929. With 20 passengers and 40 crewmembers, he flew northeast past the Statue of Liberty and headed eastward across the Atlantic Ocean. Captain Eckener brought *Graf Zeppelin* back to Lakehurst on August 29, having flown around the world in 21 days, seven hours, and 34 minutes.

The designation LZ-127 stood for Luftschiffbau Zeppelin number 127, meaning that the airship was the 127th built by the Zeppelin Company of Friederichshafen, Germany. Count (Graf) Ferdinand von Zeppelin founded the company and flew his first airship, LZ-1, in 1900. He died in 1917, aged 79. Hugo Eckener succeeded to leadership of the company.

Graf Zeppelin *(LZ 127) over Chicago on August 28, 1929, nearing the end of the eastbound round-the-world flight. (National Air and Space Museum, Smithsonian Institution SI Neg. No. 86-10070)*

USS Macon *approaches mooring site at Moffett Field, California, in 1933. The Goodyear-Zeppelin Company built the ship. NASA's Ames Research Center is based at Moffett Field. (NASA)*

The *Graf Zeppelin* honored the memory of the company's founder. The 775-foot airship, powered by five engines mounted externally, flew for the first time at Friederichshafen on September 18, 1928. After six test flights, Captain Eckener took *Graf Zeppelin* on its maiden transatlantic passenger flight to the United States in October 1928.

At the time, Eckener was the dean of airship pilots worldwide. He had made more than 3,000 flights in Zeppelin airships by the time of the round-the-world voyage, For that epic trip, Captain Eckener chose a flight route that covered 19,500 miles. He flew the first stage from Lakehurst to Friederichshafen, a distance of 4,200 miles. The next leg spanned 6,800 miles nonstop across Eastern Europe and the Soviet Union over the vastness of Siberia to Tokyo. From Tokyo, *Graf Zeppelin* crossed the Pacific Ocean 5,500 miles nonstop to make landfall at San Francisco and a stop at Los Angeles. On the final leg the airship flew 3,000 miles on a route that took it over Chicago and onward to New York and back to Lakehurst.

In the early 1930s, *Graf Zeppelin* and its sister ship *Hindenburg* (LZ-129) flew transatlantic passenger service between Germany and Lakehurst and between Germany and Rio de Janeiro. Highly flammable hydrogen gas provided the lifting power for the German airships. The *Hindenburg* burst into flames and was destroyed while approaching to tie up at Lakehurst, New Jersey, on May 6, 1937. The disaster spelled the end of the rigid airship in commercial service. The cause of the accident remains a mystery.

Following the *Hindenburg* tragedy, *Graf Zeppelin* was retired from service after having flown for more than 16,000 hours and carrying more than 13,000 passengers.

The Nazi government scrapped the airship in 1940 to use the metal for the Reich war effort.

Airship construction in the United States developed via cooperation between the Goodyear Tire and Rubber Company of Akron, Ohio, and the Zeppelin Company. In 1923 they formed the Goodyear-Zeppelin Corporation to construct rigid airships in North America under license. The U.S.

Interior of USS Macon *control cabin. (NASA)*

Navy contracted with Goodyear-Zeppelin Corporation to build the USS *Macon* and the USS *Akron* along the lines of the German design. Nonflammable helium gas lifted the airships, which were powered by eight internal engines driving external propellers. *Akron* was completed in 1931. On April 4, 1933, she went down in a storm off the coast of New Jersey. Only three persons survived of the 76 on board.

At 785 feet, the USS *Macon* was 10 feet longer than *Graf Zeppelin*. *Macon* was based at Moffett Field, California, from October 1933 until February 11, 1935. On that day, the airship flew into a severe storm off the California coast. The helium gas that provided the lift leaked out and the USS *Macon* fell into the ocean. Two crewmembers died but 81 survived. The Navy commissioned no more rigid airships after the loss of the USS *Macon*.

26 Doolittle Flies on Instruments

James H. "Jimmy" Doolittle was one of the most important aviators in the history of flight. He learned to fly in the Army Air Service in World War I.

Throughout the 1920s and the 1930s, Doolittle pioneered the development of aircraft and flying techniques, setting numerous records and stimulating progress in the pursuit of better and safer aircraft. Among his many achievements was his feat of making the first transcontinental flight within a single day. On September 4, 1922, flying a modified DH-4B aircraft powered by a Liberty 400 engine, Doolittle took off from Pablo Beach, Florida. He landed 2,163 air miles and 21 hours, 20 minutes' flying time later, at Rockwell Field, San Diego, having made just one refueling stop at Kelly Field, Texas.

Six years later, Lieutenant Doolittle flew from McCook Field near Dayton, Ohio, with Captain Albert Stevens to a record altitude of 38,000 feet, in order to demonstrate the capabilities of high-altitude aerial photography.

Flying in that era was basically a fair-weather business. Every pilot risked his or her life, and many lost their lives, when they flew into bad weather and low visibility conditions.

On September 24, 1929, Jimmy Doolittle demonstrated the way to change all that when he proved that a pilot could fly "blind" by relying solely on the instruments in his aircraft. On that morning he flew a 15-minute test flight at Mitchel Field on Long Island, New York, to show that it could be done. Doolittle flew a Consolidated NY-2 test biplane with a hood completely covering the rear cockpit so that he was unable to see outside. Lieutenant Ben Kelsey, another Army aviator, flew as safety pilot in the front cockpit, ready to take over the dual controls if anything went wrong.

Sensitive instruments made possible Doolittle's successful flight. He received directional guidance from a radio range course aligned with the airport. Aircraft attitude was displayed on the Sperry artificial horizon. A Kollsman precision altimeter provided accurate altitude information. A Sperry directional gyro provided accurate measurement of heading and turns.

Doolittle's demonstration accomplished the first "blind flight" in which a pilot took off, flew a predetermined course, and landed, using only the instruments on his dashboard to guide him. Other pilots followed Jimmy Doolittle's lead. Captain A. F. Hegenberger made the first blind solo flight without a check pilot aboard on May 9, 1932, at Dayton, Ohio. Hegenberger's further work in instrument flight led to his receiving the Collier Trophy for 1934 for development of a "successful blind landing system."

Lieutenant James H. Doolittle in cockpit of Consolidated NY-2 biplane before the first official "blind" flight solely by reference to instruments. (National Air and Space Museum, Smithsonian Institution SI Neg. No. 79-9405)

practice a pilot could fly at night or in conditions of bad weather or poor visibility. The basic principles of instrument flying pioneered by Doolittle are still applicable today, although modern instrumentation and displays have advanced considerably since 1929.

Jimmy Doolittle was more than a master pilot and aviation legend. He earned one of the early Doctor of Science (Sc.D.) degrees in Aeronautics from the Massachusetts Institute of Technology. In addition to pioneering instrument flight, he helped to develop high-octane aviation fuel and by his participation in air races influenced the design of future fighter aircraft.

During World War II Jimmy Doolittle conceived and led the surprise raid of 16 B-25 bombers on Tokyo, Japan, on April 18, 1942. He received the Medal of Honor for that mission, and then went on to lead air combat forces in Africa and Europe for the rest of the war.

27 The Link Trainer

Jimmy Doolittle's demonstration of the feasibility of flight solely by reference to instruments was a breakthrough for aviation. Manufacturers began to equip their airplanes with the devices that enabled pilots to fly on instruments and more pilots learned the techniques of instrument flight. Government installation of ground-based navigational aids such as radio beacons built vital connections with aircraft in flight.

But an essential element was missing. That was the ability to train pilots to fly, and to fly on instruments, without leaving the ground. Edwin A. Link provided the missing connection when he invented the Link Trainer, the device that enabled effective ground-based instrument flight training.

Edwin Link grew up in his father's pipe organ business in Binghamton, New York. He learned to fly in the 1920s. As Link gained more flight experience, he decided to devise a method of teaching people to fly while still on the ground. By follow-

World War II photo of interior of the Link factory where Link Trainers were being assembled. (National Air and Space Museum, Smithsonian Institution SI Neg. No. 2000-3648)

Edwin Link, inventor of the Link Trainer, at his factory during World War II. (National Air and Space Museum, Smithsonian Institution SI Neg. No. 99-41451)

ing his methods, fledgling pilots could make mistakes and learn from their errors.

Toward the end of the decade, Link used his knowledge of organ design to build a training device that gave a fair representation of the movements of an airplane in flight. The first Link Trainer was ready in 1929. The device replicated a generic airplane cockpit with the usual controls and instruments. Movements of the flight controls activated air valves and bellows to cause the trainer to respond in kind.

For instrument training, a trainee pilot sat in the enclosed cockpit with no outside references, connected to an instructor by headphones. The instructor created the outside stimuli necessary for the particular phase of training. The cues might be radio transmissions from other aircraft or air traffic control, or signals from ground-based navigation aids such as radio ranges. The trainee followed instructions and practiced maneuvers and procedures necessary for safe flight. Electrical linkages from the trainer to the instructor's table traced the flight onto a map for review and discussion after the simulated flight.

Airlines and the armed services recognized the value of the Link Trainer and began using it to train their pilots. When the advent of World War II triggered a vast expansion in pilot training, the entire production of Link Trainers went to the military.

The Link Trainer represented all aircraft, not any specific type. A pilot learned and practiced instrument flying procedures on its basic complement of instruments and controls. Once a pilot learned the basic techniques to a required level of proficiency, the procedures could be adapted to the specific cockpit layout of the aircraft the pilot actually flew.

In the decades after World War II, Link and other manufacturers began to build simulators to replicate particular aircraft. Thus, a pilot training on a modern simulator found all the controls, instruments, and switches in the right places.

As computing power became available and affordable, flight simulators gained the ability to create ever more realistic training. Virtual reality displays of the situation outside the cockpit created a realistic feel for the crewmember. Audio cues and full-motion capabilities complemented the displays and reinforced the learning. Crew members training in a modern simulator thereby experienced the sounds, feels, and sights of actually flying the airplane it represented. In addition to learning and practicing routine procedures and techniques, pilots also encountered emergency situations ranging from bothersome to catastrophic, and learned how to cope with and manage them for safe flight.

28 Supermarine and Rolls-Royce Win Schneider Trophy for Great Britain

Jacques Schneider, a French industrialist, established the Schneider Trophy for racing seaplanes in 1912. Seaplanes representing individual nations competed for speed. The first race was held in Monaco in 1913. Maurice Prevost won it for France, flying a Deperdussin monoplane at an average speed of almost 46 miles per hour.

The race was held again in 1914 when Great Britain won, but was suspended during World War I. Italy took the honors in 1920 and 1921, advancing the winning speed to 117 mph. The British won again in 1922, racking the speed up to 145 mph. A competing nation had to win three times to gain permanent possession of the Schneider Trophy.

The United States won the contest twice in succession: in 1923 at Cowes, England, and in 1925 at Baltimore, Maryland, with Navy-sponsored Curtiss biplanes. Jimmy Doolittle flew a Curtiss R3C-2 to victory in the 1925 race. He set the new world seaplane speed record at 245 mph at Baltimore on October 26. In the next contest, Italy beat the U.S. team to win the 1926 race.

The British did not enter the 1926 race, the government preferring to support the research and development to prepare for the 1927 race at Venice. The investment paid off when Flight Lieutenant S. N. Webster of the Royal Air Force flew the Supermarine S.5 designed by Reginald J. Mitchell to a new speed record of 283 mph.

The British won the next race held in 1929 at Spithead on the English south coast. Reginald Mitchell improved the S.5 design to create the Supermarine S.6. For its power plant, Sir Henry Royce of Rolls-Royce designed a new engine designated "R."

The R was a liquid-cooled V-12 engine that developed 2,000 horsepower. The combination

British team members for the 1931 Schneider Trophy contest with the Supermarine S.6B at Calshot, near Southampton, on August 11, 1931. Royal Navy Lieutenant J. N. Boothman, who won the race on September 12, is second from left. Royal Air Force Flight Lieutenant G. H. Stainforth, who set the absolute world seaplane record of 347 mph days after the 1931 race, is fourth from left. (National Archives)

Launching the Supermarine S.6 seaplane that won the 1929 Schneider Trophy. (National Air and Space Museum, Smithsonian Institution SI Neg. No. 2000-3649)

created a second victory for the British with an average speed of 328 mph.

Looking ahead to 1931, Supermarine and Rolls-Royce improved the airplane-engine combination. The airplane was designated S.6B. Rolls-Royce boosted the "R" engine power output to 2,300 horsepower. Flight Lieutenant J. N. Boothman flew the S.6B to 340 mph, another new seaplane speed record, at Spithead on September 12, 1931. With that third victory, Great Britain took permanent possession of the Schneider Trophy.

Over its lifetime, the stimulus of the Schneider Trophy led to significant advances in engine and airframe development. The Supermarine S.6B powered by the Rolls-Royce R engine was the direct ancestor of the Spitfire fighter designed by Reginald Mitchell and powered by the Rolls-Royce Merlin V-12 engine, which first flew in 1936. The Spitfire fighter proved decisive in Britain's victory over the Nazi Luftwaffe in the Battle of Britain in the summer of 1940.

Twelve-cylinder Rolls-Royce "R" engine on test stand at Derby, England, 1929. The "R" powered the Supermarine S-6 to victory in the Schneider Trophy seaplane races of 1929 and 1931, earning Britain's permanent possession of the cup. (Courtesy of the Rolls-Royce Heritage Trust)

29 Pan American Pioneers Transoceanic Service

Pan American Airways pioneered commercial airline routes from the United States over the world's oceans. Juan T. Trippe, a World War I naval aviator, led Pan Am from 1928 until he retired in 1972.

Pan American began international operations by carrying the mail from Key West, Florida, to Havana, Cuba, in October 1927. Passenger service on the route began in 1928. In 1929, Trippe engaged Charles A. Lindbergh to provide technical advice and to fly with him in surveys of new over-water routes. The Sikorsky S-38 two-engine flying boat was the airplane of choice. The airline soon expanded service to cover key destinations in the Caribbean and then Panama and onward to South America.

Igor Sikorsky followed the success of his S-38 by building the S-40 and then the S-42 flying boats to Trippe's requirements. Trippe's airline later bought flying boats from other manufacturers such as Martin and Boeing. All received a Clipper nickname. Examples included *American Clipper, China Clipper, Dixie Clipper*, and *Yankee Clipper.*

Martin's model M-130 flying boat began service with Pan American in November 1935. The Martin *China Clipper* flew the first air mail from San Francisco to Manila in the Philippines over the week of November 22–29, 1935, with stops in Honolulu, Midway Island, Wake Island, and Guam. Pan American started regular weekly passenger service between San Francisco and Manila in October 1936.

The transpacific achievement earned Pan American Airways the Collier Trophy for 1936 "for establishment of the transpacific airplane and the successful execution of extended overwater navigation in the regular operations thereof."

Juan Trippe (left) with Charles Lindbergh in British Guiana in 1929, surveying the Pan American route through the Caribbean. Aircraft is a Sikorsky S-38 flying boat. (National Air and Space Museum, Smithsonian Institution SI Neg. No. 79-10994)

Boeing's Model 314 flying boat joined the Clipper fleet in June 1939 on the transatlantic route from New York to the Azores and thence to the European continent at Lisbon, Portugal. One month later, the airline added service between New York and Southampton, England. A crew of ten staffed the giant airliner, which carried up to 74 passengers.

World War II interrupted transoceanic commercial passenger operations. Pan American and its crews and flying boats joined the war effort in long-range air transport service.

President Franklin D. Roosevelt became the first president to fly as a passenger while in office, in January 1943. He flew in the Pan American Boeing 314 *Dixie Clipper* from Miami to French Morocco for the Casablanca conference with British Prime Minister Winston Churchill.

Sikorsky S-40 flying boat taxiing. Pan American ordered the S-40 from Sikorsky in December 1929 and placed the first one in service in October 1931. The S-40, with capacity for up to 40 passengers, was the first aircraft to carry the "Clipper" designation for Pan American. (Florida State Archives)

Pan American's Boeing 314 Capetown Clipper *on takeoff from New York headed across the Atlantic for Lisbon, Portugal, via the Azores. The 314, with a range of 3,500 miles, entered scheduled transatlantic service in June 1939 and transpacific service to New Zealand in 1940. (Copyright The Boeing Company)*

Dining salon of Boeing 314 Clipper in Pan American service. The salon could be turned into a lounge and a bridal suite. Boeing built 12 Model 314s. (Copyright The Boeing Company)

Three four-engine Pan American Sikorsky S-40 Clippers fly over Miami, Florida. Sikorsky followed the S-40 with the larger and longer-range S-42, which entered service in 1934. (Florida State Archives)

U.S. Customs officers meet passengers deplaning from Fokker F-10 operated by Western Air Express. (FAA)

Industry Tries Its Wings 1930–1939

Aviation advances cascaded in the 1930s as the industry matured and responded to the needs of commerce and government. The federal government expanded the system of airways, encouraging airline development. National air races such as the Thompson and Bendix trophies offered prizes and spurred the design of speedier airplanes while stirring public excitement about aviation.

Aviators not only flew faster; they broke distance and altitude records. Female pilots showed they could fly as well as men. General-aviation manufacturers began to build affordable and safe airplanes that extended the gift of flight to ordinary people.

Passenger aircraft became larger and safer. All-metal construction replaced wood and fabric. Research by the National Advisory Committee on Aeronautics (NACA) proved the virtues of engine cowlings and mounting engines in streamlined nacelles on multi-engine airplanes.

The aeronautical technologies that created profitable airliners also contributed to development of long-range bombers, which would be needed in the next decade. Other now-familiar technologies such as radar, helicopters, and jet propulsion all came into being in the decade of the 1930s.

30 Radio Beacons Define the Airways

Glen Gilbert (right), the "father of air traffic control," with J. V. Tighe at the Newark Airway Traffic Control Station, the first in the nation. Gilbert calculated time and distance with a circular slide rule. Tighe developed the markers nicknamed "shrimp boats" that represented aircraft moving across the map. (FAA)

In its 1921 annual report, the NACA recommended establishment of a federal airways system to include provision of extended weather service "indispensable to the success and safety of air navigation."

The Aeronautics Branch of the Department of Commerce developed a practical radio navigation beam system in 1927. The system transmitted aural signals in Morse code over assigned radio frequencies. Pilots tuned radio receivers in their aircraft to the frequency for a specific beacon. By listening to the signals they could determine if they were on course, or off course to left or right, and could make the appropriate corrections to their heading.

Successful flight tests were conducted over the New York to Cleveland airway between July 1927 and February 1928. By the middle of 1929, pilots could use radio beacon service over the airway between Omaha and New York. Installation expanded through 1930 and 1931, when the radio marking of the route from San Francisco to New York was completed.

Also in 1928, the Commerce Department started sending aviation weather text information over its teletype network. The first four stations connected to the central office in Washington for this service were in Chicago, Illinois; Cleveland, Ohio; Concord, California; and Hadley Field, New Jersey. The system expanded to cover 45 states by October 1938. Experiments in sending weather maps over the teletype system succeeded in 1932 and the Aeronautics Branch began sending them to 78 air terminals.

Basic air traffic control began in the early 1930s. Cleveland Municipal Airport established a control tower equipped with radio in 1930. Other cities followed Cleveland's lead. By the mid-1930s the volume of air traffic at busy terminals such as Cleveland and Newark and Chicago threatened to become hazardous.

In 1935, a group of airlines organized a company called Air Traffic Control, Incorporated to set up airway traffic control centers and operate them until the federal government could assume the mission. The first station at Newark, New Jersey, began operation on December 1, 1935. It provided information to airline pilots about the location of other airplanes in the area. Similar centers opened in Chicago and Cleveland by June 1936. On July 6, 1936, the government took over operation of the three centers and began expanding the air traffic control system nationwide.

Air traffic controllers in action at Oakland Airway Traffic Control Center in 1939. By 1939 the Federal Airways System covered 25,500 statute miles and operated 231 radio range stations. (FAA)

31 Amelia Earhart, Trailblazer

Amelia Earhart was born in Atchison, Kansas, in 1897. She qualified as a pilot in 1921 and became a serious professional aviator in the ensuing years. She continually improved her skills and gained experience, and eventually qualified as a transport pilot, the highest rating. During her career she set many new aviation records, added glamour to aviation, and provided a stellar example for others.

Earhart became the first woman to fly the Atlantic in June 1928 when she accompanied Wilbur Stulz and Louis Gordon as a passenger on their nonstop flight from Newfoundland to Ireland. She wrote about the experience in her book titled *20 hours 40 minutes.*

The public responded to Amelia Earhart's style and achievements. She and other early female pilots competed in the Women's Air Derby in August 1929. They joined together to form the Ninety-Nines, an organization of female pilots. She served as first president of the Ninety-Nines.

In May 1932, Amelia Earhart became the first person to fly the Atlantic twice and the first woman to make the flight alone. She flew the Atlantic in her single-engine Lockheed Vega airplane on the fifth anniversary of Charles Lindbergh's solo flight from New York to Paris. She took off from Harbor Grace, Newfoundland and flew nonstop to Londonderry, Ireland, in 15 hours and 18 minutes.

Amelia Earhart discusses data on the new Lockheed Electra Model 10E airplane with Clarence L. "Kelly" Johnson, chief designer in the company's Advanced Development department. (Lockheed Martin Corporation)

Allan Lockheed holds a model of his Vega airplane. The Lockheed Vega flew for the first time on July 4, 1927. It established Lockheed's enduring reputation for excellence. (Lockheed Martin Corporation)

Two and one-half years later, Amelia Earhart flew the first nonstop solo flight across the Pacific from Hawaii to Oakland, California. She accomplished the feat on January 11–12, 1935, in 18 hours and 15 minutes.

Earhart was also determined to circle the globe. She chose a near-equatorial route, adding to the challenges and risks. Purdue University financed a new Lockheed Electra twin-engine airplane for the adventure. Her first attempt began at the west coast with a first stop in Hawaii. The adventure was cut short in Hawaii when she damaged the airplane on takeoff for the next leg. The airplane was shipped back to the United States for repair.

With her Electra repaired and ready again, she and navigator Fred Noonan departed from Miami, Florida, on June 1, 1937. They flew eastward across the South Atlantic and Africa onward to Lae, New Guinea. On July 2, 1937, Earhart and Noonan took off from Lae bound for tiny Howland Island, a speck in the Pacific Ocean more than 2,500 miles to the east. They never arrived. But Amelia Earhart's example inspired others to reach for the sky, as she had.

A jubilant Irish crowd welcomes Amelia Earhart and her Lockheed Vega on completion of her transatlantic solo flight. (Lockheed Martin Corporation)

Wiley Post Flies Far and High

32

Plenty of vivid characters peopled the aviation world in the 1930s. Wiley Post was one of the most intriguing. A Texas native, Post worked in the Oklahoma oil fields, where he lost his left eye in a drilling accident. The loss did not deter him from learning to fly. He became a barnstormer, wing-walker, and parachutist.

Post obtained a job as pilot with an oil company whose president, F. C. Hall, bought a new Lockheed Vega for Post to fly. They nicknamed the airplane *Winnie Mae* after Hall's daughter. Post flew the airplane in the 1930 National Air Races and won, setting a record of nine hours, nine minutes, and four seconds from Los Angeles to Chicago.

A record-setting flight around the world came next for Post and the Vega. He and navigator Harold Gatty took off from Roosevelt Field, Long Island, on the morning of June 23, 1931. They flew eastward along a route in the northern hemisphere that covered 15,500 miles. After eight days, 15 hours, and 51 minutes Post and Gatty landed back at their starting point.

Two years later Wiley Post took off again on a global flight, this time to do it alone. He had added an automatic pilot and radio direction finding equipment to the instrumentation aboard *Winnie Mae*. He took off from Roosevelt Field on July 15, 1933, and flew along a route similar to the one he and Gatty flew in 1931. He battled sleep and fatigue and kept going, ultimately beating his earlier time by almost a day. He arrived back at the starting point on July 22, completing the flight in seven days, 18 hours, and 49 minutes.

Post wanted to open up high-altitude flight for passengers and freight. He sought a means of maintaining pressure and providing oxygen when flying at high altitudes. His plywood Vega airplane could not be pressurized, so he chose an individual pressure suit as the solution. B.F. Goodrich built three "stratosphere suits" for Post. They answered the need for pressure and oxygen while permitting the mobility he needed to fly the airplane. In a series of research flights, he proved the existence of the jet stream as well as the potential for regular flights at higher altitudes.

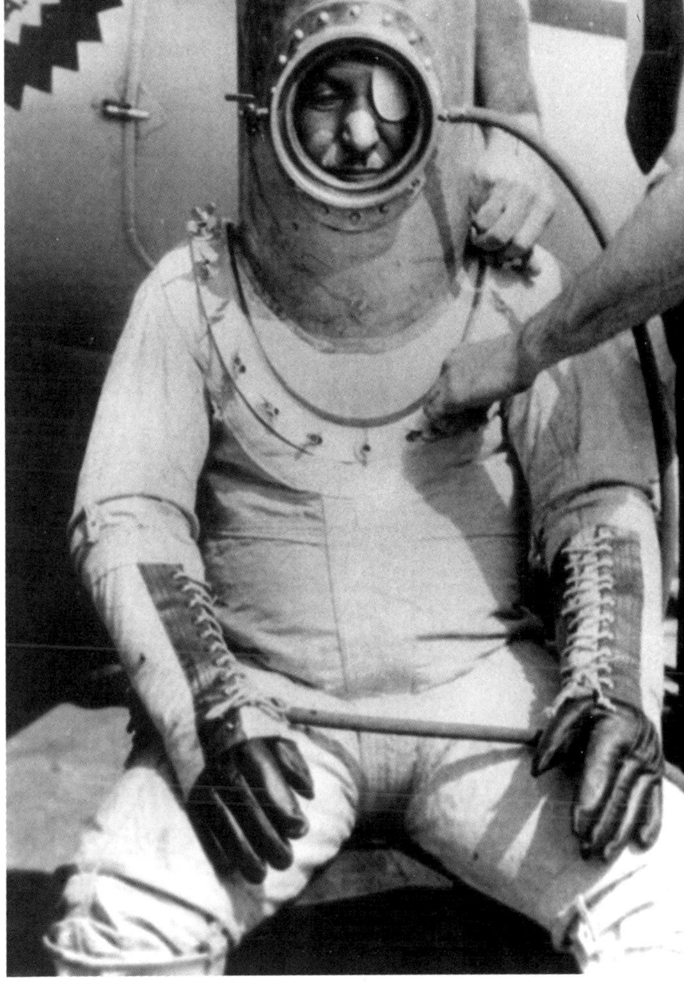

Wiley Post in his B.F. Goodrich "stratosphere suit" is ready for high-altitude flight. (Photo courtesy of Goodrich Corporation)

Wiley Post's life ended near Point Barrow, Alaska, on August 15, 1935, in a takeoff accident. His companion, the humorist Will Rogers, also died in the mishap.

Wiley Post in his B. F. Goodrich pressure suit climbs into his Lockheed Vega Winnie Mae. *He made many high-altitude flights, including a flight over Chicago at an altitude of 40,000 feet on September 5, 1934. (Lockheed Martin Corporation)*

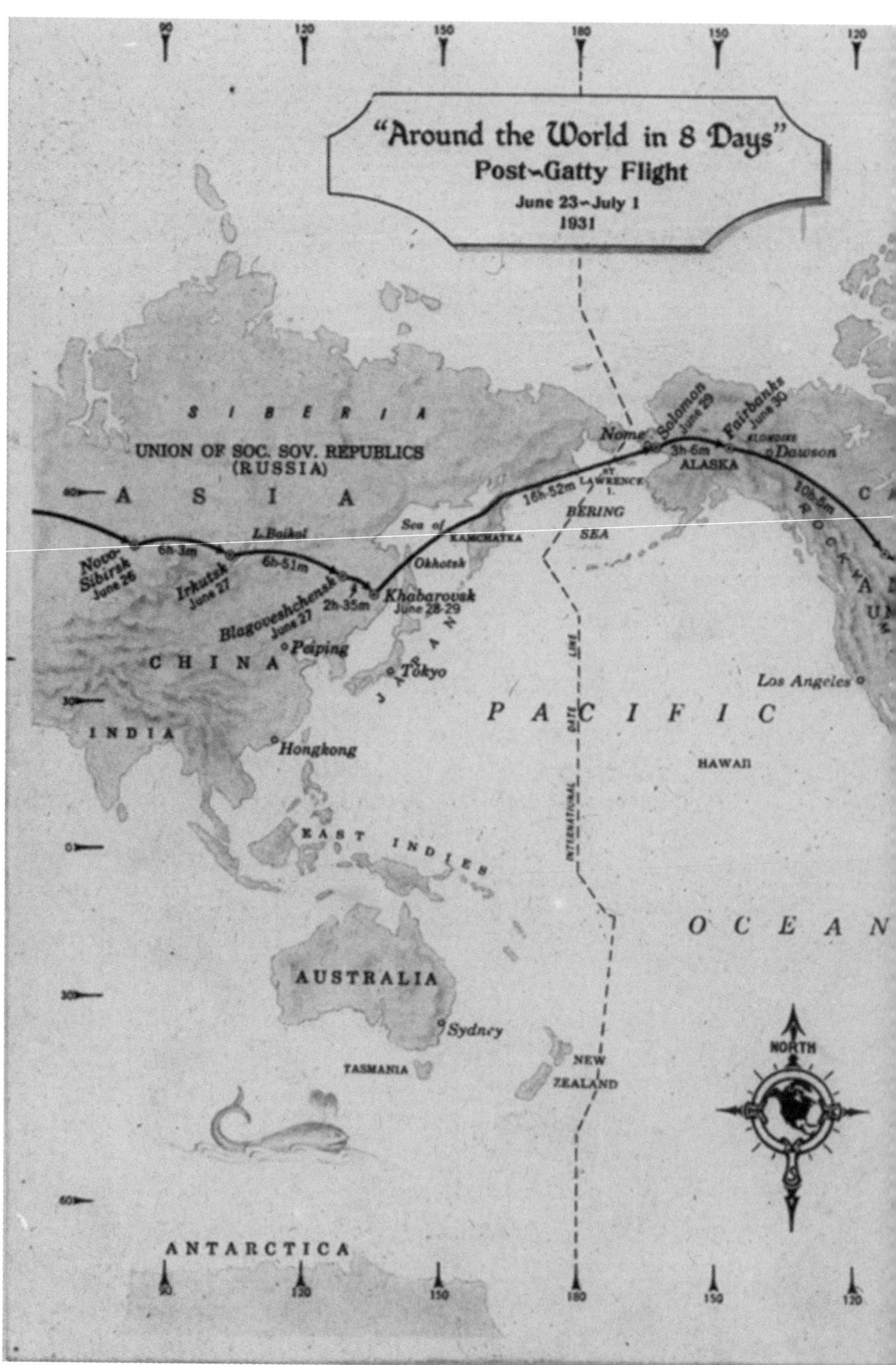

Route of the Wiley Post–Harold Gatty round-the-world flight. (National Archives)

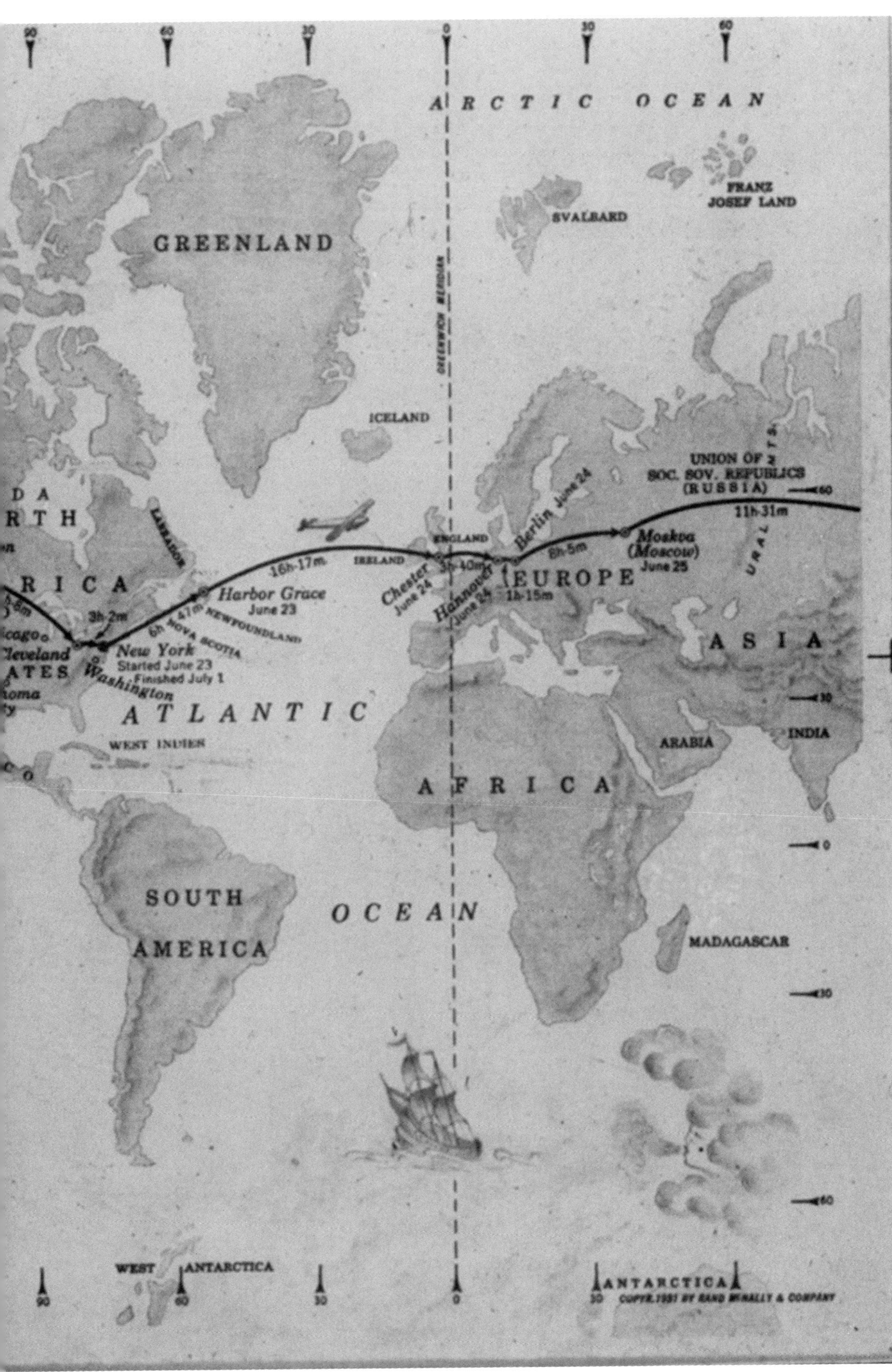
ARCTIC OCEAN
FRANZ JOSEF LAND
SVALBARD
GREENLAND
GREENWICH MERIDIAN
ICELAND
UNION OF SOC. SOV. REPUBLICS (RUSSIA)
11h-31m
Moskva (Moscow) June 25
8h-5m
Berlin June 24
ENGLAND
IRELAND
16h-17m
Chester June 24
3h-40m
Hannover June 24
1h-15m
EUROPE
URAL MTS.
LABRADOR
Harbor Grace June 23
NEWFOUNDLAND
NOVA SCOTIA
6h 47m
3h-2m
New York Started June 23 Finished July 1
Washington
ASIA
ATLANTIC
WEST INDIES
ARABIA
INDIA
AFRICA
SOUTH AMERICA
OCEAN
MADAGASCAR
WEST ANTARCTICA
ANTARCTICA
COPYR. 1931 BY RAND McNALLY & COMPANY

33 DC-3 Captures the Airliner Market

Boeing built the first truly modern airliner, the twin-engine, 10-passenger Boeing 247. Its maiden flight took place on February 8, 1933. The four airlines that later combined into United Airlines bought 60 of the 247s. Their order froze out competing airline customers and occupied Boeing's production capacity for two years.

Meanwhile, Donald W. Douglas built the Douglas DC-1 (for Douglas Commercial-1) to the order of Transcontinental and Western Air (TWA) and flew it for the first time on July 1, 1933. Douglas lengthened the DC-1 to create the DC-2, which carried 14 passengers. TWA put the DC-2 into service in June 1934.

C. R. Smith, president of American Airlines, wanted a transport that improved upon the DC-2, an airliner that could make money carrying passengers and free his airline from dependence upon government mail-carrying subsidies. Douglas designed the DC-3 in two versions for American; one with sleeper berths that carried 14 passengers for overnight flights and a standard version for 21 seated passengers.

Douglas's DC-3 airplane justified C. R. Smith's confidence in the company.

The DC-3 became the airliner that transformed commercial air travel. United Airlines followed American, becoming the second customer for the DC-3 by placing its order in November 1936. Within the next two years, 30 more airlines ordered the DC-3. By 1939, the Douglas DC-2 and DC-3 carried more than 90 percent of U.S. airline passengers. Designed initially for 21 passengers, later versions of the DC-3 carried up to 28 passengers.

The Collier Trophy for 1935 went to Donald W. Douglas and his technical and production personnel for the DC-3.

Douglas built 448 commercial DC-3s for airline customers. Its contribution to airline travel is reflected in the number of passengers carried. In 1935 all the scheduled airlines of the United States carried 679,000 revenue passengers on domestic flights. In 1941 the number of revenue passengers grew fivefold to 3,849,000.

Prototype Douglas DC-3 flew for the first time on December 17, 1935. It seated 21 passengers in the standard airline configuration. Its range was 1,495 miles. (Copyright The Boeing Company)

American Airlines bought the first Douglas DC-3 transport. The Douglas Sleeper Transport carried 14 passengers in luxury. They could sleep in berths for overnight flights. (National Air and Space Museum SI Neg. No. 91-7082)

The DC-3's military version received the designations C-47 (Army) and R-4D (Navy) and the nickname of Gooney Bird. Douglas and other manufacturers built more than 10,100 C-47s during the war. Each C-47 cost the government $85,035. General Eisenhower called the C-47 one of the most important weapons of World War II.

After World War II, surplus C-47s provided the airplanes for the expansion of commercial aviation. Domestic passenger numbers nearly tripled from 6,576,000 in 1945 to 17,345,000 in 1950.

The C-47 continued in military service through the Korean War and Vietnam conflict. During the Vietnam War, the U.S. Air Force modified the C-47 to a potent gunship, the AC-47. Hundreds of DC-3s were still in service in 2002, 67 years after the first one flew.

Ground crewmembers load freight into forward baggage compartment of a Delta Air Lines DC-3. (National Archives)

B-17 Flying Fortress

His experience in World War I led Army Brigadier General William "Billy" Mitchell to foresee the need for long-range, heavy bombers as an important contribution to victory in future wars. Mitchell demonstrated the power of air bombardment in July 1921. He led a group of Martin MB-2 bombers to drop 2,000-pound bombs against the captured German battleship *Ostfreisland* off the Virginia Capes. The battleship sank, but the Navy remained skeptical about the value of Army bombers against warships.

By the mid-1930s, the Army Air Corps invited manufacturers to propose a large multiengine bomber. Boeing financed, designed, and built its entry, the Model 299, from drawing board to first flight in less than a year. The Boeing 299 (XB-17) prototype flew for the first time on July 28, 1935. After extensive flight testing and evaluation the Army ordered the airplane into low-rate production. By the time of Pearl Harbor, December 7, 1941, the Army possessed only 131 B-17s.

With defensive armament of five .30-caliber machine guns, the B-17 was nicknamed the "Flying Fortress." The B-17's capabilities grew as successive models were modified based on combat experience. For example, the B-17E carried nine machine guns compared with five on the prototype.

The B- 17G was the final model and became the definitive "Fortress." It had a 10-man crew, was powered by four 1,200 hp Wright R-1820-97 Cyclone radial piston engines that provided a cruising speed of about 150 mph. The B-17G carried a bomb load of up to 20,000 pounds. Its crewmen defended the aircraft and themselves against enemy fighters by firing 13 heavy .50-caliber machine guns mounted to shoot in all directions.

B-17 bomber units flew in squadron formations that became building blocks for bomb

William E. Boeing founded the Boeing Company in 1916 in a boat builder's shop in Seattle, Washington. He built a flying boat and then landplanes to carry the mail and passengers. (Copyright The Boeing Company)

Boeing B-17C entered combat with the Royal Air Force in July 1941. Combat service demonstrated the need for more defensive firepower than its seven machine guns. (Copyright The Boeing Company)

Boeing B-17G was a true "Flying Fortress," armed with 13 .50-caliber machine guns. The sturdy airplane was capable of absorbing punishment from enemy fighters and anti-aircraft fire to continue its missions. (Copyright The Boeing Company)

groups of scores of airplanes arrayed horizontally and vertically for defense and for maximum impact on targets below when all the bombers in the group released their bombs at the same time.

Flying Fortresses flew and fought in every theater of World War II. On the first offensive operation of the U.S. 8th Air Force in Europe, Brigadier General Ira Eaker piloted a B-17F named *Yankee Doodle* to lead a 12-plane formation against rail yards near Rouen in northern France on August 17, 1942. B-17s formed the backbone of the 8th Air Force and the 15th Air Force in the air offensive against Germany. They dropped a total of 640,000 tons of bombs and helped to cripple Germany's ability to carry on the war.

In a wartime collaborative production effort, Boeing, Douglas, and Lockheed built a total of 12,726 B-17 Flying Fortresses. Each wartime B-17 cost $187,742. Almost all B-17s were scrapped after the war. A few have been restored and are flown by aviation heritage groups.

35

Female Aviators Excel

Amelia Earhart and 19 other female pilots flew from Los Angeles to Cleveland in the Women's Air Derby in August 1929. This was the first cross-country air race for women. At that time, only 6,000 persons in the United States held pilot licenses. However, only 40 women met the eligibility requirements for the air derby, which included possessing a current pilot license and more than 100 hours of solo flying.

The race began at Santa Monica, California, and ended at Cleveland, Ohio. After eight days of flying, 14 pilots finished the race. Louise Thaden won. Gladys O'Donnell finished second, and Amelia Earhart came in third. The Collier Trophy for 1929 was awarded to Louise Thaden for her victory.

Louise Thaden won the Women's Air Derby of 1929 flying a Beech Travel Air from Santa Monica to Cleveland. (National Air and Space Museum, Smithsonian Institution SI Neg. No. 83-2121)

Blanche Noyes (left), Vincent Bendix, and Louise Thaden at the award of the 1936 Bendix Trophy to Thaden and Noyes. (National Air and Space Museum, Smithsonian Institution SI Neg. No. 83-2174)

In 1931, millionaire Vincent Bendix offered a trophy in his name for a free-for-all cross-country air race. By establishing the trophy, Bendix intended to encourage experimental developments by airplane designers and to improve aviators' cross-country flying and navigational skills. Major James H. Doolittle won the first race by flying from Los Angeles to Cleveland in nine hours, ten minutes, and 21 seconds.

Initially, female pilots were banned from the Bendix race. The ban was lifted in 1935. Three female crews led the field in the 1936 race. On September 4, Louise Thaden and Blanche Noyes won the race, flying a Beechcraft Staggerwing C-17R from New York to Los Angeles in 14 hours, 55 minutes. Laura Ingalls came in second. Amelia Earhart and Helen Richey finished fifth.

With that triumphant showing by female pilots, no longer would people ask if women could fly as well as men. The results of the 1936 Bendix Trophy race settled the question.

Among their many aviation endeavors, Thaden and Noyes flew for the government's Bureau of Air Commerce's air marking program. Both pilots were charter members of the Ninety-Nines, the organization started in 1929 by 99 licensed female pilots (see its Web site at *www.ninety-nines.org*).

Other female pilots who made aviation history around the same time as Louise Thaden included Helen Richey, the first female airline pilot, who received the Collier Trophy in 1934; and Jacqueline Cochran, who established and led the Women Airforce Service Pilots (WASP) in World War II. Cochran also received the Collier Trophy for 1953 for being the first woman to fly supersonic.

Piper Cub Leads General Aviation Expansion

In the years immediately after World War I, former military pilots barnstormed the country with daring air shows. Their feats stimulated the enthusiasm of old and young alike. National air races and long-distance flights further fueled public interest in aviation. The barnstormers flew mostly war-surplus airplanes, cheap but past their prime. The speedsters and record-setters flew new but expensive airplanes. A safe and affordable airplane was needed so that the large numbers of people interested in flying could be turned into people who actually flew.

William T. Piper, Sr., was instrumental in the process that made flying affordable in the 1930s. His name became forever associated with the airplanes built under his leadership, the Piper Cubs.

Piper had made his fortune in the Pennsylvania oil business. In 1929, he invested in the Taylor Brothers Aircraft Company in Bradford, Pennsylvania. C. G. Taylor headed the company. Piper supported Taylor's development of a simple two-place airplane dubbed the E-2 Cub, which first flew on September 10, 1930. The E-2 became the forerunner of a long line of airplanes with the Cub nickname.

When the economy turned down, the company was forced into bankruptcy and Piper took control. C. G. Taylor stayed with the company as its chief engineer. In 1936, the company introduced an improved two-place light airplane designated the J-2 Cub. Taylor parted with Piper in that year. He moved to Alliance, Ohio, and started up another airplane company with his name, the Taylorcraft Aviation Company.

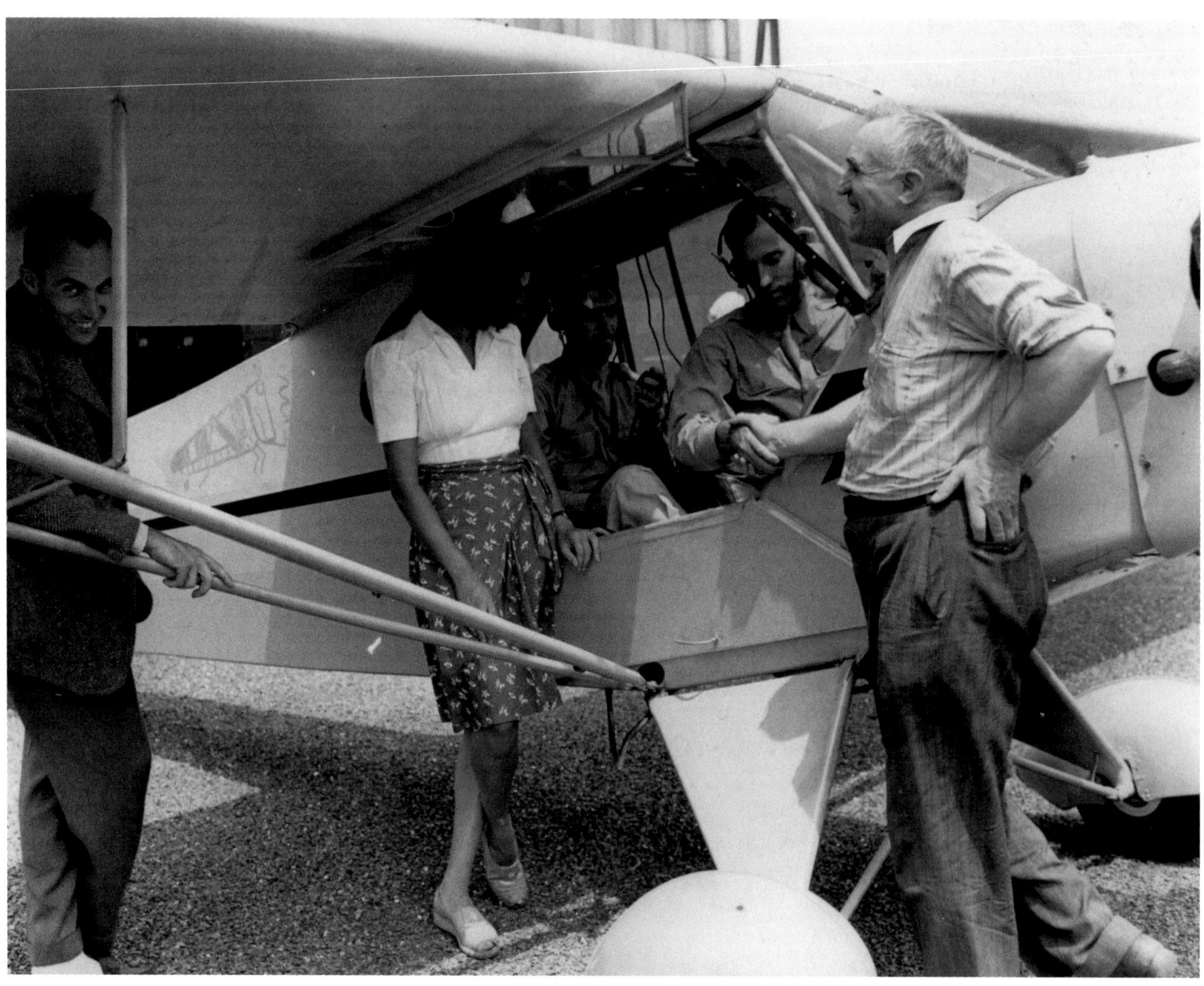

William T. Piper, Sr. (far right), congratulates his sons Pug and Tony after a demonstration flight of a Piper Cub destined for participation in Army maneuvers in 1941. Bill Piper, Jr., leans on a wing strut next to an unidentified woman. The airplane became an L-4 Grasshopper in Army service. Note the grasshopper insignia on the fuselage. Location is the Piper factory at Lock Haven, Pennsylvania. (National Air and Space Museum, Smithsonian Institution SI Neg. No. 2000-3651)

The Stinson L-5 was another general aviation airplane that was drafted into World War II military service. These two are in flight over Burma. The L-5 carried four persons, compared with two in the Piper L-4. (National Archives)

A fire destroyed the Bradford plant in 1937. William Piper reorganized the company as the Piper Aircraft Corporation and moved the operation to Lock Haven, Pennsylvania. The J-3 Cub emerged from the Lock Haven plant in 1938. Priced at $1,300, the J-3 Cub was within the reach of flying clubs and flight schools, as well as individual owners. Continental, Franklin, and Lycoming all produced engines for the J-3 Cub, ranging from 40 horsepower up to 65 horsepower.

Thousands of pilots learned to fly in Cubs in the 1930s and 1940s. Thousands of others earned their license in similar airplanes built by other manufacturers who joined Piper in meeting the demands of the general aviation market. Taylorcraft and Aeronca were second and third in production volume after Piper.

The availability of affordable and reliable light airplanes stimulated the expansion of general aviation. The growth was reflected in new airports as well as new pilots in the United States. From 1935 to 1941 the number of airports mushroomed fourfold, from 1,856 to 7,223. The ranks of licensed pilots zoomed from 18,564 in 1935 to 225,432 in 1941.

As the country began to modernize and prepare for war, the J-3 Cub filled essential roles in civilian pilot training and also as a military tool. During prewar maneuvers with the Army, the Cub earned its Grasshopper nickname. When war came in 1941, Piper and the other light airplane manufacturers stepped up production to meet the needs of the armed forces. The J-3 Cub received the military designation of L-4. It and similar airplanes performed military missions as varied as observation, artillery and naval gunfire direction, liaison and courier, delivering blood, ferrying top commanders around, and even medical evacuation. Their ability to operate from short fields or clearings or roads made them invaluable to the forces wherever they served.

William T. Piper, Sr., was to light airplanes what Henry Ford was to the automobile. To the general public, his "Piper Cub" stood for all light airplanes.

Piper Aircraft Corporation produced more than 14,000 J-3 Cubs from 1938 until the end of production in 1947. As the 21st century unfolded, Cubs still flew from airports around the nation.

37 Radar Developed in Time to Save Britain

Radar stands for "radio detection and ranging." Guglielmo Marconi, the father of radio, forecast the possibility of radar in June 1922. He said an apparatus could be designed to transmit radio waves from a ship and pick up their reflections bouncing off another ship. The apparatus would reveal the presence of the other ship and its bearing in fog or bad weather.

In the same year, scientists at the Naval Aircraft Radio Laboratory in Anacostia, D.C., confirmed that the phenomenon also worked on low-flying aircraft. Most objects reflect radio waves, thus enabling their detection by a radar system. The range to a detected object is determined by observing the time required for the radio waves emitted by the radar transmitter to return to its receiver.

Aware of the principles, scientists in Britain, Germany, and the United States in the 1930s developed devices that would lead to workable radar devices. After receiving a feasibility report in July 1935, the British government began installation of a chain of radar sites along its coastline, along with a control network that linked radar early warning control with radio direction of friendly interceptor aircraft.

The German Luftwaffe began massive air assaults against the British Isles in July 1940 as preparation for a cross-Channel invasion. The vigorous aerial offensive met determined British resistance. The British "Chain Home" warning system worked as intended. Over three months from July into October 1940, the Luftwaffe and Royal Air Force fought the Battle of Britain. By October the British had prevailed. The German invasion never came. When the onslaught subsided Prime Minister Winston Churchill paid tribute to the RAF by saying, "Never in the field of human conflict have so many owed so much to so few."

The German air assault may have succeeded without the early warning that radar provided to the British. Also, British aircraft were equipped with an electronic device called IFF (Identification, Friend or Foe) so that the radar stations could distinguish between friendly and hostile aircraft. The integrated control network made efficient use of the Royal Air Force's limited resources.

German radar developments became operational later than the British, but proved quite effective when the Royal Air Force began large-scale night bombing raids against Germany. The Luftwaffe mounted radar equipment on night fighters, which enabled them to locate and attack incoming bomber formations in the dark.

In the United States, Westinghouse led early radar development under contract from the Army for anti-aircraft purposes. By late 1941 Westinghouse had delivered 112 of its SCR-270 radar sets to the Army. Six sets were installed around the perimeter of Oahu, Hawaii.

Operators at one of the stations on Sunday morning, December 7, 1941, detected and reported large formations of aircraft approaching from the north. The radar worked, but the control system did not. Officers at the control center disregarded the warning, believing the formation to be a flight of B-17s due to arrive from the mainland. A few minutes later, waves of Japanese carrier-launched airplanes began the surprise attack on Pearl Harbor.

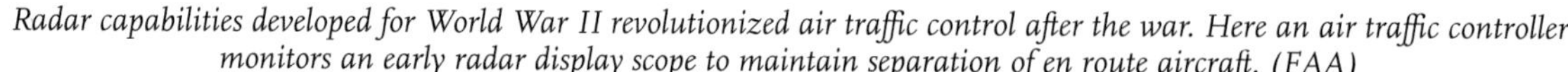

Radar capabilities developed for World War II revolutionized air traffic control after the war. Here an air traffic controller monitors an early radar display scope to maintain separation of en route aircraft. (FAA)

Three soldiers operate the radar set of an Army anti-aircraft unit in Casablanca, Morocco, June 19, 1943. (National Archives)

38 Jet Engines Take Flight

Frank Whittle became a flight cadet at the Royal Air Force College at Cranwell in 1926. His education included learning the capabilities and limitations of aircraft propulsion. He learned that internal combustion engines became less efficient at higher altitudes where the air was less dense. At higher speeds, propellers also lost efficiency.

With his nimble and inquiring mind, Whittle used the principles of thermodynamics to develop the concept of a workable jet engine. Whittle's theory was straightforward. Incoming air was compressed and burned to create thrust as it expanded and exited through a nozzle. In obedience to Newton's Third Law of Motion (every action produces an equal and opposite reaction), the thrust would propel an airplane forward. Whittle applied for and received a patent for his invention in January 1930.

After graduating from Cranwell, Whittle pursued his flying career in the Royal Air Force in the early 1930s. The military establishment showed indifference to his revolutionary means of aircraft propulsion. The engine industry also proved unenthusiastic.

By 1935, however, Whittle was able to scrape up the capital to start a firm called Power Jets Limited to build and test an actual engine based on his designs. On April 12, 1937, Frank Whittle's gas turbine engine fired up for the first time. Its success led to a government contract for an improved engine that would power an airplane. Whittle developed the W.1 turbojet engine for

Robert Stanley flew the Bell XP-59A Airacomet, the first U.S. jet-powered airplane, on its first flight on October 2, 1942, over the test base at Muroc Dry Lake, California. (Bell Aerosystems Company)

installation into an experimental airplane. The Gloster Aircraft Company built the airplane, designated E.28/39.

On the ramp at Cranwell on May 15, 1941, Flight Lieutenant P. E. G. Sayer of the Royal Air Force sat in the cockpit of the Gloster E.28/39. At 7:40 P.M. he started the Whittle engine, took off, and flew for 17 minutes. The flight marked a turning point in the history of British aircraft propulsion. The encouraging results led to the design of the Gloster Meteor twin-jet fighter, which entered service in the Royal Air Force in the summer of 1944.

Whittle received the first patent for a turbojet aircraft engine. However, a German scientist, Hans von Ohain, also began development of his own turbojet engine in the mid-1930s. Ernst Heinkel, leader of the company bearing his name,

Gloster E.28/39, the first British jet-powered airplane, on its first flight at Cranwell on May 15, 1941, under control of Flight Lieutenant P. E. G. Sayer of the Royal Air Force. (BAE SYSTEMS)

Two inventors of the jet engine with the top aviation curator. Frank Whittle (left) and Hans von Ohain (center) with Paul E. Garber in his office. For many years Garber headed the National Air Museum, the predecessor to the National Air and Space Museum. As a young boy Garber witnessed Orville Wright's flight demonstrations at Fort Myer, Virginia. (National Air and Space Museum, Smithsonian Institution SI Neg. No. 74-11297-23)

Stanley Hooker (right), Rolls-Royce Chief Engineer, with Frank Whittle (center), and John Herriott, Hooker's assistant (left), at the Barnoldswick factory in November 1944. Rolls-Royce assumed responsibility for wartime production of the Whittle jet engines. (Courtesy of Rolls-Royce Heritage Trust)

employed von Ohain to pursue jet engine development. Heinkel designed a small prototype airplane, the He-178, to fly with von Ohain's He-S3B jet engine. Piloted by Erich Warsitz, the He-178 flew for the first time on August 27, 1939, from an airfield near Rostock, Germany.

In the spirit of wartime cooperation among the Allies, the British shared the secret of Whittle's engines with the Americans. General Henry H. Arnold, head of the U.S. Army Air Forces, contracted with Bell Aircraft Corporation to build an experimental jet airplane. Bell built and flew the XP-59A Airacomet, powered by two I-A jet engines developed by General Electric from the Whittle technology. Robert Stanley flew it for the first time on October 2, 1942, from the test base at Muroc Dry Lake, California.

39

Sikorsky Perfects the Helicopter

Igor Sikorsky tried twice before 1910 to build a helicopter. The machines proved unsuccessful. However, when Sikorsky turned to designing and building fixed-wing airplanes, he succeeded. His four-engine *Grand* of 1913 was mentioned earlier, as were his series of flying boats designed for Pan American Airways.

The German aircraft designer Heinrich Focke created a working helicopter that first flew on June 26, 1936. Two counter-rotating rotors set atop outriggers built upon an airplane fuselage lifted his Focke-Achgelis Fw-61. Hannah Reitsch, a noted German test pilot, created favorable publicity for the aircraft when she flew it in Berlin's Deutschlandhalle sports arena in February 1938. She earned the distinction of becoming the world's first female helicopter pilot.

Another German designer, Anton Flettner, built a helicopter, the Fl-282 Kolibri, and demonstrated it in 1938 and 1939. Vertical lift came from counter-rotating rotors that intermeshed as they turned. The German Navy ordered 1,000 Kolibris for deployment aboard ships in the anti-submarine role, but Allied bombing raids curtailed production and service.

Meanwhile, Igor Sikorsky remained determined to build a successful helicopter. He obtained a U.S. patent for a direct-lift aircraft in 1931. He turned the design into reality and achieved his dream of vertical flight with his VS-300 helicopter. He flew it in free flight for the first time on May 13, 1940, at Stratford, Connecticut. He demonstrated it publicly to crowds who were amazed at his ability to hover, fly straight up and down, and turn on a spot.

Sikorsky's VS-300 featured a single main rotor and a smaller stabilizing tail rotor. On May 6, 1941, Igor Sikorsky set a world helicopter endurance record by flying the VS-300 for one hour, 32 minutes.

The U.S. Army awarded a development contract to Sikorsky for an improved version of the VS-300 helicopter, designating it the XR-4. The XR-4 featured side-by-side seating for two pilots in a fabric-covered fuselage. It flew for the first time on January 14, 1942.

Sikorsky delivered the XR-4 to the Army at Wright Field in Dayton, Ohio. The cross-country flight by test pilot Les Morris from Stratford to Dayton took five days. Igor Sikorsky flew on the last leg of the delivery flight, landing with Morris at Wright Field on May 18, 1942. After evaluation, the Army ordered the R-4 series into production. Part of the total production of 131 aircraft went to the Coast Guard and 50 were delivered to the Royal Air Force.

The Sikorsky R-4 demonstrated its utility and agility in missions that other aircraft could not do. Its first combat action involved evacuating wounded soldiers from jungle clearings in Burma.

Igor Sikorsky's helicopter dreams may have been thwarted in 1909–1910. However, with his VS-300 and R-4 helicopters, he established the standard for succeeding generations of vertical lift aircraft.

Igor Sikorsky (wearing his "trademark" fedora hat) demonstrates precision hovering of his VS-300 helicopter at Stratford, Connecticut. (National Air and Space Museum, Smithsonian Institution SI Neg. No. 2000-3641)

A naval engine mechanic works on a Wright Whirlwind engine in October 1942. (National Archives)

Aviation in War and Peace
1940–1949

The demands of World War II dominated the aviation agenda throughout the world in the first half of the 1940s. After the war ended in 1945, the second half of the decade saw the start of postwar economic expansion mixed with the Soviets' drawing of the "Iron Curtain" across central Europe, and the consequent beginning of the 44-year Cold War. Aeronautic research and development flourished, and the needs of the postwar world created opportunities for widespread adoption of new technologies.

As the war began in Europe in 1939 and the United States prepared for conflict, aviation was no longer a province of daredevils. Actions in the 1930s to improve aircraft and raise operating standards bore fruit in the form of safer and more reliable commercial air operations. For example, on March 26, 1940, U.S. commercial airlines completed a full year without a fatal accident or serious injury to a passenger or crewmember.

When total war engulfed the world, millions of men and women became familiar with the power of aviation. Hordes of workers built the tools of air power. Others flew or serviced the aircraft and their supporting systems. Additional millions felt the impact of air power as combatants or victims. The war saw the first use of ballistic missiles and nuclear weapons.

At war's end the nation and the world were more air-minded than ever before. Domestic and international air transport became commonplace. Airline passenger numbers in the United States tripled between 1945 and 1950 from slightly more than six million to 17,345,000. The number of certified pilots nearly doubled in the same five-year period, from 296,895 in 1945 to 525,174 in 1950. Postwar aeronautics research led to supersonic flight and innovative designs to operate in the supersonic region.

40 Northrop Flying Wings

Early in his aviation career, John K. Northrop designed airplanes for Douglas and Lockheed, including the successful Lockheed Vega. He left Lockheed in 1928 to join the Avion Corporation in Burbank, California, which eventually became Northrop Aircraft.

One of his ideas included development of an all-wing airplane. In his Wilbur Wright Lecture to the Royal Aeronautical Society in 1947, Northrop defined it as a "type of airplane in which all of the functions of a satisfactory flying machine are disposed and accommodated within the outline of the airfoil itself."

Northrop designed an all-wing airplane in 1939 and subjected it to a year of wind tunnel tests. Designated N-1M (Northrop Model 1 Mockup), the airplane flew for the first time on July 3, 1940. More than 200 flights of the N-1M provided substantial data on the special challenges of the all-wing airplane.

The Army Air Forces were persuaded of the value of pursuing the all-wing concept as the basis for a strategic bomber, and ordered four experimental flying scale models to be developed. Designated N-9M (for Northrop Model 9 Mockup), they were test airplanes to develop the intended XB-35 bomber.

John K. Northrop (right) with test pilot John Myers in the N-1M flying wing in 1940. (Northrop Grumman Corporation)

Northrop YB-49 in flight, powered by eight J35 turbojet engines. (Northrop Grumman Corporation)

The Army ordered two XB-35 prototype bombers in 1942, and in 1943 placed orders for 13 more test aircraft. Four pusher-type piston engines powered the XB-35. Problems with engines, propellers, and gearboxes delayed the first XB-35 flight until June 1946, a year after the war had ended. By then, a new generation of jet powered bombers was envisioned that promised greater capabilities. The all-wing bomber project was revived and revised in 1947 as the YB-49, with eight Allison J35 turbojet engines, each providing 4,000 pounds of thrust. It flew in October 1947. A second YB-49 broke up in flight on June 5, 1948 and all five crewmembers were killed. After intensive evaluation and review the Air Force terminated the program in November 1949.

Almost four decades later, after years of secret development, the all-wing Northrop B-2 stealth bomber was unveiled. It flew for the first time on July 17, 1989, validating an extensive test and development effort by the Air Force and Northrop.

Copilot (left) and flight engineer converse in a Stratoliner cockpit. The flight engineer operated the airplane's support systems, enabling the pilot and copilot to concentrate on flying. (Copyright The Boeing Company)

41

Boeing 307 Stratoliner, the First Pressurized Airliner

Airliners of the mid-1930s flew at altitudes below 10,000 feet in order for the crew and passengers to have sufficient oxygen. The more turbulent air at those lower altitudes made for bumpy rides and motion sickness.

Boeing overcame the altitude limitation when it introduced the 307 Stratoliner, the first pressurized airliner. The Stratoliner made its initial flight on December 31, 1938. First scheduled service began with TWA in July 1940 and with Pan American soon thereafter.

The Stratoliner design benefited from Boeing's development work on the B-17 bomber. With four engines and a larger cabin, the 307 could carry 33 passengers in comfort at altitudes up to 20,000 feet. The flight engineer operated the pressurization system and provided other system support functions, allowing the pilot and copilot to concentrate on flying.

Boeing built ten of the 307s, the prototype and nine others. Wartime military requirements put an end to further Stratoliner production. However, the pressurized Stratoliner provided an important example that influenced the entire aircraft industry. As a result of its success, future airliners would be pressurized, enabling them to fly at higher altitudes and higher speeds with greater passenger comfort.

42 Ejection Seats Save Lives

In the early days of combat flying, when an airplane became disabled the crew had little choice but to ride it down. The introduction of parachutes gave aircrews the option of jumping. However, in many cases, a pilot could not jump because he was wounded or disabled, or the stricken airplane's gyrations made a parachute jump impossible. Even when the pilot could jump, he might strike the airplane or his parachute might not work.

Ejection seats provided the answer to the problem. Combatant nations realized the vital importance of saving trained crews. Lost aircraft could be replaced, but the skills of lost airmen were gone forever.

Germany's Luftwaffe was the first air force to equip an operational aircraft with ejection seats, the Heinkel He 219 night fighter. The radar-equipped He 219 flew for the first time in November 1942 and went into combat in June 1943. It could fly higher than 40,000 feet at speeds greater than 400 mph. Heinkel developed an ejection seat that used an explosive cartridge to eject the airman and his parachute up and out of the airplane. Other ejection seats developed in Germany during World War II used compressed air for propulsion.

The British also experimented with ejection seats during and after the war. The American military learned from the British example and from captured German equipment, especially the Heinkel seat. Initially, aircraft manufacturers installed an ejection seat of their own design in their airplane. Eventually that situation ended when governments required standardized ejection seats built by companies specializing in their manufacture. The British firm of Martin-Baker Aircraft Ltd. was a leader in the business, and its name soon became synonymous with ejection seats.

Heinkel He 219 night fighter of the German Luftwaffe, the first operational aircraft equipped with ejection seats for the two-man crew. Radar antennas protrude from the nose of the two-seat airplane. (National Air and Space Museum, Smithsonian Institution SI Neg. No. 87-7688)

Ejection seats worked fine at the subsonic speeds of the late 1940s. But by the 1950s, the important question was whether airmen could survive ejection at supersonic speeds. Col. John Paul Stapp, a U.S. Air Force physician and researcher, set out to answer the question. Stapp had conducted tests on crash survival in the late 1940s, using rocket sleds for propulsion and him as the test dummy. In December 1954, he shot along the test track at a ground speed of 632 mph and withstood the windblast and sudden deceleration to prove that an ejection seat could be used at supersonic speeds.

Ejection seat developments have improved from the original simple requirement to get out of a disabled aircraft flying at altitude. Modern ejection seats work successfully at zero altitude and zero airspeed.

Martin-Baker Aircraft Company Ltd. keeps track of the cases of its ejection seats being used. From the time the company began manufacturing ejection seats in 1949 until mid-2002, its seats saved more than 6,900 lives.

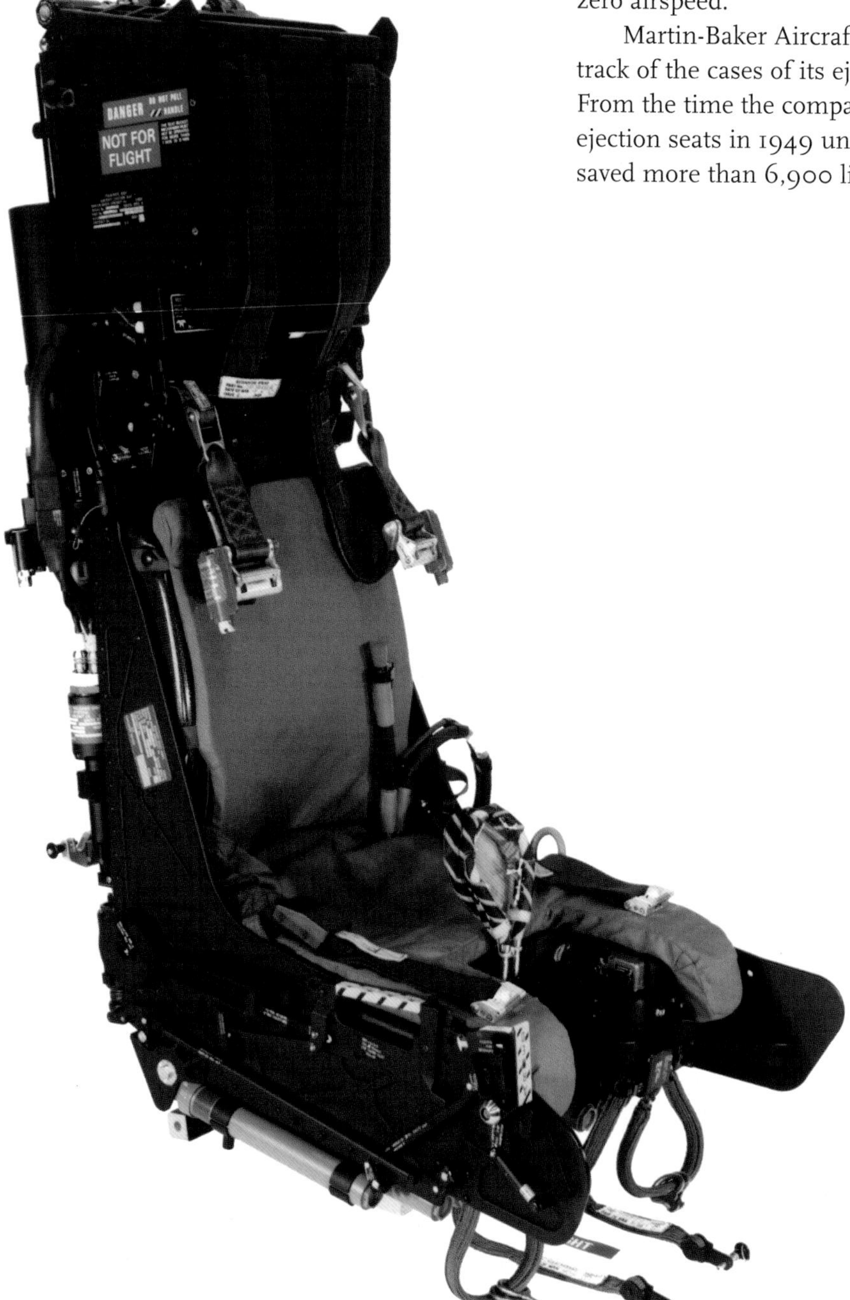

The Navy Aircrew Common Ejection Seat (NACES) is the world's first microprocessor controlled ejection seat, developed and flying in the U.S. Navy F/A-18 Hornet, T-45 Goshawk, and the F-14D Tomcat. It functions at zero speed and zero altitude, and is fully automatic. (By kind permission of Martin-Baker Aircraft Company Ltd.)

43 Lockheed Skunk Works Does the Impossible

Clarence L. "Kelly" Johnson was Lockheed's chief engineer when the Army Air Forces contracted with Lockheed to develop a jet fighter to combat the menace posed by the Luftwaffe Me-262 jet fighter. The first XP-80 airplane was to be delivered within 150 days.

Some might have considered it impossible, but Kelly Johnson accepted the challenge. He assembled a team of engineers and mechanics and got going. The project was secret and urgent. Johnson put his skilled and closely guarded group to work in a temporary setup away from the main plant.

Al Capp, a popular cartoonist of the day, drew a comic strip called "Li'l Abner." His hillbilly characters operated a liquor still called the "Skonk Works" where they secretly manufactured moonshine liquor. Members of Johnson's team were prohibited from identifying their office when they answered the telephone. They made the connection between their secret operation and Capp's characters and began answering the telephone by saying "Skonk Works." The name took hold and stuck. Lockheed later modified the name to "Skunk Works" and trademarked it.

At the time of the urgent XP-80 jet fighter requirement, Kelly Johnson had designed a succession of innovative airplanes at Lockheed. Among his creations were the Electra transport, the fast twin-boom P-38 Lightning fighter, and the four-engine Constellation transport.

Johnson and his team designed and built the XP-80 Shooting Star in 143 days, delivering seven days ahead of schedule. A single turbojet based on a British design generated 3,000 pounds of thrust. Lockheed test pilot Milo Burcham made the first flight in the XP-80 on January 8, 1944.

The war in Europe ended before the P-80 entered operational units. However, it became the first operational jet fighter in the postwar Air

Clarence L. "Kelly" Johnson (on right) shakes hands with test pilot Milo Burcham after first flight of the XP-80 on January 8, 1944. (Lockheed Martin Corporation)

Lockheed XP-80A with tail number 01 flies above the California desert in 1944. It was the predecessor of the P-80, the first U.S. operational jet fighter, and the T-33 jet trainer. (USAF)

Force. Redesignated the F-80 (for fighter) in 1948, it was ready for combat when the Korean War began. The F-80 proved victorious in the world's first jet-versus-jet aerial combat. Air Force Lieutenant Russell Brown flew an F-80 to destroy a Russian-built MiG-15 over North Korea on November 8, 1950.

The Lockheed T-33 jet trainer was developed from the P-80. Produced in thousands, the T-Bird became the standard airplane for training jet pilots.

The XP-80 project established the enduring characteristics of the Lockheed Skunk Works: secret work with technological challenges having highest priority. For example, the Skunk Works team created the U-2 strategic reconnaissance aircraft for the Central Intelligence Agency in only eight months in 1954–55. The U-2 flew higher than Soviet guns or missiles of the time could reach.

Less than a decade later the Skunk Works delivered the first of a series of fast, high-altitude strategic-reconnaissance aircraft, designated the A-11. Kelly Johnson received the Collier Trophy for 1963 for designing and directing development of the A-11.

The SR-71 Blackbird series was based on the A-11. The SR-71 made its first flight on December 22, 1964. In service with the Air Force's 9th Strategic Reconnaissance Wing, the SR-71 flew global reconnaissance missions at altitudes above 80,000 feet and speeds exceeding Mach 3 until the Air Force retired the fleet in 1990. Lieutenant Colonel Ed Yeilding (pilot) and Lieutenant Colonel Joseph Vida (navigator) set a new transcontinental speed record of 64 minutes from Los Angeles to Washington, D.C., on the final SR-71 flight on March 6, 1990.

Ben R. Rich succeeded Kelly Johnson as head of the Skunk Works. Under his leadership the Skunk Works developed the world's first operational stealth airplane, the F-117 Nighthawk.

44

Coast Guard Pioneers Helicopter Rescue

Because of wartime requirements, the U.S. Coast Guard came under Navy control during World War II. Coast Guard employment of helicopters dates back to the first Sikorsky R-4, and to those U.S. Navy needs for warfighting. When the Sikorsky R-4 went into production, the Navy ordered 23 of the new helicopters for Coast Guard use in developing helicopter antisubmarine and rescue roles. The Coast Guard designation became HNS-1 Hoverfly.

As helicopters began to emerge from the Sikorsky production line in Stratford, Connecticut, in 1943, pilot and mechanic training for all services started at the Coast Guard's nearby Brooklyn Air Station. Commander Frank Erickson led the Coast Guard helicopter activities. He oversaw the training as well as led the tactical evaluations. For the antisubmarine evaluations the USCGC *Cobb* (WPG-181) was converted into an improvised helicopter aircraft carrier.

Frank Erickson flew the world's first helicopter lifesaving mission on the night of January 3, 1944. An explosion aboard the Navy destroyer SU *Turner* sank the ship off Sandy Hook, New Jersey, at the southern reach of Lower New York Bay. Survivors were brought ashore to a hospital. The medics tending the injured survivors urgently needed blood plasma. Stormy weather included snow, sleet, gusting winds, and low visibility. Erickson took off from the Brooklyn Air Station and flew to the Battery, at the southern tip of Manhattan, to pick up two cases of blood plasma. He battled the dreadful weather and delivered the precious plasma to the hospital after a hazardous 14-minute flight.

Coast Guard Commander Frank Erickson demonstrates rescue hoist. He hovers a Sikorsky HNS-1 helicopter to bring inventor Igor Sikorsky aboard, August 14, 1944. Erickson flew the first helicopter lifesaving mission in an HNS-1. (U.S. Coast Guard Historian's Office)

In mid-1944, Commander Erickson made the first landing on the flight deck of the USCGC *Cobb*. Meanwhile, the German submarine threat had diminished. The Coast Guard shifted emphasis of its helicopter development to search and rescue.

By December 1944 Coast Guard headquarters established an Office of Air Sea Rescue to coordinate rescue operations by amphibious airplanes and helicopters along with high-speed rescue boats. The Coast Guard, along with the helicopter industry and other services, received the Collier Trophy for 1950.

Coast Guard HOS-1 helicopter (Sikorsky R-6) flown by Commander Frank Erickson approaches to land on improvised flight deck of the U.S. Coast Guard cutter Cobb *(WPG-181) during sea trials on Long Island Sound, June 29, 1944. (U.S. Coast Guard Historian's Office)*

45 Air Power Decisive in World War II

Air power struck the first blows of World War II when, on the early morning of September 1, 1939, Ju-87 Stuka dive bombers of the German Luftwaffe assaulted Polish bridges and airfields ahead of invading ground forces.

Air power brought World War II to its end in August 1945. American Boeing B-29 heavy bombers dropped the world's first nuclear bombs with devastating effects on Hiroshima (August 6) and Nagasaki (August 9). Japan capitulated within days.

Between the war's start and end points, air power proved decisive at crucial moments along the horrific path of the conflict. For example, in

Lieutenant Colonel James H. Doolittle flies his B-25 bomber off the aircraft carrier USS Hornet *to lead the raid on Tokyo and vicinity on April 18, 1942. (USAF)*

Hundreds of thousands of women joined the war production industry. Their skills made wartime industrial expansion possible. This worker installs a valve in the wing of a North American P-51 Mustang fighter. (Parker Aerospace, Parker Hannifin Corporation)

the summer of 1940, Germany launched air attacks to soften up the British Isles for an invasion across the English Channel. In the Battle of Britain, the Royal Air Force turned back the Luftwaffe in three months of fierce aerial combat. The invasion never came.

Japanese air power precipitated American entry into the war. Carrier-based aircraft of the Japanese fleet struck Pearl Harbor on December 7, 1941. The surprise attack killed more than 2,000 Americans and almost demolished the Pacific Fleet. Addressing Congress the next day, President Franklin D. Roosevelt called December 7 "a date which will live in infamy," and Congress declared war on Japan. Three days later, Germany and Italy supported Japan and declared war on the United States.

As the war spread, air power produced significant results at key moments. The United States struck back at Japan on April 18, 1942, in a surprise raid led by Lieutenant Colonel James H. Doolittle. His attack force of 16 B-25 medium bombers launched from the aircraft carrier USS

Waves of paratroopers drop on Holland in Operation Market Garden on September 17, 1944. The American 82d and 101st Airborne Divisions and the British 1st Airborne Division jumped to seize critical bridges across the lower Rhine River. (National Archives)

B-17G Mon Tête Rouge *of the 452d Bomb Group en route to bomb German installations at Châteaudun, France, on March 28, 1944. The group flew 250 missions in the 8th Air Force bombing offensive in 1944 and 1945. (USAF)*

Hornet and bombed targets in Tokyo and its vicinity. The raid shook Japanese morale and heartened the American people.

Two months later, Japanese and U.S. Navy aircraft carrier task forces engaged in the Battle of Midway, turning back Japanese expansion and beginning the end of their domination of the Pacific.

As the war intensified and spread, bombing campaigns by both sides crippled enemy industrial capabilities while carrying the horrors of war to civilian populations.

Air superiority enabled allied forces to gain a firm foothold on the beaches of Normandy and to march to victory in Europe. In the Pacific, air power was a crucial element in ejecting Japanese forces from conquered territories and islands and eventually resulted in the Japanese surrender.

At every place touched by the war, air power extended the reach and effectiveness of land and naval forces in both offensive and defensive operations. The missions varied across the spectrum of aviation capabilities such as air-to-air combat, attack, defense, reconnaissance, medical evacuation, transport, or close support of ground units. Whatever the mission, airmen and their aircraft added a potent third dimension to warfare. Air power became a necessary ingredient for victory on land or sea.

Before it could be effective in the war effort, the air power had to be created. The United States became the great "Arsenal of Democracy" as its population and industries mobilized for victory.

The 1940 census pegged the U.S. population at 132 million. More than 12 percent of them joined the armed forces. By war's end in 1945, more than 16 million men and women had served in uniform. Of that number, 291,557 were killed in combat and an additional 113,842 died of non-battle deaths. More than 671,000 members of the armed forces suffered non-mortal wounds.

Millions of men and women joined the war production effort at home, where aircraft production skyrocketed to meet the needs of the armed forces. The United States spent more than 45 billion dollars for aircraft during the war. That was about one-quarter of the total spent on munitions of all types. Aircraft production began to expand in 1940, when the industry produced 12,813 aircraft,

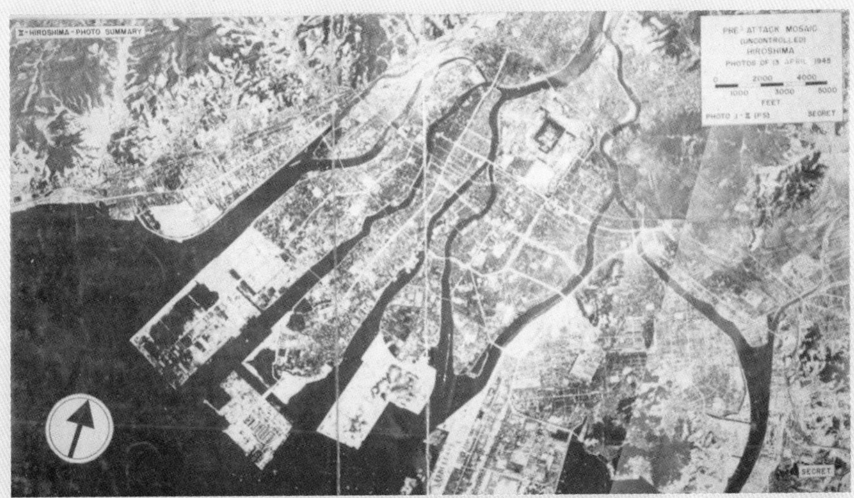

Photo mosaic of Hiroshima in late July 1945. (National Archives)

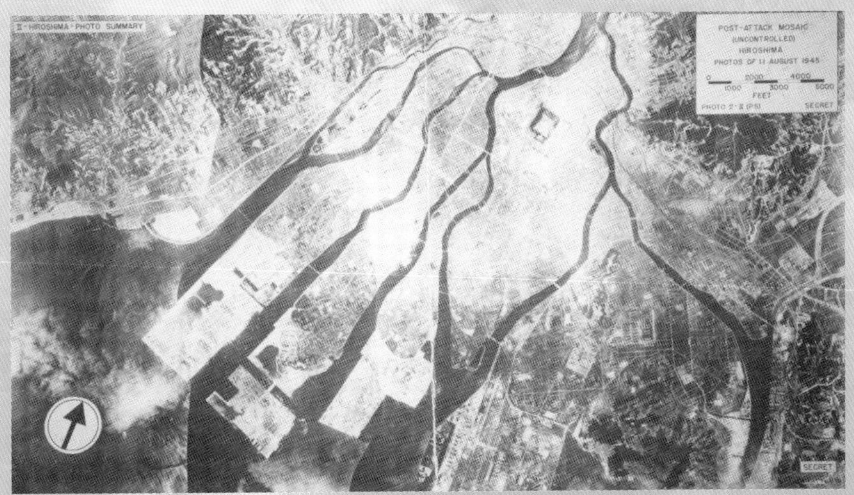

Photo mosaic of Hiroshima after the nuclear explosion on August 6, 1945, shows widespread devastation. (National Archives)

Cloud of smoke and debris rises to 20,000 feet above Hiroshima atomic bomb. (National Archives)

up from 5,856 in 1939. Production accelerated during the war years. In the peak production year of 1944, American industry produced 95,272 aircraft. In all, the nation produced more than 296,000 aircraft for the Army, Navy, and allied forces between July 1, 1940 and July 31, 1945.

By war's end in 1945, the aircraft in use were profoundly improved over those of 1939 in all aspects. Wartime technology advances took aviation from the prop-driven biplane era into the jet age. The nuclear weapons dropped on Hiroshima and Nagasaki represented the ultimate harnessing of technology for destruction. Wartime advances in other areas such as medicine and electronics were also impressive. Technologies created in the quest for victory were now ready for application in the postwar world.

46

V-2 Ballistic Missile, Terror Weapon

The German V-2 guided ballistic missile made its combat debut in World War II on September 6, 1944. On that date, German forces in the Netherlands launched the first operational V-2 against London. About six minutes after launch, the 46-foot long weapon with its 2,200-pound warhead slammed into a suburban neighborhood and established its reputation as a terror weapon.

The V-2 came into being through the leadership of Wernher von Braun, one of Germany's pioneer rocket researchers. From the mid-1930s, von Braun and his team developed a series of liquid-fueled rockets for the German Army's rocket research group, headed by Captain (later Major General) Walther Dornberger. Their A-2 flew for the first time in December 1934, from the test center near Berlin. As development activities expanded, the team needed more room, and moved in 1936 to Peenemunde, a remote island on the Baltic coast. At Peenemunde, von Braun and his colleagues continued research, development, and testing of liquid-fueled rockets, with the A-3 being next in the series.

While the developers learned from the A-3 rockets, planning for the A-4 began. The A-4 was designed as a practical and powerful long-range weapon of war, not a research tool. (A-4 stood for Assembly-4 in the nomenclature system.) After two unsuccessful launches, the third one worked as planned. On October 3, 1942, an A-4 took off from Peenemunde and flew its planned trajectory to a target 120 miles distant.

Production began in 1943. The Nazi Propaganda Ministry changed the missile's name to the Vengeance Weapon-2, or V-2.

Fueled by liquid oxygen and alcohol, the vertically launched V-2 was guided in its ballistic trajectory by an advanced gyroscopic system that sent control signals to aerodynamic steering tabs on the rocket's four fins. The V-2 could reach targets up to nearly 200 miles away. There was no way to defend against the V-2 in flight, so the Allies resorted to locating and bombing V-2 launch sites to destroy the weapons and their launching mechanisms.

German forces fired more than 3,000 V-2 missiles against targets mainly in southern England and Belgium from September 1944 until March 1945, when Allied ground forces were striking into Germany itself.

At war's end, Dornberger, von Braun, and their team of experts surrendered to American troops in Austria. The scientists were brought to the United States under a program to make use of their knowledge and experience. American forces

German General Walther Dornberger (with cigar) and Wernher von Braun (with cast) surrender to American troops in Austria on May 3, 1945, at the end of World War II. (National Archives)

American soldier guards a captured V-2 rocket in its underground assembly plant.
(With permission of the Trustees of the Imperial War Museum, London. NASM SI Neg.No. 75-15871)

also captured V-2 production facilities with components under manufacture. The components, enough for several dozen missiles, were shipped to the United States. Settled at White Sands, New Mexico, by 1946, the von Braun team and their V-2 missiles became the nucleus of the American missile and space programs.

47 Swept Wings Fly Faster

Aeronautical engineers began devoting serious attention to the virtues of swept-back wings in the late 1930s and early 1940s. They knew that as airplanes flew faster they would encounter the adverse results of the compressibility effect. As an airplane approached the speed of sound, the air ahead of its nose and wings compressed into shock waves.

Sweeping the wings back from the fuselage promised to alleviate the compressibility effects by reducing interference between the shock waves and the wings and tail. The Messerschmitt Me 262 jet fighter, which astonished allied airmen when it appeared late in World War II, employed swept-back wings.

In the immediate postwar period, NACA and the military applied lessons learned from British and German swept-wing designs. They also performed original research at the supersonic wind tunnel at the Army's Aberdeen Proving Ground, Maryland.

The first American plane to put this knowledge to use was the North American XP-86, which flew for the first time on October 1, 1947, with test pilot George Welch at the controls. XP-86 wings and tail were swept back 35 degrees. Later designated the F-86 Sabre, with a General Electric turbojet engine delivering 5,200 pounds of thrust, it set a world speed record of 670.98 mph on September 15, 1948.

Two swept-wing aircraft in research projects by the National Advisory Committee for Aeronautics (NACA) fly above California. North American F-86 Sabre (left) chases a Douglas D-558 Skyrocket. (NASA)

NAVY

Aeronautical engineers in the Soviet Union also learned from the German swept-wing developments. They designed the MiG-15 fighter with sharp sweep backs and flew it in July 1947. However, its jet engine was unsatisfactory. The Soviets bought more powerful and dependable British jet engines and sharply improved the MiG-15 performance.

The two early swept-wing jet fighters met in combat over Korea. On December 17, 1950, the 47th anniversary of the Wright Brothers' first powered flight at Kitty Hawk, an American pilot flying an F-86 shot down a Russian-built MiG-15 over

National Advisory Committee for Aeronautics (NACA) conducted many research flights with this swept-wing Boeing B-47A bomber, landing here with a drag parachute. (NASA)

High-speed research aircraft of the National Advisory Committee on Aeronautics (NACA) on the ramp at Edwards Air Force Base, California. The Douglas X-3 is in center. Others, clockwise from seven o'clock, are the X-1A, Douglas D-558-1, Convair XF-92A, Bell X-5 with variable sweep wings, Douglas D-558-II, and the Northrop X-4. (NASA)

North Korea. Throughout the air war in Korea, the F-86 ruled the skies.

Just as the F-86 Sabre was the first of a long series of swept-wing fighters, so was the Boeing B-47 Stratojet the first of a long series of swept-wing bombers. The original XB-47 first flew on December 17, 1947, from the Boeing plant in Seattle to an air base at Moses Lake, Washington. It quickly set new speed and distance records for multi-engine aircraft.

The B-47 Stratojet became the primary long-range bomber of the Air Force's Strategic Air Command until the larger Boeing B-52 Stratofortress succeeded it. More than 2,000 B-47s were built before the type was retired in 1966. In 2002, the Boeing B-52 observed its golden anniversary and continued in U.S. Air Force service.

48

First Supersonic Flight

John Stack of the National Advisory Committee on Aeronautics (NACA) proposed in 1943 that NACA create a high-speed research airplane that would explore the range of speeds in the transonic and supersonic regions. The Army Air Forces concurred, and in February 1944 contracted with Bell Aircraft to build three transonic flight research aircraft powered by rocket engines. Reaction Motors designed and built the XLR-11 rocket engine for the project. The aircraft received the designation XS-1 and later, X-1.

Mach 1.0 is defined as the speed of sound. The Mach number honors Professor Ernst Mach of Prague, who, in 1887, took the first photographs of shock waves on a body moving at supersonic speeds, a rifle bullet. The speed of an object moving through a fluid (atmosphere) can be expressed as a Mach number. It is the ratio between the body's speed through the fluid and the speed of sound through the same fluid in the same conditions. A Mach number less than 1.0 is subsonic; greater than 1.0, it is supersonic. The accepted standard for Mach 1.0 at sea level at 59 degrees Fahrenheit is 1,117 feet per second, or 761.59 mph.

The cooperation among NACA, the military, and industry in the X-1 project set the pattern for future large collaborative research projects. After

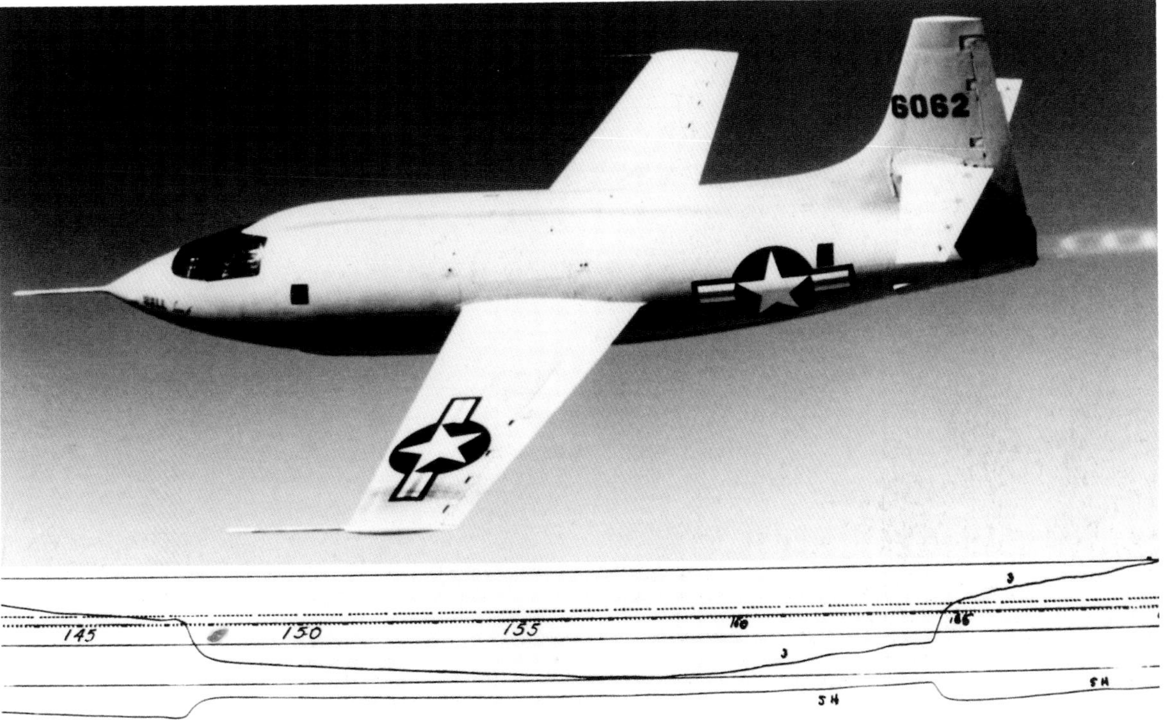

Bell XS-1 with a copy of the "Mach jump" tape that records data from the first supersonic flight, October 14, 1947. Shock waves are apparent in the exhaust plume of the Reaction Motors rocket engine. The tape displays a record of pressure altitude and airspeed against time in seconds after launch. Observers on the ground heard the crack of a sonic boom for the first time. (USAF photo by Lieutenant Robert A. Hoover via NASA)

glide tests in Florida and Muroc Dry Lake, California, the XS-1 was ready to fly supersonic. Captain Charles E. "Chuck" Yeager was designated to make the flight on October 14, 1947. A U.S. Air Force B-29 "mother ship" carried Yeager and his airplane in its bomb bay to altitude for release and flight. The XS-1 with a full load of fuel would stall at about 235 to 240 mph. Therefore, the B-29 climbed to altitude and then began a shallow 15 to 20 degree dive until it reached a speed of about 240 mph where the X-1 could be dropped safely. Yeager and his rocket craft fell clear of the bomber at 20,000 feet and he fired his rockets.

The airplane accelerated and climbed rapidly to 42,000 feet. Writing his pilot's notes immediately after the flight (classified SECRET), Yeager described the magic moment. "The needle of the machmeter fluctuated at this reading (.98 Mach) momentarily, then passed off the scale. Assuming that the off-scale reading remained linear, it is estimated that 1.05 Mach was attained at this time." Actually, Yeager and the XS-1 flew a little faster and achieved 1.06 Mach.

Yeager and the XS-1 had slipped through the mythical "sound barrier." NACA and the Air Force continued supersonic research flights with the XS-1, now designated X-1, and its descendants.

The successful supersonic flights remained secret until June 10, 1948, when the Air Force confirmed that Captain Yeager had made repeated supersonic flights in the X-1. Six months later, President Harry Truman presented the Collier Trophy to three men who represented the research team: the scientist, John Stack of NACA; the manufacturer, Lawrence D. Bell of Bell Aircraft; and, the pilot, Captain Charles E. Yeager.

Key members of the NACA-USAF XS-1 research team in 1947. From left to right: Joseph Vensel, Head of Operations; Gerald Truszynski, Head of Instrumentation; Captain Charles E. Yeager, USAF pilot; Walter Williams, Head of the Unit (holding photo); Major Jack Ridley, USAF pilot; and De E. Beeler, Head of Engineers. (NASA)

Berlin, 1948. Air Force C-47 transport aircraft unload at Tempelhof airport. Each C-47 carried 2.5 tons of cargo. The larger C-54 Skymaster aircraft replaced the C-47 and became the workhorse of the airlift. The ramp surface is composed of interlocking sections of pierced steel planking matting. (USAF)

49 Berlin Airlift: Constructive Air Power

When World War II ended in Europe, the victorious allies split Germany into two parts. The Soviet Union controlled all of the eastern part of the country. Britain, France, and the United States subdivided the western part into three zones. Berlin, the former capital of the vanquished Third Reich, lay 100 miles inside the Soviet zone. The allies also divided Berlin into four sectors and based military forces from each of the powers in their assigned sector.

In June 1948 the Soviet Union blockaded all surface travel by road, rail, or water into Berlin. The Soviets intended to force the allies out of Berlin and compel them to abandon attempts to establish an independent West Germany. Instead of mounting armed convoys or withdrawing from Berlin, President Harry Truman chose a third course. He decided to supply the western sectors of the city entirely by air.

The Berlin Airlift began in late June 1948. C-47 Skytrain transport airplanes of the U.S. Air Force flew the first sorties on June 19 to deliver fresh milk to Tempelhof airport in the U.S. sector of Berlin. The airlift began officially on June 26. Before long the Combined Airlift Task Force came into being to operate the airlift. Major General

William H. Tunner, the Air Force's preeminent authority on air transport, commanded the operation. British and American aircraft flew the bulk of the airlift missions. American flights landed at Tempelhof. The British flew into Gatow airport in their zone and their seaplanes landed on the Havel River. A third airport, Tegel, was quickly built in the French zone of Berlin.

Berlin's summertime daily survival requirement totaled 3,475 tons of all materials. The airlift met the requirements. By September, the daily average reached 4,655 tons per day. The operational tempo picked up with experience and with the arrival of squadrons of Air Force C-54 Skymaster transports and their Navy counterpart, the R-5D.

Captain Harry D. Immel commanded this C-54 on the last Operation Vittles Flight to Berlin. He and his crew flew a planeload of coal from Rhein-Main to Berlin on September 30, 1949. (USAF)

Berlin children atop rubble watch a C-54 on approach to Tempelhof airport. (USAF)

Berlin, May 1998. C-54 Spirit of Freedom *approaches to land at Berlin's Tempelhof Airport to mark the 50th anniversary of the Berlin Airlift. The airplane is owned and operated by the Berlin Airlift Historical Foundation. Its interior is outfitted with displays and artifacts about the Berlin Airlift. (Photo taken by Matthias Winkler via Berlin Airlift Historical Foundation)*

By the time the severe weather of the 1948–1949 winter set in, the daily requirements were being met and often exceeded by aircraft flowing in disciplined streams along the three air corridors into Berlin. Four years earlier, the allied air forces dropped bombs on Berlin. Now they enabled its populace to survive.

Airlift units set the record for tonnage on Easter Sunday, April 16, 1949, flying 12,941 tons of cargo on 1,383 flights. The high tempo continued for the rest of April and into May, flying an average of nearly 9,000 tons per day into Berlin.

The Soviet Union lifted the ground blockade on May 12, 1949. However, the airlift continued at a sustained reduced pace through the summer to build up stockpiles in case the Soviets reimposed the blockade. The last flight of the Berlin Airlift occurred on September 30, 1949.

The Berlin Airlift vindicated President Truman's decision and proved again the importance of air power. The airlift demonstrated determination without belligerence while providing humanitarian relief. In succeeding decades, nearly every natural disaster or political crisis has seen the speedy arrival of U.S. aircraft carrying relief goods or troops, or both.

The Berlin Airlift Historical Foundation preserves the heritage of the airlift. It is a non-profit organization with vigorous educational programs. The foundation's address is P.O. Box 782, Farmingdale, New Jersey 07727.

Computers Make Things Possible

By the time that the Wright Brothers conducted their first gliding experiments at Kitty Hawk, the 1900 Census was completed. The Census Bureau tabulated the data via a system that used holes punched in cards, a method tried for the first time for the 1890 national headcount. Herman Hollerith, an engineer from the Massachusetts Institute of Technology, invented the system and machines that allowed operators to punch, tabulate, and sort the cards. He founded a company based upon his invention and called it the Tabulating Machine Company, which later became International Business Machines (IBM).

The next major advance in machine computing happened in the 1940s. Harvard University and IBM supported Howard Aiken's research.

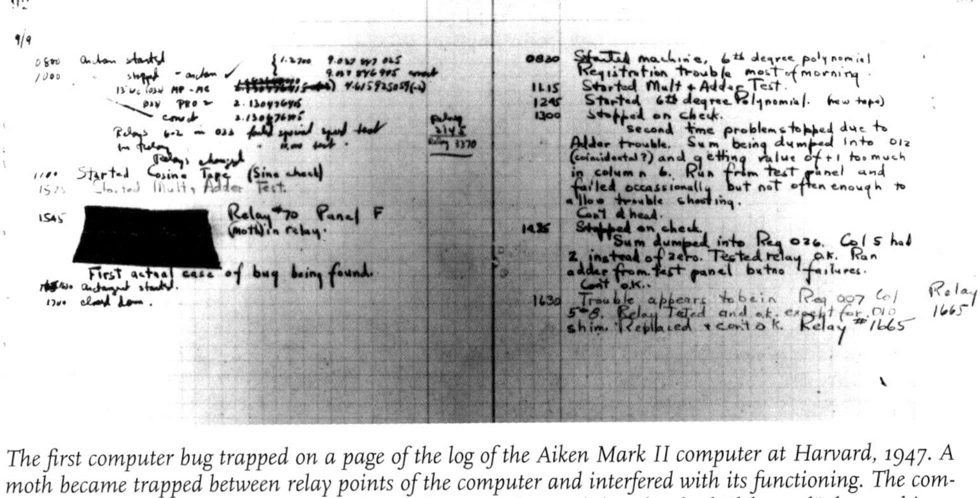

9/9

0800 Anctan started

1000 stopped - anctan ✓

1100 Started Cosine Tape (Sine check)

1525 Started Mult + Adder Test.

1545 Relay #70 Panel F (moth) in relay.

First actual case of bug being found.

1630 antangent started.

1700 closed down.

0800 Started machine, 6th degree polynomial

Registration trouble most of morning.

1115 Started Mult + Adder Test.

1245 Started 6th degree Polynomial. (new tape)

1300 Stopped on check.

second time problem stopped due to Adder trouble. Sum being dumped into 012 (coincidental?) and getting value of +1 too much in column 6. Run from test panel and failed occassionally but not often enough to allow trouble shooting.

Con't ahead.

1425 Stopped on check.

Sum dumped into Reg 026. Col 5 had 2 instead of zero. Tested relay o.k. Ran adder from test panel but no failures.

Con't o.k.

1630 Trouble appears to be in Reg 007 Col 5-8. Relay Tested and o.k. except for .010 shim. Replaced + con't o.k. Relay #1665

Relay 1665

The first computer bug trapped on a page of the log of the Aiken Mark II computer at Harvard, 1947. A moth became trapped between relay points of the computer and interfered with its functioning. The computer operators taped the moth to the log and put out the word that they had "debugged" the machine. (Naval Historical Foundation)

Aiken's machine used electromagnetic relays to perform mathematical computation on decimal numbers. His computer, dubbed the Mark I, made its debut in 1944. The huge device weighed five tons and was 50 feet long.

Meanwhile, researchers at the University of Pennsylvania worked on constructing a device that would help Army artillery crews calculate the precise angle for firing their guns to hit a target. Named ENIAC, for Electronic Numerical Integrator and Calculator, the machine was unveiled in 1946. ENIAC weighed 30 tons and was the size of a railroad freight car. More than 18,000 vacuum tubes provided the power for ENIAC's calculations.

IBM followed soon after with its own vacuum-tube computer, the IBM 701. It could perform 17,000 instructions per second, faster than any other computer on the market.

Transistors appeared in 1948 and soon began to supplant vacuum tubes. By the early 1950s transistors enabled computer makers to develop smaller and faster computers. Progress toward smaller and faster computers continued with the advent of integrated circuits in 1958.

In 1975, Steven Jobs and Stephen Wozniak founded Apple Computer, and Bill Gates and Paul Allen founded Microsoft. Personal computers became available to large numbers of people soon after 1980.

In the more than two decades since 1980, computing power has become a commodity possessed and used almost everywhere. The National Academy of Engineering assessed the engineering achievements of the 20th century and came up with a list of the top 20 that had the greatest positive effect on mankind. Neil Armstrong, a career engineer and the first human to step upon the Moon, announced the selections in February 2000. He reported that space flight was number 12. The airplane came in third. Electricity was first, because it made all the others possible. Computers ranked eighth.

Whether computers rank eighth or first or somewhere else, their power is embedded in everyday life, and especially in aerospace. To evaluate the impact of computers on everyday life, pause a moment and consider what life might be like without them.

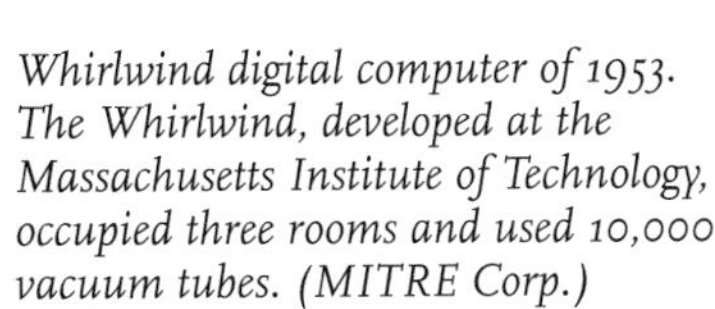

Whirlwind digital computer of 1953. The Whirlwind, developed at the Massachusetts Institute of Technology, occupied three rooms and used 10,000 vacuum tubes. (MITRE Corp.)

William H. Pickering (left), James A. Van Allen (center), and Wernher von Braun hoist a model of Explorer I *and final stage of the Jupiter-C rocket after the successful launch on January 31, 1958. (NASA)*

Jets, Missiles, and Space 1950–1959

Airline passenger travel grew rapidly in the 1950s. Jet airliners such as the de Havilland Comet, Boeing 707, and Douglas DC-8 came into service and sharply reduced the time required for long-distance travel. Customers responded. In 1950, 17.3 million persons paid to fly as revenue passengers on U.S. airlines. By 1957, the number grew to 48.6 million persons, or 28 percent of the population. More than a million passengers flew the Atlantic in 1958, surpassing Atlantic steamship passengers for the first time.

The Korean War saw the advent of jet-versus-jet in aerial combat, with U.S. jet pilots downing 984 enemy airplanes while losing 94. Throughout the decade, the Cold War between the Soviet Union and the West intensified. The Soviets launched *Sputnik* on October 4, 1957. The shock of its success was a catalyst for the U.S. space program.

Both the National Aeronautics and Space Administration (NASA) and the Federal Aviation Administration (FAA) came into being late in the 1950s. NASA gave coherence and direction to formerly scattered activities. The FAA provided new impetus for safe and orderly aviation activities in the United States.

51 Atlas, First U.S. ICBM and Space Launch Vehicle

The first U.S. intercontinental ballistic missile (ICBM) was conceived in 1951, when the Convair Division of General Dynamics began developing the Atlas ICBM for the U.S. Air Force. The Atlas had its origins in Germany's primitive V-2 ballistic rocket. Like the V-2, it was liquid-fueled. But the Atlas was a dramatically different ballistic missile, unprecedented in many respects.

Advancements in materials, electronics, and rocket propulsion made it possible for the Atlas missile to carry an exceptionally heavy payload, including a thermonuclear warhead and a computer-controlled guidance system highly sophisticated for its time. The Atlas rocket motor was powerful enough to boost the missile above the atmosphere and into ballistic flight of up to 5,000 miles downrange.

Atlas was still in development when the Soviet Union launched its first *Sputnik* satellite into orbit on October 4, 1957. The *Sputnik* launch indicated that the USSR had surpassed the United States in rocket power, and thus in ICBM capability.

The Atlas ICBM became operational in September 1959. With its thermonuclear punch, Atlas was a powerful weapon in the Cold War competition with the Soviet Union for strategic superiority. The newly deployed ballistic missile lent credibility to the "massive retaliation" policy of the U.S. government. The Air Force Atlas was succeeded by the liquid-fueled Titan ICBM and was phased out of the ICBM inventory in 1965.

Atlas rockets served as stalwart launchers of NASA's early manned space flights, propelling all Project Mercury space capsules into orbit. NASA replaced the Atlas boosters with second-generation, liquid-fueled Titan II rockets to launch all Project Gemini capsules, but kept Atlas in service to launch the maneuverable Agena rockets.

The Agena docked with *Gemini* in space to form a rigid unit. The Agena's motor then fired to propel the docked pair into a different orbit. Atlas rockets were also used through the years as boosters in numerous unmanned space programs, including the Ranger lunar mission, the *Mariner 2* Venus fly-by, and the *Mariner 4* flight to Mars.

Improved versions of the Atlas rocket built by Lockheed Martin Space Systems Company continued to provide reliable launch capabilities into the beginning of the 21st century.

An early Atlas missile rises from its pad as the service gantry (left) falls away. (USAF photo via Air Force History Support Office)

The Collier Trophy for 1959 was awarded to the team of the U.S. Air Force, Convair Division of General Dynamics, and Space Technology Laboratories for developing, testing, and putting the Atlas into operation.

52 Kaman K-225, First Turbine-Powered Helicopter

Charles H. Kaman left the position of chief aerodynamicist at United Aircraft in 1945, at age 26, to found the Kaman Corporation. He was dedicated to developing and flying his own new type of helicopter. He succeeded. The Kaman K-125 featured two intermeshing main rotors and no tail rotor. It flew for the first time on January 15, 1947.

By 1950 the Navy and Coast Guard were flying a more advanced Kaman helicopter, the K-225. It was a two-place aircraft with a tandem seating arrangement and a 225-horsepower piston engine. Piston engines powered all helicopters of that era. Although gas turbine engines were entering service in military fighter and bomber airplanes, no one had put a jet engine in a helicopter.

Charles Kaman took the bold step that changed the future of helicopter propulsion. He recommended an experiment to the U.S. Navy: to install a Boeing 502-2 gas turbine engine in one of the Navy's K-225 helicopters. The Boeing jet engine was in service aboard Navy ships. It generated power comparable to 200 horsepower, which made it suitable for the K-225.

The combination worked. Test pilot Bill Murray made the first turbine-powered helicopter flight on December 11, 1951, at the Navy's Patuxent River test installation. Subsequent flight tests of the turbine K-225 taught the Navy and industry the advantages of turbine power for helicopters.

Kaman's success emboldened the military services and helicopter industry to shift from piston engines to turbojets for all helicopters. Turbojets produced equal power for less weight, less noise, and improved reliability. By the late 1950s, the helicopter industry began incorporating gas turbine engines in all new designs.

Test pilot Bill Murray flying the world's first turbine-powered helicopter, the Kaman K-225, December 1951. (Kaman Archive Photo)

De Havilland Comet 4 of British Overseas Airways Corporation. BOAC inaugurated transatlantic jet service between London and New York on October 4, 1958. (BAE SYSTEMS)

53

World's First Jet Airliner, the de Havilland Comet

In the immediate postwar era, de Havilland of Great Britain appreciated the commercial possibilities of the jet engine and built the Comet jet airliner. Other aircraft manufacturers concentrated on building bigger and faster transports powered by piston engines. The de Havilland Comet raised the curtain on the jet age.

First flight for the DH-106 Comet 1 powered by four de Havilland Ghost jet engines occurred on July 27, 1949. After extensive flight testing and route surveys, the 36-passenger jet aircraft entered commercial service with British Overseas Airways Corporation (BOAC) on May 2, 1952. From London, the aircraft flew to Johannesburg, South Africa, with stops at Rome, Cairo, Khartoum, Entebbe, and Livingstone.

The Comet made an immediate and dramatic impact on world air travel. It surpassed the cruising speed of the fastest piston-powered airliners by 200 mph. The Comet proved more economical to operate than predicted, with lower fuel costs and lower maintenance costs on the jet engines.

BOAC ensured its competitive advantage over other airlines by extending Comet service to the Middle East and Asia, including Singapore and Tokyo.

Unfortunately, the dramatic improvement in performance demonstrated by the Comet came at a painful cost. A series of tragic accidents between October 1952 and April 1954 included two cases of the airplane disintegrating at high altitude. British aviation authorities grounded the Comet fleet.

The Royal Aeronautical Establishment (RAE) at Farnborough began an intensive accident investigation. The investigators eventually deduced that repeated compression and decompression associated with cabin pressurization caused metal fatigue in the structure, leading to the in-flight structural failures. The RAE analysis contributed greatly to establishing structural standards for aircraft manufacturers and certifying authorities worldwide. It also advanced the grim art and science of aircraft accident investigation, raising the standards far higher than before the Comet accidents.

Meanwhile, Aeroflot, the Soviet Union's state airline, began regular jet transport service between Moscow and Irkutsk in September 1956, using the Tupelov Tu-104 transport derived from the Tu-16 long-range bomber.

De Havilland incorporated the lessons learned from the Comet 1 mishaps into the first transatlantic jet airliner, the Comet 4. Passenger capacity increased from 36 to 81 compared with the Comet 1. BOAC flew the first transatlantic jet passenger service on October 4, 1958, by flying a Comet 4 from London to New York.

The hiatus forced upon de Havilland by the Comet 1 mishaps created a gap which other manufacturers, notably Boeing and Douglas, used to their advantage.

54 Boeing 707 Jet Airliner Enters Service

The Boeing 707 earned the distinction of being the first jet airliner built in the United States to enter service. The 707 traced its lineage to the swept-wing B-47 and B-52 jet bombers, and the later 367-80, its immediate predecessor.

When the company began development of the jet airliner in 1952, it took a huge risk. No airline customers had placed orders for the aircraft. The airlines showed little interest in jets. They preferred to operate postwar piston airliners such as the Douglas DC-7 and Lockheed Constellation, waiting to see how the de Havilland Comet, the world's first jet airliner, fared in the marketplace.

The Boeing development program that ultimately evolved into the Boeing 707 airliner began in 1952 as a project dubbed 367-80 and nicknamed Dash 80. The name concealed the purpose of the project by implying that it was simply an evolution of the company's prop-driven model 367 Stratofreighter transport. The company increased its risk by setting up production capabilities for the Dash 80, although it still had no customers. The 367-80 prototype aircraft flew for the first time on July 15, 1954.

Boeing's risk eased a bit when the Air Force immediately ordered a batch of 29 of the aircraft for aerial refueling and other duties. The Air Force designated its version as the KC-135 Stratotanker. Deliveries of the KC-135 to the Air Force began in June 1957, where it soon became a key element in extending the global reach of American air power.

The 707 airliner development sequence provides an example of technologies flowing to and from military and civil projects to the benefit of both. Technologies from military projects (B-47 and B-52) enabled development of a civil aircraft (Dash 80), which led to another military aircraft (KC-135) and ultimately to another civil aircraft (707).

As production of the KC-135 began, Boeing stepped up its sales campaign with the airlines, now identifying the aircraft as the 707. Meanwhile, Douglas tried to sell its first jetliner, the DC-8, to airline customers.

Pan American became the inaugural customer for the Boeing 707 when it ordered 20 on October 14, 1955. The airline hedged its bet by ordering 25 DC-8s from Douglas.

The Boeing 707 flew for the first time on December 20, 1957. The DC-8's first flight took place on May 30, 1958.

Boeing beat Douglas to the market by delivering first to the airline customers. On October 26, 1958, Pan American inaugurated scheduled service between New York and Paris with the 707. American, Continental, and TWA began domestic jet travel with the Boeing 707 in the first half of 1959. United and Delta Airlines began jet service with the Douglas DC-8 in September 1959.

First Boeing 707 airliner in flight. The 707 flew for the first time on December 20, 1957. (Copyright The Boeing Company)

BOEING 707

55 *Sputnik* Shocks the World

On October 4, 1957, the Soviet Union launched *Sputnik I*, the world's first artificial satellite, into orbit. The stunning technical achievement caught the West off guard, ushered in the space age, and started a space race between the United States and the Union of Soviet Socialist Republics that would last for more than 30 years.

Sputnik I was a relatively small sphere, about as big as a basketball. But at 184 pounds, it was much heavier than the 3.5-pound payload of the Navy's Vanguard satellite in development at the same time.

The *Sputnik I* satellite emitted a distinctive voice and captured the attention of a global audience. Its radio chirping became the symbolic signal of space telemetry around the world. *Sputnik* broadcast its signal on radio frequencies that could be received by professional and ham radio operators around the world, flouting a prior agreement among world scientists to reserve special frequencies for satellite telemetry. Its transmitter fell silent on October 26, 1957 after three weeks of operation.

On November 3, 1957, the Soviet Union launched *Sputnik II*, a larger and heavier artificial satellite than its predecessor. The increased payload included a dog named Laika. Laika became the first living organism to orbit Earth. *Sputnik II* ceased transmission on November 10, 1957.

Sputnik III shot into orbit on May 15, 1958. *Sputnik III* weighed 2,926 pounds and the Soviets claimed it could carry a man. The vehicle remained in orbit for two years.

Sputnik I *was the first manmade satellite in space. (NASA)*

Lifting the lid provides a look inside Sputnik I. *(NASA)*

56 Federal Aviation Administration Established

Air traffic in the United States grew rapidly in the 1950s, and the skies became crowded. In June 1956, two airliners collided over the Grand Canyon, killing 128 people. That catastrophe and other accidents, plus a general awareness that existing systems for keeping aircraft separated were inadequate, spurred Congress into action. Congress enacted the Federal Aviation Act of 1958 and President Dwight D. Eisenhower signed it into law on August 23. The act, Public Law 85-726, created a new federal organization named the Federal Aviation Agency (FAA), which came into being on November 1, 1958. (The name changed to Federal Aviation Administration in 1967 when it became part of the newly created Department of Transportation.)

Elwood R. "Pete" Quesada took the oath as the first administrator of the FAA. Quesada had been President Eisenhower's primary advisor on civil aeronautics. As an Army pilot, he was a crewmember of the *Question Mark*, the Army Air Service airplane that in January 1929 set a new endurance record of 150 hours for continuous time aloft.

Quesada and his staff were given the independence and authority to take complete responsibility for domestic airspace. The responsibilities included operating a nationwide air traffic control system to ensure safe separation of commercial aircraft during all phases of flight from departure through the en route phase to safe arrival.

The FAA also took charge of all aviation safety matters, ranging from aircraft certification and aircrew standards to maintenance and training. The Civil Aeronautics Board (CAB) transferred several major functions to the new FAA. The CAB was created in 1940 to make safety rules, conduct accident investigations, and perform economic regulation of the airlines. After the FAA was activated the CAB retained only the airline economic matters such as routes and rates.

Key events in the evolution of aviation in the United States are presented in *FAA Historical Chronology: Civil Aviation and the Federal Government, 1926–1996*, edited by Edmund Preston (Washington: Federal Aviation Administration, 1998).

President Dwight D. Eisenhower presides over Elwood Quesada's oath taking as first FAA Administrator. (FAA)

57 Integrated Circuits

Just as transistors supplanted vacuum tubes beginning in the 1950s, so did integrated circuits supersede transistors beginning in 1958.

Transistors did the work of vacuum tubes, but consumed less power, were more reliable, and much smaller—transistors of the early 1950s were as small as postage stamps. But for all their virtues, transistors shared a limitation that afflicted vacuum tubes: They had to be connected in circuits requiring thousands of soldering operations to create a device run by transistors. This created a "tyranny of numbers." The more circuits and connections required, the higher probability that one or more connections would be defective or fail in use.

Two electronics engineers working in different locations overcame the tyranny of numbers at about the same time. Jack St. Clair Kilby at Texas Instruments had the idea for a monolithic circuit in the summer of 1958. He theorized that all elements of a circuit, such as resistors, capacitors, and transistors could be made of a single material and interconnected in place, obviating the need for the soldering and attendant difficulties. Kilby built the first integrated circuit from a wafer of germanium. It was about half the size of a paper clip and it worked. Kilby demonstrated his integrated circuit to his colleagues at Texas Instruments on September 12, 1958.

At about the same time, Robert N. Noyce, a founder of Fairchild Semiconductor Company, concentrated on the notion of putting multiple electronic components on a chip of a single substance. Noyce approached the challenge differently from Kilby. In early 1959, Noyce connected the elements of a circuit by overlaying a thin strip of metal atop a silicon wafer. His concept worked and enabled Fairchild to produce the first commercial integrated circuits. Noyce co-founded Intel Corporation in 1968 with his colleague Gordon E. Moore.

Both Kilby and Noyce received patents for their inventions. Their companies fought over possible patent interference. After a long period of litigation, the issues were resolved. Kilby received credit for integrating components on a single chip and for a working demonstration. Noyce was recognized for designing a practical planar circuit and a method of interconnecting its components.

The integrated circuits created by Kilby and Noyce spawned great industries worldwide and revolutionized society and culture everywhere. Noyce received the National Medal of Technology in 1987. Kilby received the medal three years later. Also in 1990, they were co-recipients of the engineering profession's highest honor, the Charles Stark Draper Prize. In presenting the prize to Kilby and Noyce, President George Bush said, "Integrated circuits have enabled us to do the unimaginable."

58 NASA Established; Creates Focus on Aeronautics and Space

The National Aeronautics and Space Administration (NASA) opened for business on October 1, 1958, under the leadership of T. Keith Glennan, almost exactly one year after the Soviet Union launched *Sputnik I* into space on October 4, 1957.

The Sputnik series had plunged the United States into a crisis of confidence. Congress reacted directly to the Sputnik spectaculars by passing the National Aeronautics and Space Act. President Dwight D. Eisenhower signed the Act on July 29, 1958. As Public Law 85-568, the legislation transformed the National Advisory Committee for Aeronautics into the nucleus of the National Aeronautics and Space Administration, or NASA.

NASA was established to manage all civilian aeronautical and space programs, and "to provide for research into the problems of flight within and outside the Earth's atmosphere." The National Advisory Committee for Aeronautics (NACA) formed the core of the new agency.

NASA took over leadership of NACA's Langley Aeronautical Laboratory, the Ames Aeronautical Laboratory, and the Lewis Flight Propulsion Laboratory. Also blended into NASA were the Naval Research Laboratory's space science group, the California Institute of Technology's Jet Propulsion Laboratory, and the Army Ballistic Missile Agency, where Wernher von Braun's engineering team was developing large booster rockets to compete with those of the Soviet Union. Numerous other NASA centers were established around the country through the succeeding decades.

Under the leadership of Keith Glennan and Hugh Dryden, his deputy, NASA defined policies for space activities and developed goals and programs in support of those policies. Glennan and his colleagues built the foundation for future work in aeronautics and space. At the same time, the new agency immediately undertook a number of aeronautic and space programs.

By the time NASA came into being, the United States had already launched its own first Earth satellite named *Explorer I*, on January 31, 1958. NASA's most notable early endeavor in human spaceflight was Project Mercury. On May 5, 1961, astronaut Alan B. Shepard, Jr., rode his *Mercury* capsule in a 15-minute suborbital flight, thus becoming the first American to fly in space. On February 20, 1962, Mercury astronaut John H. Glenn, Jr., became the first American to orbit Earth. Project Mercury was followed by Project Gemini and then by Project Apollo, which took men to the Moon and finally dispatched the specter of *Sputnik*.

Although the new NASA quickly came to be called the "space agency," it placed considerable emphasis on aeronautical research right from the start in the best tradition of its distinguished predecessor, the National Advisory Committee on Aeronautics. The successful rocket-powered X-15, for example, flew above the atmosphere at hypersonic speeds, contributing valuable information for the manned space flight programs.

59 *Explorer I*, the First U.S. Satellite

Explorer I, the first U.S. Earth-orbiting satellite, rocketed into space on January 31, 1958. The satellite constituted a major part of the United States' program for the International Geophysical Year 1957–1958. It also represented a rapid reaction to the Soviet launch of *Sputnik I* almost four months earlier.

Immediately after *Sputnik I* went into orbit, three organizations were harnessed as a team to move rapidly with the Explorer satellite program as an alternative to the Navy's languishing Vanguard satellite program.

A team at the Jet Propulsion Laboratory at Pasadena, California, led by William Pickering, designed and built the satellite. James Van Allen led a team of scientists, engineers, and students at the State University of Iowa to create the satellite's instrument package. Wernher von Braun at the Ballistic Missile Agency at Huntsville, Alabama, headed a team that modified a Jupiter-C rocket to launch the satellite into orbit. The entire process took less than three months.

Explorer I was a small satellite. It weighed 30.7 pounds and measured 80 inches long by six inches in diameter. The instrument payload accounted for more than half the weight of the satellite. Small in size it might be, but its large purpose transcended scientific exploration.

Officially designated Satellite 1958 Alpha, *Explorer I* was sent aloft to seek out radiation in space. The data returning from *Explorer I*'s instruments surprised the scientists who received them. Geiger counters on board *Explorer I* indicated a much lower cosmic ray count than had been anticipated. Van Allen theorized that the satellite's radiation-finding instruments had been saturated and overwhelmed by radiation greatly exceeding their capacity to record it. He theorized that the radiation came from charged particles encircling the Earth, trapped in space by Earth's magnetic field.

The *Explorer III* satellite, launched on March 26, 1958, confirmed the existence of the radiation belts that Van Allen hypothesized. They were named the Van Allen Belts in his honor.

William H. Pickering (left), James A. Van Allen (center), and Wernher von Braun hoist a model of Explorer I *satellite and the final stage of the Jupiter-C rocket after the successful launch on January 31, 1958. (NASA)*

Gemini 4 *pilot James McDivitt photographed astronaut Ed White over New Mexico during the first American space walk. (NASA)*

Race to the Moon 1960–1969

The decade of the 1960s saw acceleration of the race to space as well as continued expansion of aviation activities on Earth. Yuri Gagarin's single orbit of Earth in April 1961 electrified the world and galvanized renewed U.S. activities in space. The Soviet Union was first to hit the Moon with an object sent from Earth, but two American astronauts became the first humans to set foot on the Moon. Global communications via satellite developed during the 1960s.

To achieve preeminence in space, the United States committed increasing resources. Government outlays for space activities (NASA, Department of Defense, and others) rocketed upward from $960 million for the 1960 fiscal year to $6.3 billion in 1969.

Aviation activities also picked up the pace in the 1960s. American aircraft manufacturers dominated the global market for airline transport. In 1960, more than 81 percent of the transport aircraft operated by world civil airlines (aside from China and the Soviet Union) were built in the United States.

More people flew aboard commercial airlines, which supplanted steamships for international travel and railroads for domestic trips. Domestic airline passengers in 1960 totaled 52.3 million. The number nearly tripled by 1969, to 142.3 million. The number of international passengers also tripled during the decade, growing from 5.4 million in 1960 to 16.8 million in 1969.

The number of certified pilots in the United States grew in similar fashion, from nearly 360,000 in 1960 to more than 691,000 in 1969.

60 Delta Expendable Launch Vehicle

The first successful space launch by a Douglas Aircraft Delta rocket took place on August 12, 1960, boosting the *Echo I* satellite into orbit. *Echo I*, an inflatable sphere 100 feet in diameter, was the first passive communications satellite in space. Passive satellites reflect radio waves. By contrast, active satellites receive, process, and retransmit signals. President Dwight D. Eisenhower sent a radio message to *Echo* that was reflected nationwide, demonstrating the feasibility of satellite communications.

NASA's Goddard Space Flight Center managed the *Echo I* launch in conjunction with the NASA Langley Research Center. It was the first of 21 consecutive, successful Delta launches, earning the Douglas Delta an early reputation as an extraordinarily reliable workhorse of a rocket.

Delta rockets boosted several other first-of-their-kind satellites into orbit. They included *Ariel I*, the first international satellite; *Telstar I*, the first privately owned satellite; *Syncom II*, the first synchronous orbiting satellite; the *Orbiting Solar Observatory; Tiros II*, the first weather satellite; *Explorer XVIII*, the first Interplanetary Monitoring Platform; and the first Global Positioning System (GPS) satellite. A Delta also launched the *Pioneer 6* space probe.

The Delta was derived from the Thor intermediate-range ballistic missile that Douglas Aircraft developed for the Air Force in the 1950s. The Delta was conceived as an "interim launch vehicle" to be employed only until rockets with greater thrust, then being developed for NASA's manned space program, came into service. But the Delta performed so well that NASA kept it around and modified it to launch ever-larger payloads.

The earliest Delta rockets lifted payloads of about 100 pounds into relatively low orbits. Their modified successors in the 1960s were capable of boosting satellites weighing more than 800 pounds into orbits of roughly 1,000 nautical miles. Delta II rockets have launched many navigation, communications, and space-exploration satellites, including the entire GPS constellation for the Air Force.

Boeing assumed ownership of the Delta program on absorbing its longtime proprietor, McDonnell Douglas. At the beginning of the 21st century, the Delta family of launch vehicles included the Delta II, Delta III, and Delta IV variants, each more powerful than its predecessor.

Delta II space launch vehicle awaits liftoff to carry a Global Positioning System satellite into orbit. March 27, 1996. (Department of Defense)

61

Yuri Gagarin, the First Human in Space

The Soviet Union announced to the world on April 12, 1961, that 27-year-old Major Yuri A. Gagarin had orbited Earth and returned safely. Gagarin flew aboard the Soviet 5-ton spacecraft *Vostok I.* He described the spherical shape of our planet and the blue halo that is its atmosphere. Upon landing, Gagarin joined the pantheon of great explorers. He became a global hero. Gagarin perished in an airplane accident in 1968.

On the day of Gagarin's historic flight, President John F. Kennedy held a regular news conference. He said he was tired of seeing the United States second to the USSR. He said, "We are behind." Soon after, President Kennedy congratulated Soviet premier Nikita Khrushchev on the feat. Khrushchev replied to Kennedy on April 30: "I express the hope that the Soviet Union and the United States may work together on the matter of mastering the universe, considering the mastering of the universe as a part of the great task of creating peace without armaments and war."

Soviet cosmonaut Yuri Gagarin, first human to orbit the Earth, April 12, 1961. (Courtesy of RIA Novosti)

Soviet cosmonaut Valentina Tereshkova was the first woman in space. She inspects an Apollo command module with U.S. astronaut Alan Bean during a tour of the Johnson Space Center on May 5, 1977. (NASA)

Three weeks later, on May 25, 1961, President Kennedy appeared before a joint session of Congress to present his message on urgent national needs. He referred to *Sputnik* and Gagarin and acknowledged the Soviet lead and head start in space. He stressed the need for the United States to "take longer strides."

President Kennedy set forth an accelerated program for space, and set this objective for the nation: "I believe that this nation should commit itself to achieving the goal, before this decade is out, of landing a man on the Moon and returning him safely to Earth. No single space project in this period will be more impressive to mankind, or more important for the long-range exploration of space; and none will be so difficult or expensive to accomplish."

Valentina Tereshkova was the first woman to fly in space. She made 48 orbits of Earth during her flight aboard *Vostok VI* from June 16 through 19, 1963. Two days before she launched, cosmonaut Valery Bykovsky went into orbit aboard *Vostok V.* He made 81 orbits to her 48. At one point their spacecraft passed within five kilometers of each other. They landed on the same day. Before becoming a cosmonaut, Valentina Tereshkova was an experienced parachutist.

62 First American in Space

Alan B. Shepard, Jr., will be remembered as the first American in space. His suborbital flight in the *Freedom 7* capsule on May 5, 1961, occurred three weeks after Yuri Gagarin had made his one-orbit flight. Shepard's flight lasted 15 minutes and took him 302 miles downrange from Cape Canaveral to a safe splashdown in the Atlantic Ocean. Brief it may have been, but Alan Shepard's flight showed that America was ready to get into space. He was the first American astronaut into space as part of Project Mercury.

NASA started the Mercury program in October 1958, a year after the Soviet Union launched *Sputnik*. Mercury engineers created a capsule to protect the crew from the frigid vacuum of space and exposure to radiation, as well as tolerating the high temperatures of reentry into the atmosphere. Of utmost importance was testing the Redstone rockets designed by Wernher von Braun's team in Alabama, which safely launched the first suborbital Mercury flights.

Shepard's *Mercury Redstone 3* flight proved an astronaut could work comfortably in space, survive weightlessness, and maneuver the spacecraft. Virgil I. "Gus" Grissom flew the second suborbital mission of the Mercury program on July 24, 1961.

The suborbital missions by Shepard and Grissom, and the four Mercury orbital flights that followed, demonstrated the value of skilled human crewmembers as crucial to the space program's success.

The seven original U.S. astronauts inspect a model of the Mercury *capsule and rocket assembly at NASA on April 30, 1959. They are (from left) Virgil I. Grissom, Alan B. Shepard, Jr., M. Scott Carpenter, Walter M. Schirra, Jr., Donald K. Slayton, John H. Glenn, Jr., and L. Gordon Cooper, Jr. (NASA)*

63 Orbital Flights of Project Mercury

On February 20, 1962, John Glenn, Jr., became the first American to orbit the Earth. An Atlas rocket launched his Mercury capsule named *Friendship 7* on a flight that included three orbits and lasted for nearly five hours. When he splashed down safely in the Atlantic, the primary goal of Project Mercury was demonstrated. John Glenn became an immediate national hero. An enthusiastic nation embraced the manned spaceflight program, which he epitomized.

Astronaut Glenn performed eight basic functions during his orbital flight, which NASA listed as falling into two basic groups. The first comprised systems management, sequence monitoring, control of vehicle attitude, navigation by ground reference and the stars, communications, and research observation. The second group required staying in good condition under the stresses of acceleration and weightlessness, and being patient during the pre-launch period and while waiting for pickup after splashing down in the ocean.

Six of the *Mercury 7* astronauts flew missions into space. (A heart condition grounded Donald K. "Deke" Slayton at the time.) Glenn was the first human to see a sunrise and sunset in space and to take photographs of Earth. M. Scott Carpenter's three-orbit mission of May 24, 1962, focused on science experiments. Walter M. Schirra, Jr., followed his colleagues into orbit on October 3, 1962, in a six-orbit flight that dealt with the capsule engineering. On the final Mercury flight on May 15–16, 1963, L. Gordon Cooper, Jr., orbited Earth 22.5 times in 34 hours. During the flight he released the first satellite from a spacecraft. The satellite was a six-inch sphere intended to test how well an astronaut could see objects in space.

By the program's end in 1963, with six manned launches and a total of 52 hours in space, Mercury proved that a human could be successfully launched into space, operate and survive spaceflight, and return safely to Earth, thus providing the foundation for the Gemini and Apollo programs that followed.

Grissom, Cooper, and Schirra went on to fly in the Gemini program. Shepard, Schirra and Slayton returned to space in the Apollo program. John Glenn became the first senior citizen in space, flying as a crewmember on the STS-95 (Space Transportation System-95) *Discovery* shuttle mission in the fall of 1998.

The seven Project Mercury astronauts received the Collier Trophy for 1962 for pioneering manned space flight in the United States.

For summaries of flights in the Mercury and succeeding programs through June 1998, see the NASA publication *U.S. Human Spaceflight: A Record of Achievement, 1961–1998*, compiled by Judy A. Rumerman. It is number nine in NASA's Monographs in Aerospace History Series.

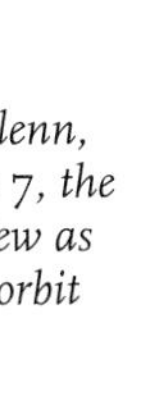

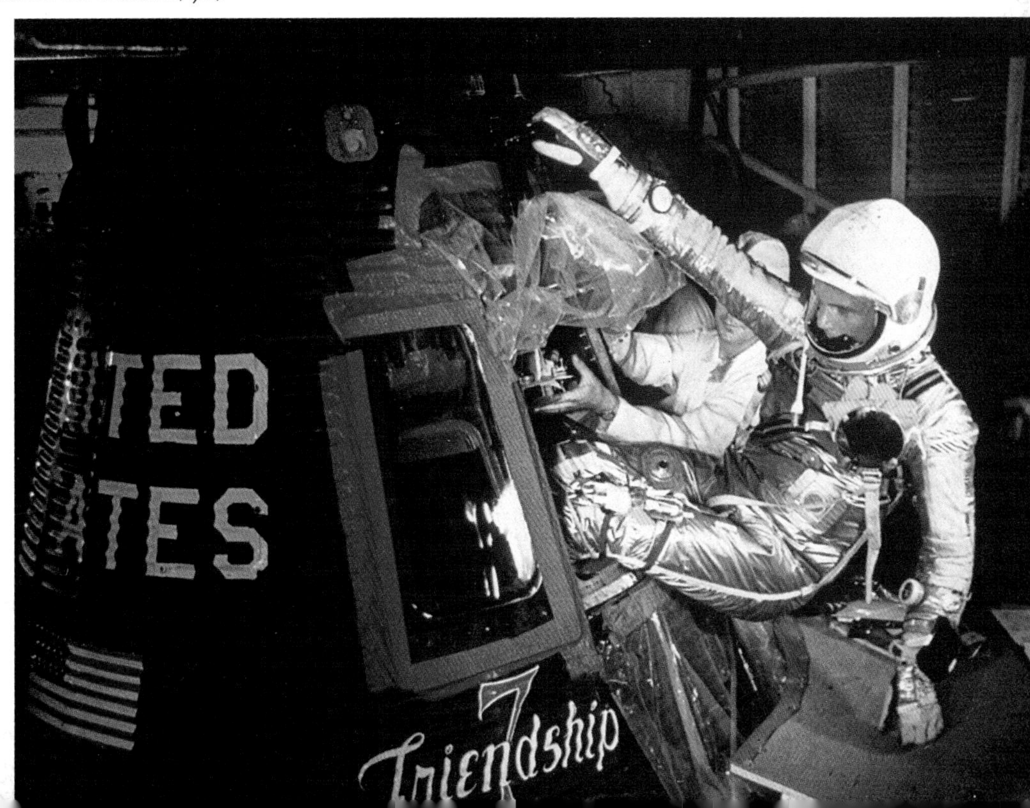

Astronaut John H. Glenn, Jr., enters Friendship 7, *the Mercury capsule he flew as the first American to orbit Earth. (NASA)*

Test pilot Bill Bedford hovers the P1127 V/STOL aircraft on its first tethered flight, October 21, 1960. (BAE SYSTEMS)

64 Harrier: the Vertical/Short Takeoff and Landing Aircraft

The notion of a practical V/STOL (vertical/short takeoff and landing) aircraft developed in the late 1950s at Hawker Siddeley Aviation in Great Britain. The concept envisioned an aircraft that could both hover like a helicopter and transition into level flight. It was made possible through vectoring the thrust from its jet engine through four rotatable nozzles. Hawker and Rolls-Royce collaborated in building a prototype V/STOL aircraft designated P1127.

Test pilot Bill Bedford flew the P1127 on its first flight at Dunsfold, Surrey, on October 21, 1960. Bedford's broken ankle was wrapped in a cast. Since no medical regulations existed for the new type of aircraft, he made the flight and many others in the development program that followed.

Improvements made to the P1127 during the development program led to an aircraft named the Kestrel, after a British bird of prey that hovers and swoops. Kestrel's first flight occurred on March 7, 1964. The British, German, and U.S. military forces decided to evaluate the Kestrel for military use. A tripartite evaluation squadron was formed in 1965. Extensive flight tests led to endorsement of the Kestrel's value for military service.

The Royal Air Force (RAF) became the first customer for the V/STOL aircraft. Renamed the Harrier, it flew for the first time on August 31, 1966. Harriers entered service with the RAF in 1969 and by 1972, four frontline squadrons were equipped with it for the ground attack, close support, and reconnaissance roles.

A naval version called the Sea Harrier entered service with the Royal Navy in 1979. Both the RAF and Royal Navy took Harriers into combat for the first time in the Falklands War of 1982. The aircraft and their crews performed vital roles in aerial engagements and ground support.

The U.S. Marine Corps became the first export customer by ordering 102 Harriers, the Marine version being designated the AV-8A. The first Marine Squadron so equipped was formed in South Carolina in 1971, developing the doctrine and tactics

AV-8B Harrier launches at Marine Attack Training Squadron 203, 2d Marine Aircraft Wing, Marine Corps Air Station Cherry Point, North Carolina. (L/Cpl C.E. Sellers, USMC)

Kestrel XV-6 aircraft of the Tripartite Evaluation Squadron in 1965. Kestrel evolved into the Harrier. (BAE SYSTEMS)

for V/STOL operations from austere land bases and at sea from helicopter assault ships.

Boeing, British Aerospace, and Rolls-Royce worked together to develop the AV-8B, an upgrade of the AV-8A model. The first one was delivered in 1983. The Harrier II Plus, a night attack version for the Marine Corps, entered the inventory in July 1993.

Harriers were the first Marine Corps tactical aircraft to arrive in the Persian Gulf during Operation Desert Storm. They flew from small strips and from warships at sea. During 42 days of combat operations, 86 USMC Harrier II aircraft flew 3,380 combat sorties, compiling 4,112 combat air-hours and delivering more than six million pounds of ordnance. Harrier II squadrons attained an aircraft readiness rate of better than 90 percent, unprecedented in a wartime environment.

Harriers fly in service with the RAF and Royal Navy, the U.S. Marine Corps, Indian Navy, Italian Navy, and Spanish Navy.

Syncom Communications Satellites

65

NASA started a program in the early 1960s called Syncom to demonstrate the feasibility of communications via satellites stationed in synchronous orbits. Arthur C. Clarke had proposed the concept in a magazine article in 1945. Clarke speculated that three satellites spaced evenly around Earth (120 degrees apart) in synchronous orbits could provide communications for the entire populated world.

A synchronous satellite orbits at 22,300 miles altitude. Because its orbital speed matches Earth's rate of rotation the satellite stays in position above a location on the Earth below.

Hughes Aircraft built three Syncom satellites for NASA. The satellites weighed 78 pounds when deployed and had a diameter slightly larger than 2 feet. NASA launched three Syncoms using Delta boosters. *Syncom 1* went up on February 14, 1963, but lost contact with ground stations. *Syncom 2* was launched on July 26, 1963, and went into orbit over the Atlantic Ocean. It operated as intended and became the world's first successful synchronous communications satellite. President John F. Kennedy used *Syncom 2* to speak with, and exchange facsimile images with, Nigerian Prime Minister Abubakar Balewa. *Syncom 2* was later moved to a position above the Indian Ocean.

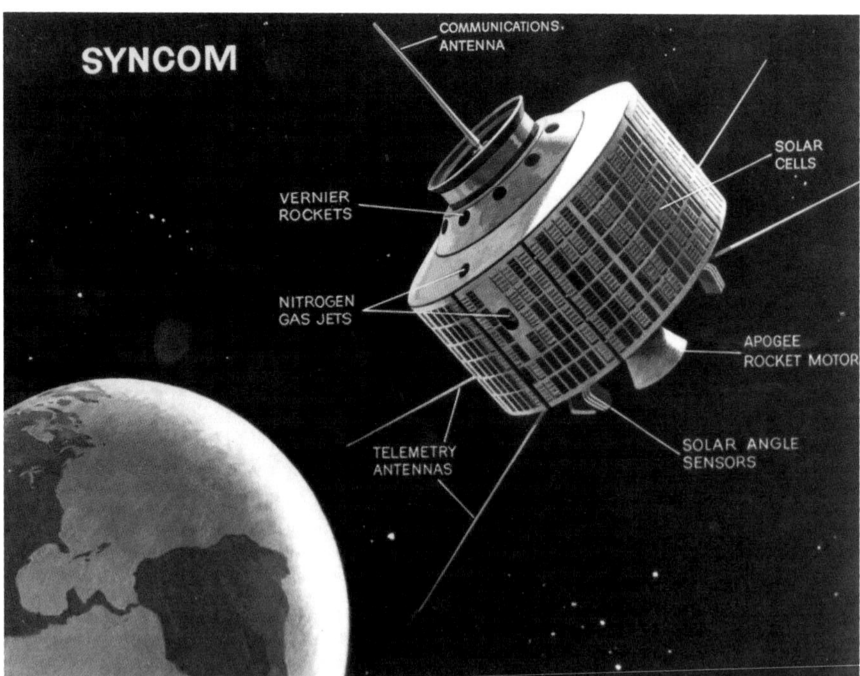

Components of Syncom 2, *the world's first synchronous communications satellite. (NASA)*

Syncom 3 followed its siblings into orbit on August 19, 1964, to a spot over the Pacific Ocean near the International Date Line. Shortly after beginning operation, *Syncom 3* transmitted a TV relay of the Olympic Games in Tokyo to viewers in the United States.

Syncom 2 and *Syncom 3* operated for five more years before being decommissioned in April 1969. Their success ushered in a new era of satellite communications for the people of the world.

Harold Rosen and Allen Puckett of Hughes Aircraft received the National Medal of Technology in 1985 for leadership in initiation and development of geostationary communications satellites.

66

X-15 Flies Highest and Fastest

NASA's research with the Bell X-1 series of rocket planes explored the supersonic flight regime and led to a new generation of supersonic research aircraft. The entire X-1 series of tests ended at the end of 1958 after a total of 237 flights.

Looking ahead, the Air Force and the National Advisory Committee for Aeronautics (NACA) asked North American Aviation to build a rocket plane that would explore the regime of hypersonic flight (five times the speed of sound). The highest speed ever attained in the X-1A (by Charles E. Yeager) was Mach 2.44 (1,650 mph) on December 12, 1953. To fly two or three times faster seemed a difficult goal. North American took the challenge.

North American finished the first of three X-15s by late 1958 as the X-1 program was ending. Reaction Motors built the rocket engines for both planes. The engine in the X-1 could not be throttled back once it was ignited, and burned at top power for only five minutes. The improved rocket engine on the X-15 could be speed controlled over one hour of flight.

Research pilot Scott Crossfield made the first powered X-15 flight on September 17, 1959. He clocked a speed of 1,393 mph, or Mach 2.11 at an altitude of 52,341 feet.

Inside view of the X-15 cockpit. The stick and rudder pedals are conventional controls for flight in the atmosphere. Controls on each side use gas jets for controlling the aircraft outside the atmosphere. (NASA)

The X-15 drops away from the B-52 mother ship and its rocket motors ignite. (NASA)

The X-15 team continued to strive to fly higher and faster. On the eighteenth X-15 flight on August 18, 1960, research pilot Joe Walker set a new speed record of 2,196 mph, or Mach 3.31. On the flight after that, Air Force Major Robert White reached an altitude of 136,500 feet. (Highest altitude reached in the X-1 program was 90,440 feet.)

The X-15 program set records that exceeded expectations. In March 1961, Major White became the first person to exceed Mach 4 and in June 1961, he exceeded Mach 5. As for altitude, Joe Walker reached 246,700 feet in April 1962 on the X-15's 52nd flight. Major White flew to a higher altitude in July 1962, when he reached 314,750 feet. A year later, on August 22, 1963, Joe Walker reached 354,200 feet or 68 miles above Earth.

Since those flights and 11 others were actually above Earth's atmosphere, the pilots received astronaut's wings.

In all, the three X-15s logged 199 flights. More than half of the missions flew faster than Mach 5 and four exceeded Mach 6. Research pilot Pete Knight flew the fastest, reaching 4,520 mph or Mach 6.7 on October 3, 1967, almost 20 years after Yeager in the Bell X-1 passed through the sound barrier. The pioneering achievements of the X-15 program paved the way for NASA's manned space programs from Mercury to Gemini to Apollo to the Space Shuttle.

President John F. Kennedy presented the Collier Trophy for 1961 to the X-15 pilots for their contributions to the advancement of flight and their skill and courage as test pilots.

President John F. Kennedy, Scott Crossfield, and Major Robert White with the 1961 Collier Trophy, July 18, 1962. (NASA)

67

Alexei Leonov, the First Human to Walk in Space

Orbiting high over Earth on March 18, 1965, Alexei Leonov opened the airlock of his spacecraft *Voskhod 2* and stepped into the cold vacuum of space. He floated outside the vehicle for 12 minutes, connected to it only by a tether cord.

When Leonov reeled himself along the cord and worked his way back through the airlock into the *Voskhod 2,* he had established another first for the human race and for the Soviet Union's space program. Once again the Soviets had set down a marker to claim primacy in space.

Alexei Leonov was 25 years old and an experienced fighter pilot and parachutist when he became one of the first 20 members of the Soviet cosmonaut corps. After the *Voskhod 2* flight, Leonov served in a series of challenging positions within the Soviet Air Force and space program. Leonov returned to space in 1975 as commander of *Soyuz 19*, the craft that participated in the Apollo-Soyuz Test Project with NASA.

Soviet cosmonaut Alexei Leonov walked in space on March 18, 1965, the first human to do so. (Courtesy of RIA Novosti)

68

Ed White, the First American to Walk in Space

Astronaut Edward H. White II earned the distinction of being the first American to walk in space. He emerged from the two-man *Gemini 4* spacecraft during its third orbit after launch on June 3, 1965. White remained outside for 22 minutes while he and the spacecraft flew across the breadth of North America. Although linked to the spacecraft by a tether, White used a handheld gasjet device to maneuver himself in the vacuum of space. Pilot James A. McDivitt flew the spacecraft and photographed White's activities.

The *Gemini 4* astronauts remained aloft for four days, a new record.

The Gemini program built upon the knowledge from the single-pilot Mercury flights and created a bridge to the Apollo lunar missions with three crewmembers. Developing longer-endurance missions and experimenting with extravehicular activities contributed to the Gemini program's objectives. However, its main goal was to prove the techniques for rendezvous and docking in orbit.

The important first rendezvous occurred during the *Gemini 7* mission, flown by astronauts Frank Borman and James A. Lovell, Jr., during December 4 through 18, 1965. The crew of *Gemini 6*, Walter M. Schirra, Jr., and Thomas P. Stafford launched on December 15. Pilot Schirra brought his and Stafford's capsule into formation with *Gemini 7* and they flew together for five hours.

The crew of Gemini 6 *photographed the* Gemini 7 *spacecraft during the first rendezvous in orbit, December 1965. (NASA)*

Gemini 8 astronauts Neil A. Armstrong and David R. Scott accomplished the first orbital docking on March 16, 1966, with an Agena rocket target already in orbit. However, the mated craft started to roll continuously when a thruster on the capsule fired and stuck open. Armstrong and Scott undocked from the target and used their reentry thrusters to stop the roll and make an emergency descent to Earth.

Gemini missions *9, 10, 11,* and *12* followed. *Gemini 10* proved that radiation at higher orbits was not a problem and also achieved the first

Gemini 4 *pilot James McDivitt photographed astronaut Ed White in first American space walk on June 3, 1965. (NASA)*

double rendezvous in orbit. *Gemini 11* astronauts conducted multiple dockings and more spacewalks. On *Gemini 12*, November 11 through 15, 1965, astronaut Edwin E. "Buzz" Aldrin, Jr., made a tethered spacewalk lasting two hours and 20 minutes, the longest to date.

Twenty astronauts flew ten *Gemini* missions between March 1965 and November 1966, logging nearly 1,000 hours of spaceflight time. The program accomplished its objectives, and provided the necessary next steps to the Apollo lunar program, already well along in development.

Ed White, Gus Grissom, and Roger Chaffee perished in a fire aboard an Apollo command module during training on the ground on January 27, 1967.

69 Lunar Orbiters Shoot the Moon

On August 14, 1966, *Lunar Orbiter 1* lived up to its name by becoming the first U.S. spacecraft to orbit the Moon. It went there to photograph the surface of the Moon in preparation for the Apollo landings. *Lunar Orbiter 1* was the first of five successive spacecraft that performed the same mission through 1967. Their photos included highly detailed images of 20 areas pre-selected by NASA as possible safe landing sites for Apollo astronauts.

NASA awarded a contract to Boeing in 1964 to design and build the Lunar Orbiters. *Lunar Orbiter 1*, launched at Cape Canaveral, Florida, on August 10 by an Atlas-Agena booster, took more than 200 photos, including a shot of the Earth and the Moon together in space. That photo gave the Apollo astronauts a preview of Earth as they would see it from lunar orbit.

Lunar Orbiter 5, the last in the series, was launched on August 1, 1967. It photographed the Moon from August 6 through 18. When its mission was finished, on command the spacecraft departed from orbit and crashed into the lunar surface.

All five Lunar Orbiter missions were successful. They resulted in more than 1,000 photographs covering more than 14 million square miles, or 99 percent of the lunar surface, including the far side of the Moon invisible from Earth. The Lunar Orbiters captured images of objects as small as three feet across. They also gathered data on micrometeors and radiation in space and on the Moon's gravitational field.

Clifford Nelson, NASA's manager for the Lunar orbiter missions, examines a section of the 30-foot square mosaic composed of 127 photographs taken by one of the five Lunar orbiters. (NASA)

Final assembly of Boeing 747 in the world's largest building (by volume). (Copyright The Boeing Company)

70

Jumbo Jets Enter Service

Lockheed and Boeing competed in the mid-1960s for an Air Force requirement to develop a very large long-range transport airplane. Lockheed won the competition in 1965 and eventually built the C-5 Galaxy transports.

Boeing lost the Air Force bid. However, it adapted knowledge from the military competition to create a new civilian airliner, the successful 747 jumbo jet. The initial design of the 747 that Boeing offered to airlines contemplated its use either for passengers or cargo. The flight deck was placed above the passenger cabin, allowing cargo for the freighter version to be loaded through the nose. The characteristic hump behind the flight deck could be used for passenger seats or as a lounge. In the passenger configuration, the wide-body fuselage featured two aisles instead of the single aisle then standard. Pan American Airways became the launch customer for the 747, placing an order for 25 of the jumbos in April 1966.

On its first flight on February 9, 1969, the 747-100 flew 5,100 miles. After extensive flight-testing and FAA certification at the end of the year the 747 was ready to begin airline service. Pan American put it to work on the heavily traveled route between New York and London on January 22, 1970.

By mid-May 1970, Boeing had booked more than 200 orders for the 747. Additional orders flowed in as its virtues became apparent. For passengers, the airplane was more comfortable than the narrow-body jets. For airlines, the jumbo 747 reduced the cost of flying a passenger across the Atlantic by 30 percent.

McDonnell Douglas followed with its own wide-body DC-10 in 1970. Two of its three engines were mounted on the wings and the third on the tail. Lockheed's entry in the jumbo field was the L-1011, with three engines mounted as on the DC-10. The DC-10 and L-1011 were smaller than the 747, each carrying about 250 passengers.

With the advent of the jumbos, a new era of affordable air travel began. The Boeing Company received the Collier Trophy as leader of the industry-airline-government team that successfully introduced the 747 into commercial service. The citation expressly recognized the contributions of Pratt & Whitney for the turbofan engines and Pan American as the first customer.

Pike's Peak provides a scenic backdrop for Air Force One. Boeing modified two 747-200s (delivered in 1990) for the presidential fleet. The Air Force designation is VC-25A. (Department of Defense)

Boeing continuously upgraded the 747 from the original dash 100 version. The 747-200 was introduced in the mid-1970s and the 747-300 in the early 1980s. The 747-400 was introduced in 1988. Each model featured incremental improvements and refinements that took advantage of scientific advances in aerodynamics and structural materials as well as advances in propulsion and avionics. The 747-400 carried from 400 up to 550 passengers, depending on the configuration the customer ordered. Besides the passenger version, Boeing offered the 747-400 as a freighter or as a combination freighter and passenger model.

By the beginning of the 21st century, Boeing had produced variations of its 747 jumbo continuously for 30 years and the world's airlines continued to order them.

Airbus Industrie, the European aircraft consortium, entered the market later. By the beginning of the 21st century, Airbus had mounted vigorous competition for Boeing in the wide-body field and challenged it for share of the global wide-body market.

71

Concorde Introduces Supersonic Passenger Travel

The British and French governments agreed in November 1962 to cooperate to develop a supersonic passenger transport to be named Concorde. Concorde would fly at Mach 2.0. British Aircraft Corporation and Sud Aviation would divide the work equitably in a joint effort. Rolls-Royce and SNECMA were prime contractors for the jet engines. Construction got under way early in 1965.

At about the same time, the Tupelov design bureau in the Soviet Union began work on a supersonic transport designated Tu-144. The Concorde and Tu-144 designs were similar, featuring a long slender fuselage, delta wings, and four powerful turbojet engines with afterburner. On both types the nose section dropped hydraulically for better crew vision during takeoff and landing.

The Tu-144 flew first, taking to the air on December 31, 1968. The French Concorde prototype flew on March 2, 1969, followed by its British counterpart on April 9. Nineteen Concorde aircraft were built. A U.S. supersonic transport project began in 1963 but was abandoned after several years. A Tu-144 crashed at the Paris Air Show in

British Airways and Air France inaugurated supersonic passenger service from London and Paris into Washington Dulles International Airport on May 24, 1976. Concorde service into New York began on November 22, 1977. (BAE SYSTEMS)

1973, and the type never became a commercial passenger liner. The field of supersonic airline travel was left to Concorde.

British Airways and Air France began the first scheduled supersonic passenger service in the world on January 21, 1976, with simultaneous takeoffs from London and Paris bound for Bahrain and Rio de Janeiro respectively. Concorde airliners carried 100 passengers in luxury at the promised Mach 2.0 airspeed. Both airlines began Concorde service into Washington Dulles International Airport on May 24, 1976. Concorde service into New York was delayed until November 22, 1977, by environmental concerns and lawsuits.

The Concorde was a technological marvel but its economic performance was less spectacular. Nevertheless, it represented another advance in the history of flight and a milestone of technological prowess.

British Airways and Air France operated the Concorde on scheduled and charter services for nearly a quarter-century without a fatal accident. On July 25, 2000, an Air France Concorde crashed soon after takeoff from Paris, killing all 109 persons on board and five persons on the ground.

Intensive investigations into the accident led to modifications and recertification. The Concorde returned to British Airways and Air France transatlantic service in November 2001.

72 Apollo Program Sends Men to the Moon and Back

President John F. Kennedy's declaration that the United States would land a man on the Moon and return him safely by decade's end shifted the space program's goal from lunar orbit to manned lunar landing. The goal was achieved on July 20, 1969. *Apollo 11* astronauts Neil A. Armstrong and Edwin E. Aldrin, Jr., stepped out of their lunar module craft and walked on the Sea of Tranquility while Michael L. Collins remained in orbit in the command module.

President John F. Kennedy kicks off the Apollo lunar program when he urges Congress on May 25, 1961, to achieve the goal, "before this decade is out, of landing a man on the Moon and returning him safely to the Earth." In the background are Vice President Lyndon B. Johnson (left) and House Speaker Sam Rayburn. (NASA)

Apollo 11 *crew (right to left) Neil A. Armstrong, Michael Collins, and Edwin E. Aldrin, Jr. (NASA)*

Eleven missions were flown in the Apollo program. Two missions checked out equipment in Earth orbit, two flew lunar orbits, one aborted mission swung around the Moon, and six missions landed men on the Moon.

Three major components comprised the Apollo package: three-stage Saturn rocket launch vehicles, Apollo command/service module, and the lunar module. The lunar module had no aerodynamic qualities and was designed to fly in the vacuum of space. It separated from the command module and descended carrying two astronauts to the lunar surface. A small rocket launched it back to dock with the orbiting command module.

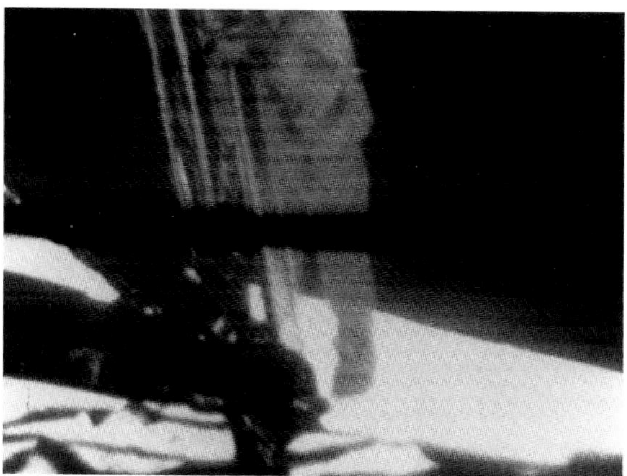

Astronaut Neil A. Armstrong descends lunar module ladder to become the first human to set foot on the Moon, July 20, 1969. (NASA)

Technical requirements and training were much more complex than in Mercury and Gemini. Ground control had to track two separate spacecraft after the lunar module separated. Astronaut training ranged from working in simulations of lunar gravity to learning geology and practicing landing and launching the lunar module.

Tragedy struck the Apollo program on January 27, 1967. Virgil I. Grissom, Edward H. White II, and Roger B. Chaffee were training inside an Apollo command module when a fire ignited and they lost their lives. The accident delayed the launch of *Apollo 7* until October 1968. However, the 11-day earth-orbiting mission of *Apollo 7* rebuilt the confidence of NASA and the American people in the space program.

Launch of *Apollo 8* on December 21, 1968, gave a Christmas present to the nation. The command module (with no attached lunar module) entered lunar orbit on Christmas Eve with Frank Borman, James A. Lovell, Jr., and William A. Anders aboard. *Apollo 9* successfully tested the lunar module, undocking and redocking it with the command module in lunar orbit, and tested the first spacesuit with its own life-support system. *Apollo 10*, a dress rehearsal for the Moon landing, broadcast the first live color television pictures from space.

The *Apollo 11* landing on the Moon was the pinnacle of the U.S. space program. Soon after-

Apollo 11 *astronauts appear before a joint session of Congress on September 16, 1969. Michael Collins is speaking. Neil A. Armstrong and Edwin E. Aldrin, Jr., listen from their seats on the right. In the background are Vice President Spiro T. Agnew (left) and House Speaker John McCormack. (NASA)*

launch on July 16, 1969, the third stage of the Saturn V propelled *Apollo* out of Earth orbit and on its outward journey to the Moon. *Columbia,* the command/service module, then separated from the Saturn, turned around, and connected nose to nose with the lunar module, the *Eagle,* which had been stored in the third stage.

The attached vehicles entered lunar orbit on July 19. Armstrong and Aldrin landed the *Eagle* on the Sea of Tranquility at 4:17 P.M. EDT on July 20. Armstrong reported to Houston, "The *Eagle* has landed." When he stepped onto the lunar surface six hours later, he said, "That's one small step for a man, one giant leap for mankind." A global television audience of 600 million people saw the grainy black and white images transmitted live from Tranquilly Base.

Armstrong and Aldrin took off from the Sea of Tranquility the next day and rejoined the *Eagle* to the *Columbia,* in which Collins had waited in lunar orbit. The *Columbia* descended into Earth's atmosphere and landed safely in the Pacific Ocean on July 24.

The second lunar landing in *Apollo 12* was precisely targeted for the astronauts to land near a robot module that had landed on the Moon two years earlier. They brought back pieces of the module; collected rocks; and took seismic, solar wind flux, and magnetic field readings, as well as many photographs on the surface and from orbit.

Apollo 13 proved the program's ability to weather a major crisis and bring the crew back safely from an aborted mission. Soon after launch an oxygen tank in the service module exploded, forcing the astronauts to use the lunar module to swing around the Moon to gain a trajectory back to Earth.

Apollo 14, 15, 16, and *17* spanned 1971 and 1972. The program ended in December 1972, having achieved all of its goals. The National Academy of Engineering ranked the Apollo program with the construction of the Pyramids and the Panama Canal as outstanding engineering achievements of all time.

The Apollo program earned two awards of the Collier Trophy. The trophy for 1969 was presented to Neil A. Armstrong, Edwin E. Aldrin, Jr., and Michael L. Collins for "the epic flight of *Apollo 11* and the first landing of man on the surface of the Moon." The *Apollo 15* mission received the Collier Trophy for 1973. Astronauts David R. Scott, James B. Irwin, and Alfred M. Worden were cited for their superb skill and courage. Dr. Robert T. Gilruth was cited as representing the engineering genius of the manned space flight team.

Apollo 17 *on the Moon. Astronaut Eugene Cernan checks Lunar Rover at Taurus-Littrow landing site before loading it with equipment. Scientist-Astronaut Harrison Schmitt took the photo. Schmitt was the last human to set foot on the Moon. (NASA)*

Simulated Mercury encounter by NASA's Mariner *Venus/Mercury spacecraft. (NASA)*

Aerospace Bounds Unlimited 1970–1979

In the decade of the 1970s, aerospace developments proved again that their potential was unlimited.

New spacecraft created and operated by the National Aeronautics and Space Administration (NASA) soared upward to discover new information about the world we live in and the universe in which our world exists. Satellites became routine tools of communications and remote sensing. Spacecraft of the United States and Soviet Union proved that humans could work and live in space for long periods and also that their host nations could cooperate in space.

New airplanes and helicopters were developed and put into service, surpassing the capabilities of their predecessors.

Airline passenger numbers nearly doubled in the decade. Domestic airlines carried 170 million passengers in 1970 and 317 million in 1979. International airline passenger traffic in the free world grew at the same pace, from 311 million worldwide in 1970 to 652 million in 1979.

Airline deregulation enacted late in the decade increased domestic competition and variety, often with unexpected results.

73 Landsat Looks at Earth

On July 23, 1972, America's first environmental satellite, called the Earth Resources Technology Satellite (ERTS), rose into orbit from Vandenberg Air Force Base, California, atop a Delta rocket. The launch was the start of a long-duration remote-sensing program of considerable importance to the United States. The ERTS name became Landsat in 1975, and it is remembered by that title. Landsat satellites have been in operation ever since the first launch, continuously supplying the world with images of the planet's surface.

Landsat 1 carried a television camera and an experimental digital sensor called the multi-spectral scanner that delighted NASA with its images transmitted from space. Multi-spectral scanners were also aboard *Landsat 2*, launched on January 22, 1975, and *Landsat 3*, launched on March 5, 1978, the year in which *Landsat 1* was retired. By then, *Landsat 1* alone had produced more than 300,000 images of Earth.

Landsat 4, the first of NASA's second-generation remote-sensing satellites, was launched on July 16, 1982, with a new sensor, the Thematic Mapper. It outperformed its predecessor, providing images of much greater resolution in the visible and near-infrared regions of the spectrum. *Landsat 5*, launched on March 1, 1984, also carried a Thematic Mapper and was still in operation at the turn of the

NASA Administrator James Fletcher (seated), and Charles Mathews, Associate Administrator for Applications, review first Earth Resources Technology Satellite photos. July 26, 1972. (NASA)

New views of Earth. NASA scientists examine early imagery from Landsat *satellite on large projection viewer. (NASA)*

century, many years beyond its design lifetime. Earth Observing Satellite Company (EOSAT), a commercial company, managed *Landsat 5*. EOSAT also managed *Landsat 6*, which failed to reach orbit after launch in October 1993.

NASA launched *Landsat 7*, the latest in the distinguished family, on April 15, 1999. The U.S. Geological Survey manages sales of its images.

Landsat satellites have recorded millions of images for use in business, science, industry, education, and government, including national security. Landsat established and sustained the United States as the world leader in land remote sensing.

The Landsat program also encouraged a new generation of very-high-resolution commercial satellites and revolutionary commercial applications of data from remote sensing in space. Examples include continuous weather observation leading to timely and more accurate forecasts, agricultural forecasts, and mineral exploration.

At mid-2002, NASA and the U.S. Geological Survey were planning the next mission in the series, called the Landsat Data Continuity Mission, with the goal of receiving the first data in 2006.

NASA and General Electric, representing the whole government and industry team, received the 1974 Collier Trophy for the development of Landsat.

74 Microprocessor: Computer on a Chip

Just as integrated circuits succeeded transistors, microprocessors represented the next step over integrated circuits in the evolution of computing. The progression from integrated circuit to microprocessor stemmed from a commercial order.

A Japanese company named Busicom came to Intel in 1971, requesting 12 separate chips that it would use in producing advanced calculators. Marcian E. (Ted) Hoff led the Intel team to develop a solution. Hoff and his crew came up with the answer. They created an off-the-shelf processor on a chip that would handle many functions and also be programmable. They assembled 2,300 transistors onto a chip measuring only 1/8 inch wide and 1/6 inch long. The device contained a central processing unit that controlled a random access memory, along with a read-only memory and a shift register.

The tiny but powerful device was named the Intel 4004. It could perform 60,000 operations per second and possessed the computing power of the 30-ton ENIAC of 25 years earlier. Even better, it was easily programmable. Busicom soon started selling calculators using the 4004. Intel bought back the rights from Busicom. Beginning at the end of 1971, Intel began selling the 4004 for $200, calling it "affordable computing power."

TRW Incorporated installed the Intel 4004 in the *Pioneer 10* spacecraft it was constructing for NASA to investigate the interplanetary space beyond Mars and the environment around the planet Jupiter. *Pioneer 10* took off on its mission on March 2, 1972. *Pioneer 10* reached its closest approach to Jupiter on December 3, 1973, at a distance of about 125,000 miles. It performed the assigned scientific missions as planned, including transmission of images of Jupiter's Red Spot.

After passing Jupiter, *Pioneer 10* began a trajectory out of the solar system. When it passed the orbit of Pluto in 1983, it continued into deep space. It is heading toward the red star Aldebaran in the constellation Taurus. NASA estimates *Pioneer 10* will traverse the 68 light years to Aldebaran in about two million years.

NASA maintained occasional communication with *Pioneer 10* with its Intel 4004 microprocessor through the 1980s and 1990s, and in April 2001 and March 2002. *Pioneer 10* is the farthest-traveled manmade object in the universe.

While *Pioneer 10* performed its scientific missions over a span of three decades, microprocessors on Earth became ever more powerful and found applications everywhere. The combination of microprocessors and ready-made software made the personal computer possible, bringing computing power within reach of nearly everyone.

75 F-14 Tomcat, Durable Navy Fighter

The Grumman F-14 Tomcat, the U.S. Navy's foremost interceptor and strike fighter, flew for the first time on December 21, 1970. The Tomcat made its first catapult launch and first carrier landing in June 1972 and entered service in the fleet in 1973.

Primary missions for the twin-engine F-14 include air superiority, fleet air defense, and precision strike against ground targets. Its fighting system is able to track 24 targets at the same time and engage six targets simultaneously. The Tomcat is armed with a mix of Phoenix, Sparrow, and Sidewinder missiles plus 20mm cannon. The varied armaments enable the F-14 to prevail in close air-to-air combat and strike aerial targets as far as 100 miles away.

The F-14 features variable-sweep wings. The wingspan for takeoff and landing is 64 feet. When swept back for supersonic flight (Mach 2.0) the wingspan is reduced to 38 feet.

Successive improvements have maintained the F-14's premier capabilities. For example, its original engines each produced 20,900 pounds of thrust. The two General Electric F110-GE-400 turbofan engines in the latest F-14D create 27,000 pounds of thrust, one-third more power. Upgrades have also been incorporated in the Tomcat's radar, fire control, and avionics systems. The Navy has configured the Tomcat to take on more combat roles. Besides the fighter mission, the F-14 has been equipped to become a medium-range strike aircraft.

The Navy expects the F-14 Tomcat to remain a potent element of naval air power until at least 2010.

First flight of the F-14 Tomcat at Calverton, Long Island, on December 21, 1970. Robert Smyth, Grumman chief test pilot, and project pilot William Miller flew the airplane. (Northrop Grumman Corporation)

Carrier takeoff. F-14A Tomcat aircraft of Fighter Squadron Fourteen (VF-14), its afterburners aglow, roars down the catapult track on takeoff from USS Dwight D. Eisenhower *(CVN-69). (Department of Defense)*

103
AC

76

Mariner Spacecraft Visit Venus and Mercury

NASA's Mariner series of spacecraft produced significant scientific information about nearby planets and interplanetary space. Examples from two of the missions highlight the successes achieved in the Mariner program.

Mariner 2 was the first spacecraft to encounter another planet successfully. It visited Venus on December 14, 1962, and returned data about the planet's mass, atmosphere, and magnetic field.

Mariner 10 was the seventh and last launch in the series. It was launched on November 3, 1973. The spacecraft carried 177 pounds of instruments, including two television cameras, an ultraviolet spectrometer, an infrared spectrometer, and two magnetometers.

During its mission, *Mariner 10* visited both Venus and Mercury. It was the first spacecraft to use the gravitational pull of one planet (Venus) to reach another (Mercury). Main objectives of the *Mariner 10* mission were to validate the gravity-assisted technique for changing course and measure the atmospheric and surface characteristics of Venus and Mercury.

After launch by an Atlas Centaur booster, *Mariner 10* followed an orbit around the Sun on its path to Venus. While en route to Venus, *Mariner 10* captured television and ultraviolet images of the comet Kohoutek. The spacecraft flew by Venus on February 5, 1974, at a distance of 2,600 miles. It accelerated upon entering the planet's gravitational field and used the gravity to its advantage in changing course toward Mercury.

Mariner 10's ultraviolet imagery of Venus displayed swirling clouds in a massive weather system blanketing the planet. Its infrared sensors measured extremely hot surface temperatures of up to 900 degrees Fahrenheit.

Continuing onward, on March 29, 1974, *Mariner 10* flew past Mercury at about 440 miles altitude and took the first close-up photos of the planet nearest the Sun. The images revealed rugged cratered terrain similar to the Moon.

Mariner 10 orbited the Sun once again, and revisited Mercury. The spacecraft made its second Mercury flyby on September 21, 1974, and visited Mercury for the third time on March 16, 1975. All three visits were productive. *Mariner 10* ran out of attitude-control fuel eight days later, and its mission was terminated. It remains the only spacecraft to have visited Mercury.

Mariner 10 *Venus-Mercury flight path showing positions of Earth and the planets on key dates. (NASA)*

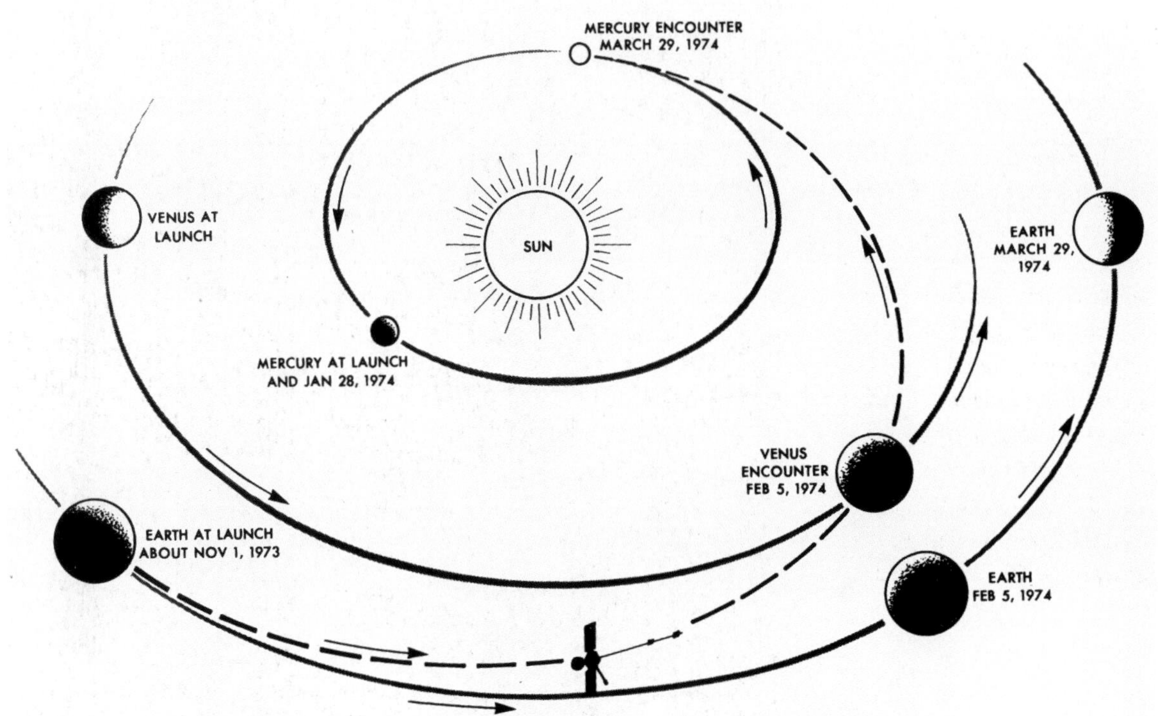

Skylab Is First U.S. Space Station

NASA's three Skylab missions proved that astronauts could work and survive in missions of long duration of one, two, and three months while conducting experiments and observations from space.

The orbital workshop was the main component of the Skylab space station. It was made from the upper stage of a Saturn rocket. Crew accommodations aboard Skylab were relatively spacious compared with the cramped capsules of the Mercury, Gemini, and Apollo programs. Its two sections consisted of an upper floor with storage lockers and workspace, while the lower section provided living space and an additional work area.

Three Skylab manned missions were flown from May 1973 to February 1974. *Skylab 2* lasted 28 days, from May 25 to June 22, 1973. First task for its crewmembers Charles "Pete" Conrad, Jr., Paul J. Weitz, and Joseph P. Kerwin was to repair the workshop launched on May 14 on the unmanned *Skylab 1* mission. After fixing the damage to the workshop the trio of astronauts conducted medical experiments and collected solar and Earth science data for the remainder of their time in orbit.

The *Skylab 3* mission extended to 59 days, from July 28 to September 25, 1973. Its crew of Alan L. Bean, Jack R. Lousma, and Owen K. Garriott continued a busy regime of experiments. Garriott and Lousma conducted a 6.5-hour spacewalk during the mission.

The last mission, *Skylab 4*, lasted the longest. Gerald P. Carr, William R. Pogue, and Edward G. Gibson flew the mission for more than 84 days, from November 16, 1973, through February 8, 1974.

Crews of the three Skylab missions logged 513 person-days in orbit, exceeding the combined totals of all of the world's previous space flights up to that time. The empty Skylab spacecraft reentered the atmosphere and burned up on July 11, 1979.

The Skylab program received the Collier Trophy for 1973.

Which way is up? Astronauts William Pogue (arms folded) and Gerald Carr demonstrate weightlessness during the 84-day Skylab 4 *mission. (NASA)*

78 Apollo-Soyuz Test Project

The Soviet Union embarked on its Soyuz manned spacecraft development project in 1962 as the first step toward its objectives of orbiting a manned space station and flying cosmonauts to the Moon. The Soviet lunar program fell into limbo after the *Apollo 11* astronauts landed on the Moon in 1969. However, the Soyuz program led to a succession of Soviet space stations and to a history-making American-Soviet rendezvous in space, the Apollo-Soyuz Test Project.

Apollo-Soyuz had its genesis in a goodwill agreement between the United States and the Soviet Union in 1972. The three-man Apollo command module and the Soviet two-man Soyuz module were the spacecraft for the mission.

The Apollo and Soyuz spacecraft lifted off from their respective pads on July 15, 1975. Soyuz went up from Baikonur Cosmodrome with cosmonauts Alexei Leonov and Valery Kubasov on board. Apollo launched almost seven hours later from Kennedy Space Center, carrying astronauts Thomas P. Stafford, Donald K. "Deke" Slayton, and Vance D. Brand.

The two spacecraft docked on July 17. Three hours after docking, Stafford and Leonov reached from their respective modules and shook hands.

Apollo mated with Soyuz by means of a docking module designed by NASA to serve as an airlock passageway between the two craft. The docking module played a central role in the Apollo-Soyuz Test Project mission: to demonstrate and test a universal docking system for use in future U.S.-Soviet cooperative space ventures, including joint rescue operations.

The Apollo-Soyuz mission spanned nine days from initial liftoff to return to Earth. It occurred during a period of U.S.-Soviet détente. The mission marked a lessening of tensions between the superpowers and opened the possibility of teamwork between the two nations in space.

According to the National Aeronautic Association publication, World and United States Aviation and Space Records (as of December 31, 2001), the Apollo-Soyuz crews hold the absolute world record for distance traveled in linked flight: 1,309,974 kilometers.

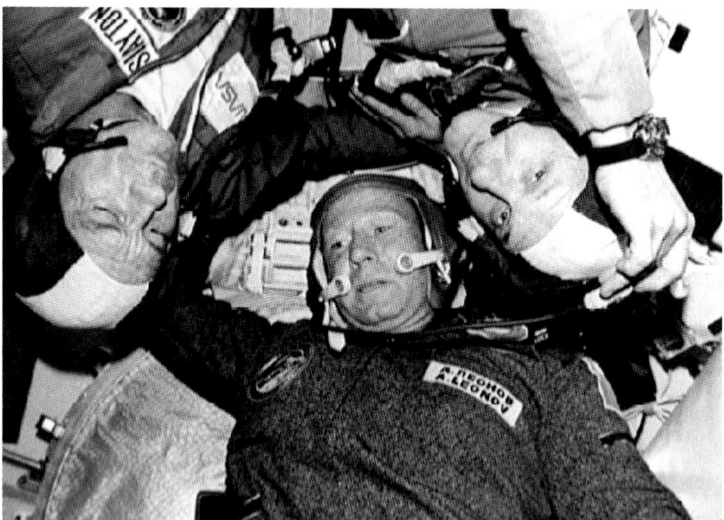

Putting their heads together. Cosmonaut Alexei Leonov and astronauts Donald K. "Deke" Slayton and Thomas P. Stafford during the Apollo-Soyuz mission. Stafford took the photo. (NASA)

79 F-16 Fighting Falcon

The F-16 Fighting Falcon originated through an Air Force competition in the early 1970s for a new lightweight fighter airplane. The Fort Worth Division of General Dynamics won with its design for the YF-16. (The company later became Lockheed Martin Aeronautics Company.)

Harry Hillaker led the team that designed and built the YF-16. They applied the technologies of the day to keep things simple and small and to create exceptional maneuverability. The YF-16 was light and small but sturdy, being able to take 9.0 Gs of stress, much more than other aircraft in the skies then and foreseen.

Test pilot Phil Oestreicher flew the first prototype YF-16 on January 20, 1974. He and other General Dynamics and Air Force test pilots continued the flight testing and evaluation program.

Meanwhile, four NATO air forces opened a competition for a new fighter aircraft. Belgium, Denmark, Norway, and The Netherlands stipulated that the airplane they chose must have part of its production performed by companies in their countries.

General Dynamics test pilot Neil Anderson and two other pilots flew the YF-16 on demonstrations for the buying NATO nations in May 1975.

The F-16 Fighting Falcon has retained its sleek external lines even as its internal systems have progressed through seven major upgrades. (USAF)

The competition came to a climax during the Paris Air Show in June 1975. Near the end of the exposition, the four NATO countries announced their choice of the F-16. The coproduction agreement worked, and became a model for similar cooperative international projects.

The first production F-16 for the U.S. Air Force flew in December 1976. The airplane went into operational service with the Air Force in January 1979. The F-16 has participated in all Air Force combat actions since its introduction. During Operation Desert Storm in 1991, F-16s flew more strikes than any other aircraft.

More than 4,000 F-16s had been produced by 2002, and the aircraft served in the air forces of a score of countries.

The Collier Trophy for 1975 went to the General Dynamics Corporation and the F-16 Air Force-industry team for development of the F-16.

80

AH-64 Apache Attack Helicopter

U.S. Army AH-64 Apache attack helicopters made the first strike of the Gulf War against Iraq. Attacking in the early morning hours of January 17, 1991, Apache crews knocked out Iraqi early-warning radar stations, creating gaps for coalition air forces to penetrate and begin the air campaign of Operation Desert Storm.

Apaches performed essential attack missions in the ground campaign that began on February 24, 1991. Throughout the lightning war that followed, Apache firepower devastated Iraqi armored and artillery units. They were credited with destroying more than 500 tanks and hundreds of other vehicles. During the sustained war in Afghanistan in 2001 and 2002, U.S. Army AH-64 Apaches performed vital roles in support of U.S. and allied combat actions against Taliban and Al Qaeda enemy forces.

The AH-64 Apache was developed to meet the U.S. Army's need for an advanced attack helicopter. Hughes Helicopters (absorbed into McDonnell Douglas and later Boeing) developed the aircraft and flew it for the first time on September 30, 1975. Hughes won the Army flyoff competition in 1976. After more than five years of development and testing, production of the AH-64A began in 1982.

The AH-64A Apache was equipped with laser and infrared systems that gave it the ability to conduct routine operations around the clock and in poor weather. Two General Electric T700 turbine engines powered the aircraft. Armament consisted of a combination of Hellfire missiles, 70mm rockets, and a 30mm automatic cannon. It operated

Soldiers of the Army's 102d Quartermaster Company refuel an AH-64 Apache attack helicopter during Operation Desert Storm. (Department of Defense)

Apache Longbow attack helicopter fires Stinger missile during Army tests. The Stinger adds a "fire and forget" capability to the aircraft's armament set. (Courtesy of Raytheon Company)

effectively in combat in Panama in December 1989, where much of the activity was at night. The night capabilities of Apaches and their crews proved invaluable in combat in the war in Afghanistan beginning in the autumn of 2001.

The addition of a Longbow fire control radar created a new model of the aircraft designated the AH-64D Apache Longbow Attack Helicopter. The Longbow radar is mounted on the Apache's rotor mast. It detects air and ground targets and is integrated with the Hellfire missile system, the Apache's main armament. Boeing delivered the first Apache Longbow to the U.S. Army in March 1997. Production for the U.S. Army is expected to continue for the next decade. Boeing is also producing AH-64D Apache Longbows for The Netherlands and, via teaming with Westland Helicopters, for the United Kingdom.

The U.S. Army and the Hughes AH-64A Apache team received the Collier Trophy for 1983.

The Boeing E-3 Sentry is the premier air battle command-and-control aircraft in the world. (USAF)

81

E-3 Sentry Controls the Air Battle

Boeing adapted the 707-320 aircraft to meet an Air Force need for an airborne air defense monitoring system. Modification included mounting a rotating radar dome on two struts extending 11 feet above the fuselage as well as packing advanced computing, control, and communications capabilities inside. Engineering test and evaluation with the Air Force began in October 1975. The first E-3 Sentry went into service in March 1977.

Inside the aircraft a team of 13 to 19 specialists, depending on the mission involved, keep up surveillance of the situation in all weather conditions. The radar system presents a 360-degree view of the situation from surface to high altitudes. The radar can detect low-flying aircraft out to 250 miles and farther for targets at medium to high altitude.

Besides maintaining continuous awareness of the air situation, the E-3 Sentry gathers information about positions of friendly and enemy ships as well as the location of friendly air, naval, and ground forces. This information is relayed in real time to commanders to enable them to control the action. The Sentry's operators also direct friendly aircraft to engage enemy aircraft within its zone. The electronic equipment aboard the E-3 is resistant to enemy electronic countermeasures.

Since its entry into the force in March 1977, the E-3 Sentry has become a necessary and vital component of national air power. It was among the first aircraft to deploy to the Persian Gulf during Operation Desert Shield in August 1990, where it kept Iraqi forces under round-the-clock surveillance. During the combat operations of Desert Storm in January and February 1991, E-3 crews logged more than 5,000 hours on station. They controlled more than 2,200 coalition aircraft sorties per day without mishap. They provided timely information for commanders and assisted in 38 of the 41 air-to-air kills recorded in that conflict.

The U.S. Air Force operates 33 E-3 Sentry Aircraft. NATO, France, Saudi Arabia, and the United Kingdom all have acquired E-3 Sentry aircraft. After the terrorist strikes on September 11, 2001, the North Atlantic Treaty Organization deployed several NATO E-3 Sentry aircraft to assist in combat air patrols in the skies over the United States.

82

Viking Missions to Mars

On July 20, 1976, a spacecraft landed on Mars for the first time in history, followed by another one less than two months later, on September 3. They were the *Viking 1* and *Viking 2* landers, conceived and operated by NASA. Their pioneering flights made 1976 an illustrious year in the annals of space exploration.

NASA embarked on its Viking Project in 1968 after canceling its more ambitious and much more expensive Voyager mission to Mars. Viking's success was especially poignant in view of the Soviet Union's previous repeated failures to land unmanned spacecraft on Mars.

The two Viking spacecraft combinations consisted of an orbiter and a lander. *Viking 1* was launched on August 20, 1975, and *Viking 2* on September 9, 1975. Both Viking landers touched down on the northern hemisphere of Mars after a voyage from Earth that took less than a year.

Once established in orbit around Mars, the orbiters photographed and transmitted images of the Martian surface that enabled NASA to select safe landing sites. Upon command, the unmanned *Viking 1* and *Viking 2* landers each detached from its orbiter and touched down gently

Viking 1 *orbiter photograph of the Martian surface taken on July 25, 1976. The* Viking 1 *orbiter photos enabled NASA to select a landing site for the* Viking 2 *lander, which landed in September. Shadows create the illusion of eyes, nose, and mouth of a human head on the huge rock formation in the center of the photo. (NASA)*

First photograph of the Martian surface, taken by the Viking 1 *lander minutes after it settled onto the Martian surface on July 20, 1976. Center of the image is about five feet from the camera. (NASA)*

on the Martian surface at different locations. The orbiters continued circling Mars.

Landing safely on Mars required a tricky descent through an atmosphere only one percent as dense as Earth's. Each orbiter fired its retro-rockets and descended beneath a parachute. NASA selected landing sites in low-lying regions of the Martian surface so the landers could decelerate to land softly.

The Viking orbiters reconnoitered Mars and its atmosphere remotely via photographs and radio signals. The Viking landers employed their instruments in physical contact with the atmosphere and the surface. Each lander came equipped with two cameras and a sampler arm with a collector head, a magnet, and a temperature sensor. Each of them also carried a seismometer, a spectrometer, and a meteorology boom with wind-direction and wind-velocity sensors.

The *Viking 2* orbiter powered down on July 24, 1978, after making 706 orbits. The *Viking 1* orbiter was shut down two years later on August 7, 1980, after more than 1,400 orbits. The *Viking 2* lander stopped communicating on April 11, 1980. The *Viking 1* lander lasted longer, but fell silent two and one-half years later on November 13, 1982.

A large photo mosaic displays the images that the Viking 2 *orbiter captured of this massive dust storm almost completely covering the southern hemisphere of Mars on June 7, 1977. (NASA)*

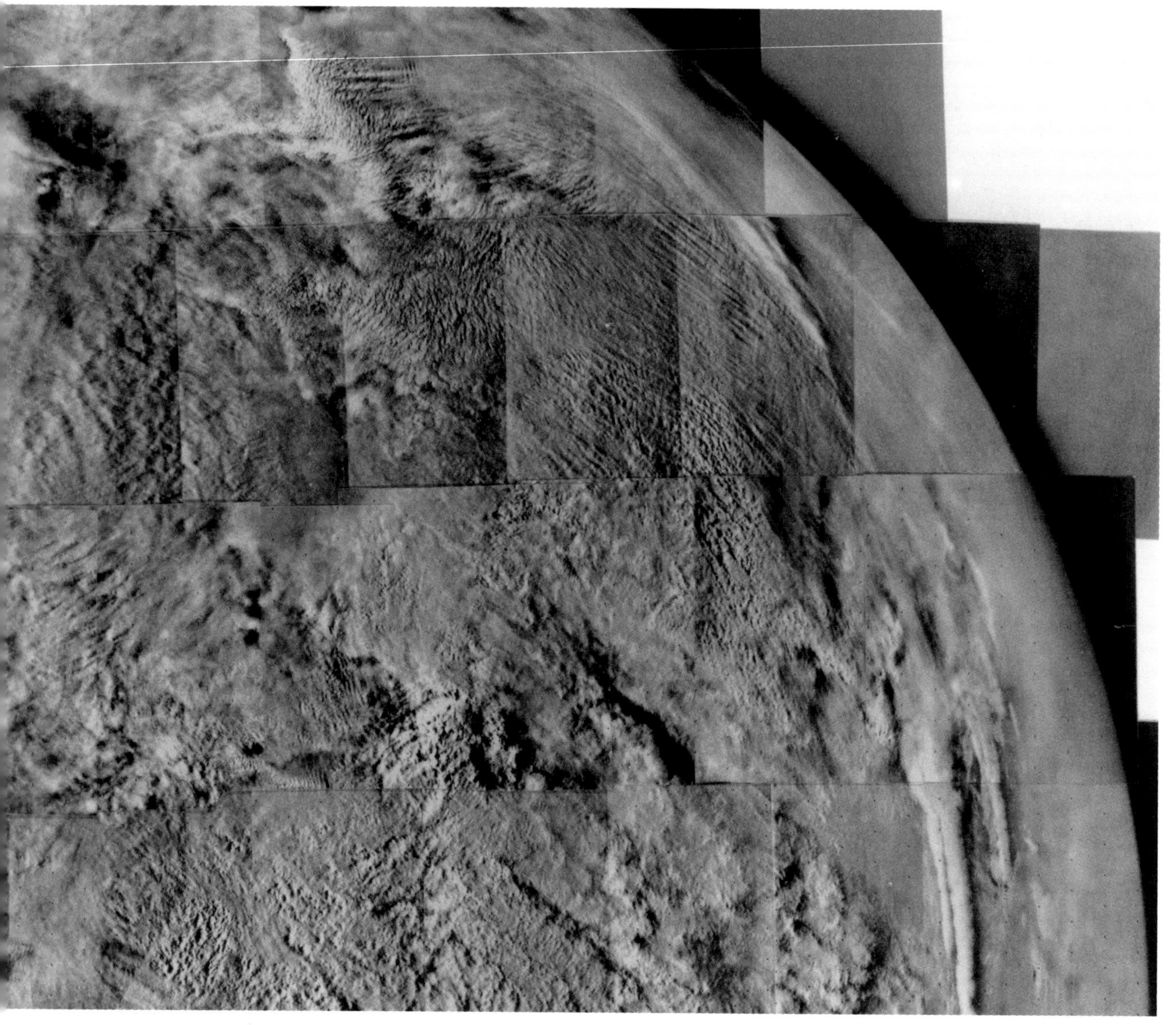

83 Deregulation Spurs Domestic Airline Competition

President Jimmy Carter signed the Airline Deregulation Act of 1978 into law on November 24, 1978. Public Law 95-504 freed passenger airlines to reduce fares by up to 70 percent and to serve new routes not protected by other carriers without having to seek permission from the Civil Aeronautics Board (CAB).

Deregulation affected the airline industry dramatically. Route and rate restrictions previously imposed by the CAB were to be phased out over the next four years, with all restrictions on routes and new services ended by December 31, 1981. Once started, the process moved much more quickly than that. By the end of 1978, the CAB awarded 248 new routes to airline applicants. Existing carriers established service on new routes and new airlines were organized to compete for passenger business.

The CAB itself ceased to exist on January 1, 1985. The Department of Transportation (DOT) assumed some of its functions, such as international routes and landing rights and review of airline mergers. DOT also assumed responsibility for ensuring continued airline service to smaller communities.

The number of air carriers jumped sharply after deregulation. At the time of deregulation, the FAA certified 36 major carriers. By 1984, the number had grown to 123.

With freedom to pick routes, the major airlines quickly began developing "hub and spoke" networks. Hubs emerged at major cities where flights from outlying areas arrived at the airport around the same time. Passengers and baggage transferred to a choice of outgoing flights departing from the hub soon afterward.

Airline profits slumped during the shakeout that followed deregulation. Airline passenger traffic increased at first but then dropped. From a base of 222 million in 1977, the number of passengers enplaned increased to 292 million in 1979, then decreased to 265 million in 1981. The scheduled airline industry experienced the worst financial losses in history in 1981. Operating costs remained high and fare competition spurred by deregulation reduced revenues.

After two decades of airline deregulation, the Federal Aviation Administration evaluated its effects. In its report, *Twenty Years of Deregulation: 1978 to 1998*, the FAA noted that the Airline Deregulation Act "envisioned that the traveling public and the air carrier industry would both benefit. Twenty years have since passed and, for the most part, it appears that the Act has accomplished its intended purpose."

However, the blessings were not universal. The affiliated phenomena of full airplanes and busy airports degraded the quality of airline travel. As time passed, some smaller airlines and a number of startups went out of business or merged. Stronger airlines survived and rebounded, only to experience serious revenue losses due to the effects of global economic problems at the turn of the century. Nevertheless, airline use continued to grow, and, by the year 2000, 627.5 million passengers flew on U.S. domestic airlines.

Technicians service an SR-71 Blackbird strategic reconnaissance aircraft. The Blackbird fleet flew missions at speeds greater than Mach 3.0 and altitudes above 80,000 feet for a quarter-century before retirement was announced in 1990. Among its many records is a transcontinental dash from Los Angeles to Washington, D.C., in 64 minutes on March 6, 1990. (USAF)

Technology Thrusts Forward 1980–1989

The excitement of new developments in aviation and space activities continued throughout the decade of the 1980s. NASA's Space Shuttle program proved the concept of reusable space vehicles. New computer applications enabled manufacturers to create complete virtual aircraft designs that could be manufactured into real airplanes. Additional advanced computer technologies enabled designers to improve aircraft control systems.

Larger turbofan engines gave more power to aircraft while reducing noise and exhaust pollution. Low-observable (stealth) technologies emerged into the open after years of development in secret.

The epitome of aviation achievement in the decade came in 1986, riding on the wings of an airplane that embodied humankind's highest technology and oldest dreams. A small aircraft company in California and its cadre of volunteers created the *Voyager* airplane. *Voyager*'s two pilots achieved one of aviation's ultimate goals by flying around the world nonstop and unrefueled.

84 Space Shuttle Begins Era of Reliable Human Space Travel

President Richard M. Nixon proposed development of a reusable space transportation system on January 5, 1972. Nine years later, on April 12, 1981 astronauts John W. Young and Robert L. Crippen flew *Columbia* for the first Space Shuttle flight.

Columbia's flight opened a new age of space travel with a vehicle that can be launched and brought back many times and can retrieve and repair cargoes, satellites, and other vehicles that previously had been abandoned in orbit. During the more than two decades since *Columbia* first flew into space, Shuttle crews have proved that humans can live and work comfortably in space for long periods of time.

Columbia was the first of a fleet. *Challenger* joined in 1983, *Discovery* in 1984, and *Atlantis* in 1985. *Endeavour* arrived in 1991. The fleet soon became workhorses of space.

The Space Shuttle orbiter is the heart and brains of the system. Part spacecraft and part airplane, it is also home to the crew. The orbiter's cargo bay carries payloads into space and back. It also features a Remote Manipulator System—a long crane built by the Canadian Space Agency that functions like a large and powerful human arm to move things into and out of the cargo bay. The large external fuel tank and the two solid rocket boosters complete the major components of the system. Two minutes after launch, the solid rocket boosters drop away, followed by the external fuel tank separating at 8.5 minutes after launch.

Space Shuttle crews performed the first of the program's spacewalks during *Challenger's* debut flight, launched on April 4, 1983. The crew evaluated new space suits and worked outside in the shuttle's cargo bay. *Challenger*'s crew grew to five persons for its next mission on June 18, 1983. Sally K. Ride, the first American female astronaut, flew as one of three mission specialists. Guion S.

Shuttle Enterprise *separates from NASA Boeing 747 for approach and landing tests. The research flights proved the orbiter's flying qualities and ability to land safely. It did not fly into space. (NASA)*

April 12, 1981. Space Shuttle Columbia *ascends from the pad at Kennedy Space Center, Florida, on the first flight of the Space Transportation System. Astronauts John W. Young and Robert L. Crippen flew* Columbia *on the historic first mission. (NASA)*

Bluford, the first African-American astronaut, flew on *Challenger*'s next mission on August 30, 1983.

From the original crew of two, Space Shuttle crews grew to five, then seven, and finally eight members. The usual crew size is five to seven members. Crewmembers were divided initially into two categories. Pilots took responsibility for flying and maintaining the orbiter. Mission specialists were responsible for experiments and payloads. Eventually another category was added; that of payload specialist. Payload specialists looked after specific experiments and were not necessarily career astronauts.

After 24 successful missions, tragedy struck. *Challenger* exploded 73 seconds after launch on January 28, 1986. All seven members of the crew perished. The program paused while the causes were investigated. Primary cause of the disaster was a seal that failed in one of the Solid Rocket Boosters. The boosters were redesigned and safety procedures revised. The program resumed on September 29, 1988 with the launch of *Discovery*.

Since its rebirth, the STS program has concentrated on scientific and defense missions, conducting a number of historic space science projects. They include the Hubble Space Telescope launch and subsequent repairs and upgrades, the Galileo Jupiter spacecraft, and the Gamma Ray Observatory. Shuttle crews staged nine dockings and five crew exchanges with the Russian Mir space station in preparation for deployment of the International Space Station.

By mid-2002, NASA had flown 109 Space Shuttle missions. A replacement vehicle to fly humans into space is unlikely until the year 2012 or later.

Four awards of the Collier Trophy were presented to the Space Shuttle program. The trophy

Robert L. Crippen (center, first row) commanded the Space Shuttle Challenger *for mission STS-7, the first to have a five-member crew. Pilot Frederick H. Hauck is on the right. Sally K. Ride, John M. Fabian, and Norman E. Thagard are the mission specialists. The crew flew* Challenger *in orbit June 18 through 24, 1983. (NASA)*

Boeing 777 in flight. Boeing received the Collier Trophy for 1995 in recognition of its 777 accomplishment. (Copyright The Boeing Company)

for 1981 was awarded to NASA and the entire government-industry team responsible for proving the concept of manned reusable spacecraft.

The 1984 Collier Trophy was presented to NASA and Martin Marietta Corporation for developing the Manned Maneuvering Unit, which allows astronauts to walk in space without a tether.

Richard H. Truly received the Collier Trophy for 1988 in recognition of his leadership for the successful return of America to space after the *Challenger* tragedy.

The Collier Trophy for 1994 again was presented to NASA, this time to its Hubble Space Telescope Recovery Team. The crew of *Endeavour* carried out one of the most demanding missions when it serviced the Hubble Space Telescope to put it into top shape and correct deficiencies that impaired its ability to "see" the universe.

Astronaut Shannon M. Lucid holds a women's world absolute record for accumulated space time. She flew on four Space Shuttle missions and worked aboard the Russian Mir space station to accumulate more than 5,354 hours in space. Shannon Lucid became NASA's Chief Scientist in February 2002.

85

Boeing 777: Working Together

In the late 1980s, the Boeing Company aimed to build a new airplane that would fit into the airliner market between the 747 jumbo and smaller 767. Boeing employed an innovative approach to creating its new 777 airliner.

Two aspects of the Boeing 777 creation were especially important. First, the company brought its airline customers into the project early in the design phase. The process also involved pilots, engine manufacturers, suppliers, and maintenance people, among others. The program was dubbed "Working Together."

Second, the airplane was designed entirely on computers. It was the first time no paper plans or engineering mockups were prepared in advance of manufacture. The airplane was preassembled on computers. The Boeing designers used a digital system called CATIA (for Computer-Aided Three-Dimensional Interactive Application). The CATIA system enabled everyone to visualize all the designs as three-dimensional objects. The process ensured that subassemblies mated properly before a single piece of hardware was employed. The designers were organized into 238 coordinated teams.

Airline orders for the new 777 justified Boeing's pioneering approach. United Airlines placed the first order for 34 aircraft in October 1990. Other airlines followed suit. Boeing flight-test pilots John Cashman and Ken Higgins flew the 777 on its first flight on June 12, 1994.

Following an intensive flight certification program, both the Federal Aviation Administration and the European Joint Aviation Authorities granted type and production certification for the 777 on April 19, 1995. United took delivery of the first production 777 one month later and began carrying passengers in June 1995. The first model 777-200 seated from 305 to 328 passengers in three classes (first, business, and economy). The stretched model 777-300 seated 328 to 394 passengers. By mid-2002, Boeing had delivered more than 400 of the 777 to customers.

86

Voyager Circles the Globe Nonstop without Refueling

Elbert L. (Burt) Rutan gained renown in the aviation world as an innovative designer who made exceptional use of composite materials in the structures of his aircraft. He designed and built *Voyager*, the airplane that in 1986 captured the absolute record for a nonstop nonrefueled flight around the world.

Burt Rutan and his colleagues at the small Rutan Aircraft Factory and Voyager Aircraft of Mojave, California, proved the exception to the notion that only giant government or industry establishments could build record-shattering aircraft. Rutan created *Voyager* to achieve a single goal—global flight.

The Rutan team began pursuing the global flight dream in 1982. Burt Rutan's design made maximum use of lightweight but strong composite materials and also created maximum volume for the fuel load required for the voyage. The tiny cylindrical fuselage fit into the center of a structure of two wings and two booms. Two reliable Teledyne Continental piston engines powered the propellers. One engine (a tractor) was mounted

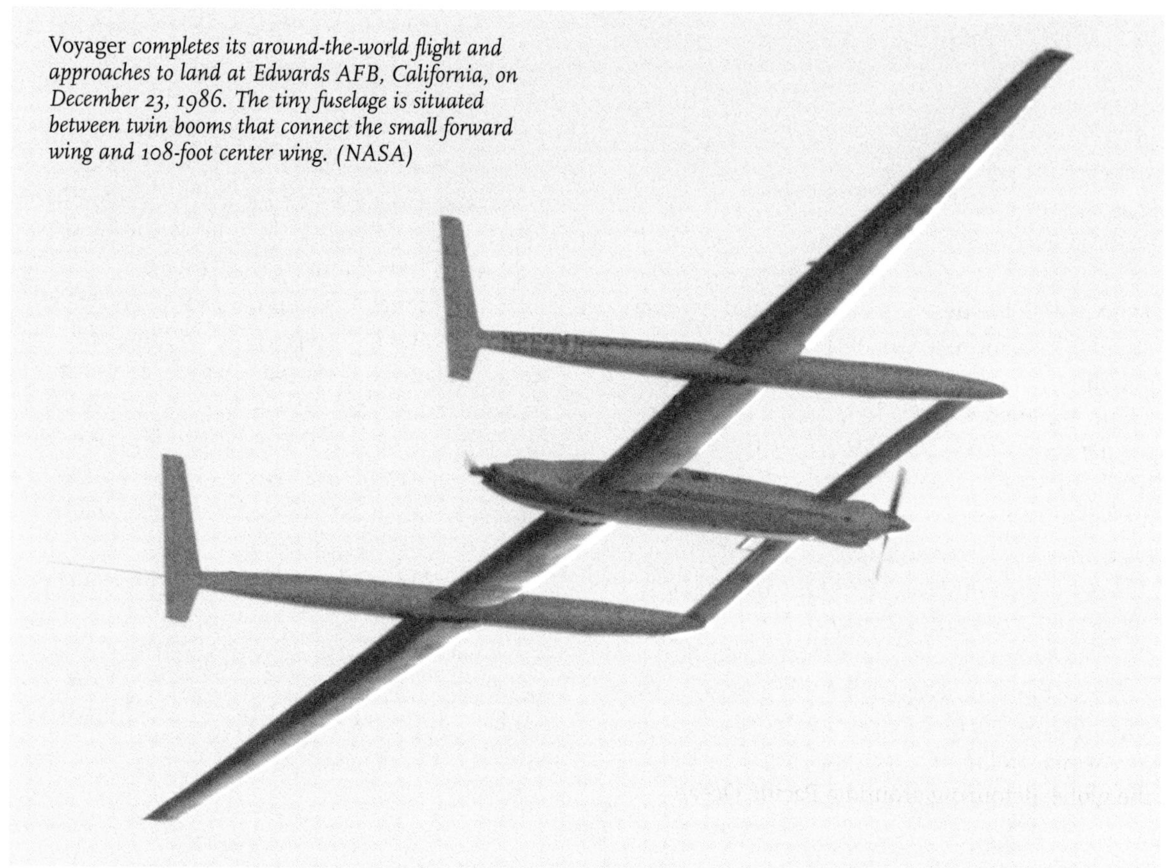

Voyager completes its around-the-world flight and approaches to land at Edwards AFB, California, on December 23, 1986. The tiny fuselage is situated between twin booms that connect the small forward wing and 108-foot center wing. (NASA)

Burt Rutan (left), Jeana Yeager, and Dick Rutan display the citations for the Presidential Citizens Medal they received from President Ronald Reagan at the White House on December 27, 1986. (Mark Greenberg/Visions)

forward and the other (a pusher) was mounted aft on the fuselage.

Dick Rutan, Burt's brother, and Jeana Yeager piloted *Voyager*. Their tiny combination cockpit and cabin in the fuselage measured only 7.5 feet long by 3.3 feet wide and three feet high.

Voyager flew for the first time on June 22, 1984. Subsequent flight tests over the next two years proved the design's efficiency and produced valuable data on fuel consumption and handling qualities. Concurrently, the Voyager organization set up a ground support network for the flight.

By early December 1986, everything was ready. Dick Rutan and Jeana Yeager lifted *Voyager* off the runway at Edwards Air Force Base, California, one minute after 8:00 A.M. Pacific Standard Time on December 14, 1986. *Voyager* weighed 2,250 pounds empty. When it took off from Edwards, the airplane carried more than 7,000 pounds of fuel plus the pilots and minimal supplies and equipment.

Voyager followed a great circle route around the globe, detouring around a Pacific Ocean typhoon and avoiding thunderstorms along the way. It returned to land at the start point at Edwards Air Force Base, California, nine days, three minutes, 44 seconds after takeoff.

Once again the American public became excited about aviators striving for lofty goals. Burt Rutan, the designer, and the pilots received well-deserved acclaim for the achievement.

The National Aeronautic Association (NAA) awarded the Collier Trophy for 1986 to Jeana Yeager, Dick Rutan, and Burt Rutan, along with *Voyager*'s team of volunteers. The citation recognized the ingenious design and development of the *Voyager* aircraft and skillful execution of the flight. The NAA also certified *Voyager*'s establishing three absolute world records:

Speed around the world nonstop, unrefueled: 115.65 mph.

Great circle distance without landing: 24,986.727 miles.

Distance in a closed circuit without landing: 24,986.727 miles.

87

V-22 Osprey Tiltrotor

The V-22 Osprey tiltrotor aircraft descends directly from earlier tiltrotor experimental aircraft such as the XV-3 and XV-15. In the 1950s and early 1960s, the Bell XV-3 demonstrated the feasibility of a new concept; an aircraft that could take off and land vertically like a helicopter and then tilt its rotors and fly like a conventional airplane. Bell Helicopter Textron took the concept to the next step with the XV-15 Tiltrotor and conducted research with NASA in 1980 and 1981 to demonstrate the technology.

The next development in tiltrotor evolution came in 1982, when Boeing and Bell teamed to build the V-22 Osprey. Boeing was responsible for the fuselage, subsystems, avionics, and fly-by-wire controls. Bell was responsible for the wings, transmissions, empennage, rotor systems, and engine installations.

The first of the new V-22s flew on March 19, 1989. Development continued through the 1990s while the military services decided how to take advantage of the aircraft's special capabilities. The Marine Corps decided to buy the Osprey as an assault transport to replace its aged fleet of medium lift helicopters. The Navy saw the Osprey's value in combat search and rescue, special operations, and fleet logistic support missions. The Air Force wanted it for long-range special operations missions.

The V-22 Osprey has a crew of three and can carry 24 combat troops or up to 20,000 pounds of cargo. Two Allison gas turbine engines power it. While it can hover and rise vertically like a helicopter, the Osprey can cruise at 317 mph in the airplane mode and climb to altitudes above 20,000 feet. The rotors can be folded and the wings rotated to save space in the hangar deck of an aircraft carrier.

The National Aeronautic Association awarded the Collier Trophy for 1990 to the Bell-Boeing team for development of the V-22 Osprey.

A crewmember aboard USS Saipan *guides the pilots of a Marine Corps MV-22 Osprey in the helicopter mode approaching to land during training exercises at sea. (PH1 Benjamin Olvey/Naval Air Systems Command V-22 Integrated Test Team)*

MV-22 Osprey tiltrotor aircraft flies in airplane mode over the Chesapeake Bay. (Vernon Pugh/Naval Air Systems Command V-22 Integrated Test Team)

Predator Unmanned Aerial Vehicle during joint-service evaluation, 1995. Predator flies at speeds up to 80 mph and altitudes up to 25,000 feet. (Department of Defense)

After two fatal V-22 accidents killed 23 persons in 2000, the program stood down. The Department of Defense and NASA performed two independent reviews that assessed the safety of the aircraft and the validity of the technology. Both reviews concluded that the tiltrotor design contained no inherent flaws and recommended engineering changes and improvements to the aircraft.

V-22 developmental flight-testing resumed in May 2002.

88 Unmanned Aerial Vehicles

During World War II the military forces used small pilotless drone aircraft as aerial targets. They had been developed from radio-controlled model airplanes flown by enthusiasts. By the time of the Vietnam War, drones were renamed "remotely piloted vehicles," or RPVs. Instead of serving as passive targets, the RPVs became active participants in several roles. They performed missions such as photo-reconnaissance and communications intelligence.

In the early 1980s, U.S. military leaders saw requirements for additional inexpensive pilotless aircraft. The Navy took the lead, deciding to speed up the process through purchase of existing systems that could be further developed. The name for pilotless aircraft changed again, and became unmanned aerial vehicle, or UAV. The Pioneer UAV, developed by Israel Aircraft Industries, won the Navy business. Tests aboard ship and with Marine Corps ground units in 1986 and 1987 proved Pioneer's value. The U.S. Army joined the Pioneer program in 1990.

Pioneer unmanned aerial vehicles performed effectively during the Gulf War in 1991. Six operational units from the Army, Marine Corps, and Navy flew hundreds of missions to support combat operations. The Navy credited Pioneer UAV aircraft with particular success in supporting naval gunfire missions against enemy defenses along the Kuwait coastline. Pioneers assisted with target selection, adjustment of naval gunfire, and battle-damage assessment. In one instance, Iraqi troops actually surrendered to a Pioneer UAV. They believed its presence meant they would soon be targets for the 16-inch guns of Navy battleships.

RQ-4 Global Hawk flies over Edwards Air Force Base, California, on first flight, February 28, 1998. (Department of Defense)

First flight of Boeing X-45A Umanned Combat Air Vehicle at Edwards Air Force Base, California, on May 22, 2002. The technology demonstration program includes NASA Dryden Flight Research Center, Boeing, the U.S. Air Force, and the Defense Advanced Research Projects Agency. (NASA)

Building upon Pioneer's success in the Gulf War, the Department of Defense in the mid-1990s accelerated selection of a new UAV called Predator. A joint armed services team worked with the contractor, General Atomics Aeronautical Systems of San Diego, California, to evaluate and test Predator.

After successful test and evaluation, the Secretary of Defense designated the Air Force to direct further Predator development and service. Predator received the designation of RQ-1. (The "R" stands for reconnaissance and the "Q" for unmanned.) The Air Force operates the RQ-1 Predator, flying its missions in support of all services in a theater of operations. Sensors aboard Predator include video cameras, an infrared camera, and a synthetic aperture radar. With those sensors, it operates effectively day or night and through smoke, clouds, or haze. The Predator's endurance exceeds 24 hours and it performs at altitudes up to 25,000 feet. Predator aircraft became a vital part of the combat team during the war in Afghanistan that began in October 2001.

Another unmanned aerial vehicle, the RQ-4 Global Hawk, flew into combat in the war in Afghanistan while still in the advanced development phase. The prime contractor for Global Hawk is the Ryan Aeronautical Center of Northrop Grumman in San Diego, California. Global Hawk's endurance can range up to 40 hours at altitudes reaching 65,000 feet.

Demand for UAVs is expected to grow, both for the military and for civilian missions. They can fly into hazardous places and perform essential tasks with less risk to human life and at lower costs.

The National Aeronautics Association awarded the Collier Trophy for 2000 to Northrop Grumman Corporation and its teammates on the Global Hawk. The team included Rolls-Royce, Raytheon Company, L-3 Communications, U.S. Air Force, and Defense Advanced Research Projects Agency.

89 Digital Fly-By-Wire Controls

For the first seven decades of aviation, pilots manipulated the control surfaces of their aircraft by applying direct force. Pilots moved control wheels or sticks with their hands and pushed rudder pedals with their feet. Those flight controls connected to rods and cables that conveyed pilot pressure to the control surfaces on wings and tails.

As airplanes became faster and larger, hydraulic systems gave added power to control inputs from the pilot. Control systems grew in size, weight, and complexity. With the advances in computers and electronics in the late 1960s, new possibilities for flight controls became evident.

Engineers at NASA's Dryden Flight Research Center developed a program to explore the potential of the new concepts. The Navy transferred a supersonic Vought F-8C Crusader fighter to NASA for the project. The Dryden engineers took out the

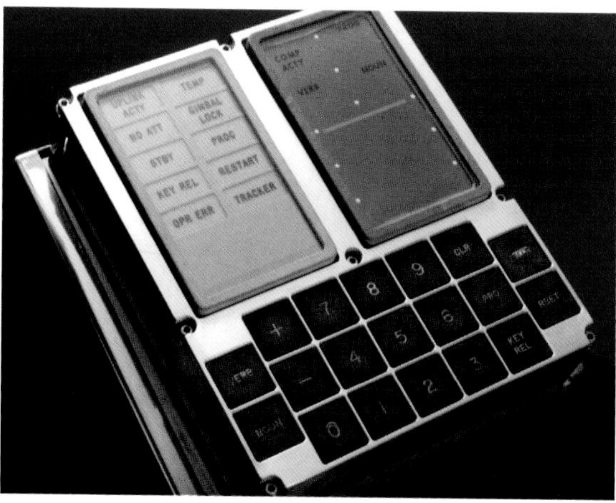

Display and Keyboard Unit computer interface box from the Apollo program was used in the first phase of the NASA F-8 Digital Fly-by-Wire research program. (NASA)

The supersonic Vought F-8 Crusader aircraft was modified to become the first Digital Fly-By-Wire aircraft in the world. (NASA)

entire mechanical flight control system in the F-8C. Gone were the cables, rods, and cranks. A digital flight control computer from the Apollo program connected to a network of wires that ran from the computer to actuators at the airplane's control surfaces.

NASA research pilot Gary Krier flew the modified F-8C on its first flight on May 25, 1972. The system worked. NASA progressed to the next phase of its research by replacing the Apollo system with a new triple-redundant digital flight control system. That system functioned effectively over a long period of fruitful research that lasted until 1985.

The NASA fly-by-wire results were applied in development of the U.S. Air Force F-16 Fighting Falcon. The F-16 was the first U.S. high-performance aircraft with a digital fly-by-wire flight control system.

The Airbus Industrie consortium applied European digital fly-by-wire research to the flight controls of its A320 airliner. The A320 became the first commercial airliner with full digital fly-by-wire controls when it was introduced in 1988. Boeing incorporated digital fly-by-wire controls for the first time with its 777 transport. By the 21st century, most high-performance aircraft and large transport aircraft were equipped with digital fly-by-wire systems.

The Digital-Fly-By-Wire control systems in modern aircraft are redundant. That is, the primary system is backed up by three or even four similar systems to ensure reliability and safety.

Cockpit of the Airbus A330 airliner. Side-stick controllers on the ledges at left and right replace control yokes. Bright full-color situation displays on the panel replace banks of instrument dials. (Airbus)

90

High-Bypass Turbofan Engines

High-bypass turbofan jet engines offer many advantages over basic turbojets. Both types swallow and compress incoming air, which is burned. The combustion creates a hot, rapidly expanding gas that is expelled through the exhaust to produce thrust. The exhaust also turns a turbine that spins the compressor.

The high-bypass turbofan creates more thrust by taking advantage of the thermodynamic phenomenon that a large volume of slow-moving air generates more thrust than a small volume of fast-moving air. The high-bypass engine adds a large fan up front to pull in a larger volume of air that bypasses the combustion chamber and blends with the hot exhaust gases at the rear. The volume of bypass air exceeds the volume of burned air by ratios of five to one ranging up to eight to one.

High-bypass turbofan engines are easy to recognize because their cowlings are "fatter" by comparison with a slender turbojet. They offer significant advantages over the straight turbojet. Most importantly, they improve operating costs by deliv-

A Pratt & Whitney engineer inspects the fan blades of the company's PW4000 112-inch fan engine. This was the launch engine for the Boeing 777 airliner. Pratt & Whitney developed the PW4000 family of high-bypass turbofan engines to serve a range of customer requirements. The 100-inch fan version was developed specifically for the Airbus A330 wide-body twinjet airliner. The engine entered service in December 1994. (Pratt & Whitney, a United Technologies Company)

ering up to twice the thrust per pound of engine weight, while burning less fuel. They are also much quieter, with noise levels sharply lower than earlier engines.

The U.S. Air Force specified brand-new General Electric high-bypass turbofan engines for its huge Lockheed C-5A Galaxy transport, which first flew on June 30, 1968. Since then, high-bypass turbofan engines manufactured by Pratt & Whitney, General Electric, and Rolls-Royce have become the engine of choice for large transport aircraft.

Air Force specialists prepare an F-117A Nighthawk for its next mission during Operation Desert Storm, 1991. Note the myriad flat surfaces and radar-absorbent skin coating. (USAF)

91 Nighthawks Own the Night

Ben R. Rich succeeded Clarence L. "Kelly" Johnson in leadership of the Lockheed Skunk Works in 1975. He managed the creation of the world's first operational stealth aircraft, the F-117A Nighthawk. Before the Air Force gave the production go-ahead in 1978, the Rich-led team had already proved the feasibility of low-observable technologies that make the airplane nearly invisible to radar. From production decision to first flight took only 31 months. The rapid response resulted from a combination of streamlined management, ultra-tight security, and innovative engineering.

First flight of the F-117A Nighthawk occurred on June 18, 1981. The airplane flew mainly at night during its test program, both to maintain rigorous security and to prove the night attack capabilities of the airplane and its systems. The Air Force began receiving production Nighthawks beginning in 1982 and continuing into 1990, when a total of 59 aircraft had been delivered.

In November 1988, the Air Force lifted the security lid to reveal the Nighthawk's existence. A year later, Nighthawk pilots flew combat missions for the first time during Operation Just Cause in Panama in December 1989.

Before its unveiling in November 1988, the F-117A Nighthawk stealth fighter seldom flew in daylight. With a wingspan of more than 43 feet, the airplane's radar signature matches that of a big bird. The wings and fuselage shield the engine air intakes and exhaust nozzles from infrared detectors below. (USAF)

F-117A Nighthawk stealth fighter of the 37th Tactical Fighter Wing departs on a strike mission during Operation Desert Storm, 1991. (Department of Defense)

F-117s contributed greatly to the successful air campaign of Operation Desert Storm against Iraq. Beginning on the night of January 16–17, 1991, Nighthawk pilots flew attacks against the most heavily defended Iraqi targets. They flew more than 1,250 sorties, dropped more than 2,000 tons of bombs, and flew more than 6,900 hours during Desert Storm.

They were the only aircraft to bomb valuable strategic targets in heavily-defended downtown Baghdad. The stealth characteristics of the F-117A made them virtually immune to Iraqi air defenses, and their precision-attack capabilities blasted strategic targets with accuracy, while minimizing casualties among civilians near the targets.

Not one F-117A was touched by Iraqi defenses during Desert Storm. Eight years later, one was lost during Operation Allied Force in Yugoslavia in March 1999.

The National Aeronautic Association presented the 1989 Collier Trophy to Ben Rich, Lockheed, and the U.S. Air Force team for development of the F-117A.

92 B-2 Spirit Stealth Bomber

The first B-2 Spirit stealth bomber appeared publicly on November 22, 1988, when it rolled out of the Northrop Corporation hangar at Palmdale, California. Six months earlier, the Air Force had confirmed the existence of the long-range heavy bomber and released an artist's drawing of the aircraft. Eight months after rollout, the B-2 flew for the first time on July 17, 1989.

The Air Force selected Northrop (later Northrop Grumman) in October 1981 to begin development of an advanced-technology bomber that would become the B-2. The Air Force, Northrop, and its partners on the industry team incorporated the latest low-observable technologies into designing a brand-new airframe. They used advanced computer-aided design and computer-aided manufacturing capabilities to ensure a successful "first fit" of all the components.

The shape of the B-2 owed much to John K. Northrop's original successes with the flying wing design. The B-2 brought together advances in technology in engines, materials, avionics, and especially low-observables. The resulting airplane combined high aerodynamic efficiency with a stealthy ability to penetrate defenses of virtually any type.

The Air Force described the B-2's low-observable capabilities as thwarting many types of sensors, including acoustic, infrared, electromagnetic, visual, and radar. Although most of its special characteristics remain classified, the Air Force noted that its flying wing design and construction of composite materials with special coatings all contributed to the B-2's stealthiness.

As a strategic long-range bomber, the B-2 can fly halfway around the world on one refueling, carrying up to 20 tons of conventional and nuclear weapons to deliver precisely on target any time, day or night, in any kind of weather. The crew of two flies the airplane at subsonic airspeeds and altitudes up to 50,000 feet to strike targets anywhere on the globe.

The first production B-2 entered Air Force service on December 17, 1993, 90 years after Kitty Hawk. Since then the fleet has grown to 21 aircraft. The B-2 saw its first combat in March 1999 against Serb targets during Operation Allied Force.

The team led by Northrop and the Air Force received the 1991 Collier Trophy for designing and producing the B-2. Other team members included Boeing Military Airplane Co., General Electric Aircraft Engine Group, and Hughes Aircraft.

First flight of the B-2 Spirit stealth bomber, July 17, 1989. Bruce Hinds, Northrop's chief test pilot, and Air Force Colonel Richard S. Couch flew the airplane on the historic occasion. (Northrop Grumman Corporation)

(Background) The B-2 bomber in its fifth test flight. Northrop Chief Test Pilot Bruce Hinds and Air Force Lieutenant Colonel John Small were at the controls. (USAF)

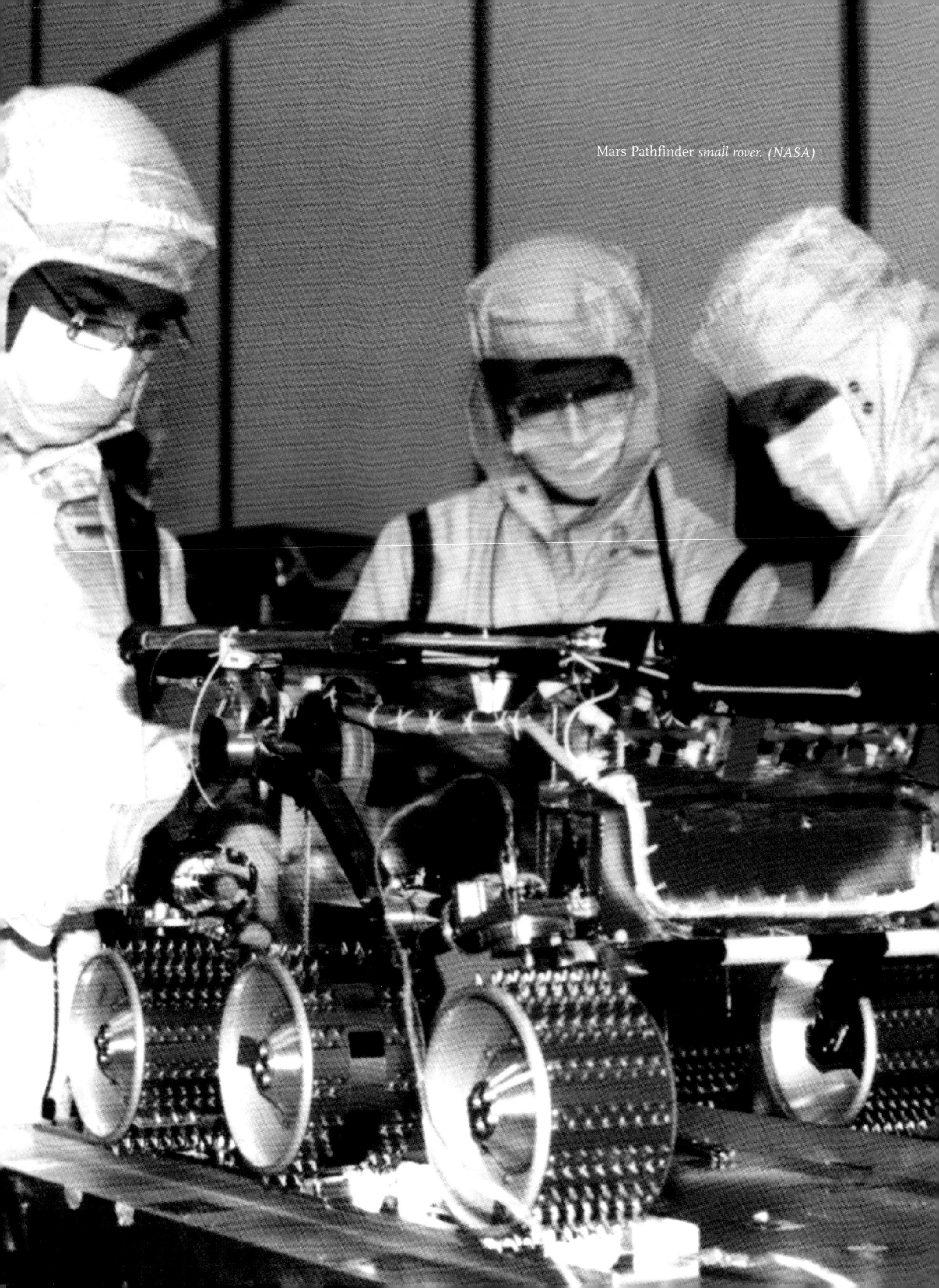

Mars Pathfinder *small rover. (NASA)*

Our Unfettered Future 1990 to the Present

During the decade of the 1990s, space programs sustained the pace of progress through examples such as the Hubble Space Telescope, *Mars Pathfinder*, and the beginnings of the International Space Station. The Space Shuttle proved its reliability and utility as the tool to make other orbital programs possible.

Here on Earth, everyday applications of space technologies spread wide and far among the world's population. The space tools that enabled millions of users to make wireless telephone calls or connect on the Internet or know their location with precision were invisible and taken for granted.

Airline passenger traffic continued its steady growth throughout the decade. The annual number of passengers enplaned on U.S. domestic airlines grew from more than 423 million in 1990 to 627.5 million in 2000. At mid-decade in June 1995, the scheduled airlines of the United States carried their 10 billionth passenger, as counted from the beginning of record keeping in 1926.

Aerospace progress during the 1990s built momentum and motivation for developments in the 21st century.

93

Hubble Space Telescope

A new age of astronomy dawned on April 24, 1990, with the launch of NASA's Hubble Space Telescope aboard Space Shuttle *Discovery*. Released into Earth's orbit on the following day, the 12.5-ton Hubble has astounded the world with its unprecedented and revolutionary images of the cosmos.

The Hubble Space Telescope, a cooperative project of NASA and the European Space Agency, was designed to be a durable observatory in space whose capabilities serve the international astronomical community.

The orbiting observatory's name honors the American astronomer Edwin P. Hubble. Early in the 20th century, Edwin Hubble discovered galaxies beyond the Milky Way and made the first measurements of the universe's expansion rate.

Earliest images obtained from the Hubble Space Telescope were blurred because of a flaw in its main mirror that resulted from a faulty prescription. The system was able to function fairly well despite the flaw. Its positioning above the atmosphere, which distorts images in space, gave Hubble an optical advantage that partly compensated for its imperfect mirror. The orbiting observatory made a number of major discoveries in space even before it was repaired.

Space Shuttle *Endeavour* astronauts, commanded by Richard O. Covey, repaired and upgraded Hubble during the first servicing mission in December 1993. Two teams of astronauts made five spacewalks to the Hubble, a record number for the time. They installed a new Wide Field Planetary Camera and sets of corrective optics for all other optical instruments, and replaced solar arrays, gyroscopes, magnetometers, and electrical components. Then *Endeavour* re-boosted the restored space observatory back into orbit.

The Collier Trophy for 1993 was awarded to the Hubble Space Telescope recovery team for the dramatic and successful first servicing mission.

After the servicing mission, Hubble immediately began producing a stream of clear images of objects and events in space, including massive black holes, the previously unobserved surface of Pluto, the birth of stars in enormous stellar clouds, and galaxies at the edge of the universe. When the Comet Shoemaker-Levy collided with Jupiter in July 1994, the Hubble's Planetary

Image of planet Saturn and its rings captured by the Hubble Space Telescope. (NASA)

December 4, 1993. The Hubble Space Telescope (HST) is berthed in Space Shuttle Endeavour*'s cargo bay and is ready for servicing. The seven-member* Endeavour *crew performed planned repairs and upgrades on the HST and corrected a flaw in its main mirror. (NASA)*

Camera captured and relayed to Earth color images of the comet's breakup into eight fragments and their impact on the planet.

Additional servicing missions to the Hubble Space Telescope involving multiple spacewalks by the astronauts occurred in February 1997 and December 1999. During those missions, Space Shuttle astronauts modernized systems and performed maintenance and repair work on its components. Astronauts performed further servicing missions in 2001 and 2002.

NASA plans another servicing mission to Hubble in 2004. After that, the Hubble Space Telescope is scheduled to be decommissioned in 2010 and replaced by the Next Generation Space Telescope.

94 Kaman K-MAX, the Aerial Truck

Charles H. Kaman opened new opportunities in the 1950s when he brought out the first helicopter powered by a gas turbine engine, the Kaman K-225. Four decades later, his Kaman Aerospace Company introduced another pioneering concept; that of a helicopter's being a dedicated vertical lifter, an omnipresent utility aircraft. They called it K-MAX, the "aerial truck."

Kaman Aerospace created the K-MAX for repetitive lift requirements of industries such as logging, oil and mineral exploration, and construction as well as special purposes such as firefighting and reforestation.

First flight for K-MAX came on December 23, 1991. After an extensive flight test program, the helicopter received certification in the United States and Canada in 1994. Deliveries to customers also began in 1994.

An Allied Signal T53-17A-1 gas turbine engine powers the K-MAX. The aircraft's main rotors intermesh. It has no tail rotor. Thus, according to Kaman Aerospace, all the engine power goes directly to the main rotors, creating "the highest lifting efficiency of any rotor configuration." The aircraft and engine combination provides a workhorse helicopter capable of daily multiple cycles of lifting heavy loads over extended periods.

Charles H. Kaman in front of the K-MAX helicopter. K-MAX is the first helicopter specifically designed, built, and tested for medium to heavy external load repetitive lift operations. (Kaman Archive Photo)

K-MAX is a registered trademark of Kaman Aerospace.

95 Global Positioning System Revolutionizes Navigation

The U.S. Department of Defense developed the Global Positioning System, or GPS, for the armed services to provide continuous all-weather navigation capabilities to forces on land, sea, or air. By national policy, the GPS has become a dual-use system available to both military and civilian users.

Three major elements comprise the GPS system: a space segment, a control segment, and users. The space segment consists of a constellation of 24 satellites in orbit about 11,000 nautical miles above Earth. Five ground stations located around the world make up the control segment. The user segment consists of everyone with a GPS receiver. Civilian GPS receivers can pinpoint a user's location to an accuracy as precise as one to three meters.

Each of the 24 GPS satellites continuously transmits radio signals that tell its location and the exact time each signal is transmitted. The time is accurate to one ten-billionth of a second. Six satellites are within reach of any point on the globe at any time. By comparing the signals from at least four satellites, a GPS receiver can determine its precise three-dimensional location and calculate its velocity.

The Department of Defense began developing the system in the 1970s, with Rockwell International leading the industry team. The first satellite was launched on February 22, 1978. Ten more satellites went into orbit by late 1985 to prove the feasibility of the system. Launches of the 24 second-generation operational satellites began in February of 1989 and continued through March 1994. Delta II expendable launch vehicles take the satellites into orbit from Cape Canaveral Air Force Station, Florida.

Military and civilian users began using the GPS system even before all 24 satellites were in position. More than 9,000 civilian GPS receivers

NAVSTAR Global Positioning System satellite mounted on outdoor test stand. The satellite measures 8 feet by 8 feet by 12 feet and weighs more than 2,100 pounds. The widespread solar arrays provide power. (Department of Defense)

were distributed to American ground forces during the Gulf War, providing invaluable navigation tools as units moved around the trackless desert.

The number of civil users grew into the millions as the receivers became smaller and less expensive. The airlines and aviation communities installed GPS receivers in their aircraft for more accurate aerial navigation. The Federal Aviation Administration has developed and published GPS approach procedures so that aircraft equipped with GPS receivers can approach and land at airports under adverse weather conditions. Among the major civil uses, beyond those of air and sea navigation, are fleet management; mineral and resource exploration; intelligent vehicle systems; public safety and services such as police, fire, and rescue; surveying and mapping; open pit mining; precision agriculture; and construction on land and sea. Automobile manufacturers began offering GPS-based navigation displays as optional equipment beginning in the mid-1990s.

The Department of Defense designated the Air Force as the executive service for managing the GPS system. On the civil side, the Department

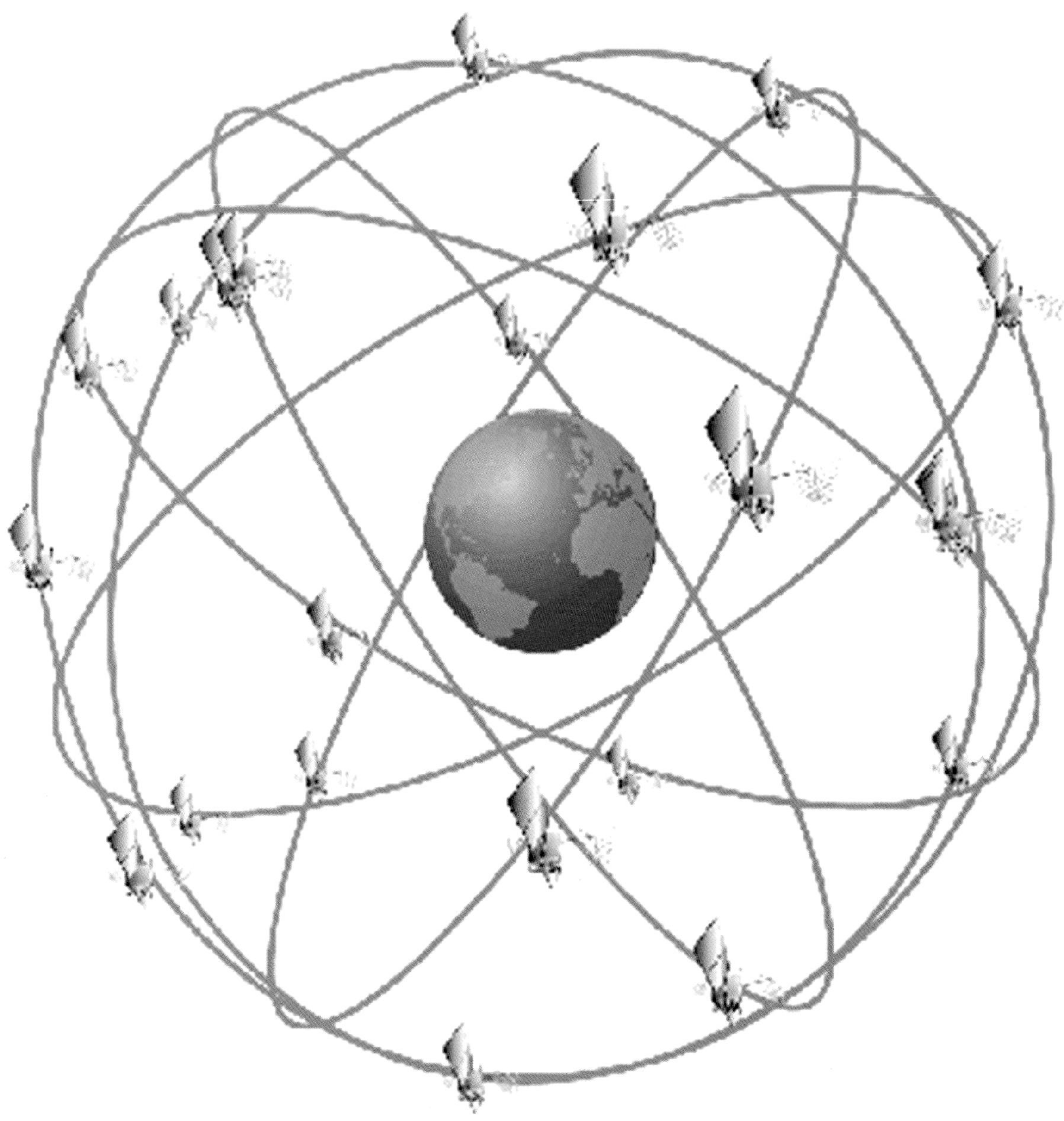

The Global Positioning System constellation consists of 24 satellites orbiting about 12,500 miles above the Earth. They are positioned in six planes, with four satellites in each plane. Each satellite completes an orbit every 12 hours. (Department of Transportation)

of Transportation is the lead agency for all federal GPS matters. The Defense and Transportation Departments are committed to continue improving GPS capabilities, accuracy, and reliability. At the same time, the GPS industry continues to find new applications while shrinking receiver size and lowering their cost, making the capability available to even more users.

The National Aeronautic Association awarded the Collier Trophy for 1992 to the Global Positioning System team consisting of the U.S. Air Force, U.S. Naval Research Laboratory, the Aerospace Corporation, Rockwell International Corporation, and IBM Federal Systems Company.

96 *Mars Pathfinder* Enhanced Knowledge of Earth's Neighbor

NASA gave the United States an Independence Day gift when the *Mars Pathfinder* landed on Mars on July 4, 1997. Eight months earlier, NASA had launched the *Mars Pathfinder* for its journey to the neighboring planet. The scientific objective was to gain understanding of the characteristics of the Martian environment as a prelude to further exploration. The Jet Propulsion Laboratory (JPL) designed, built, and operated the *Mars Pathfinder* for NASA.

NASA technicians prepare Mars Pathfinder *Sojourner Rover for its mission. It arrived on Mars on July 4, 1997, aboard the* Pathfinder *lander. The lander remained in position while the Sojourner roved and analyzed rocks and soil. An operator on Earth controlled the rover's activities. (NASA)*

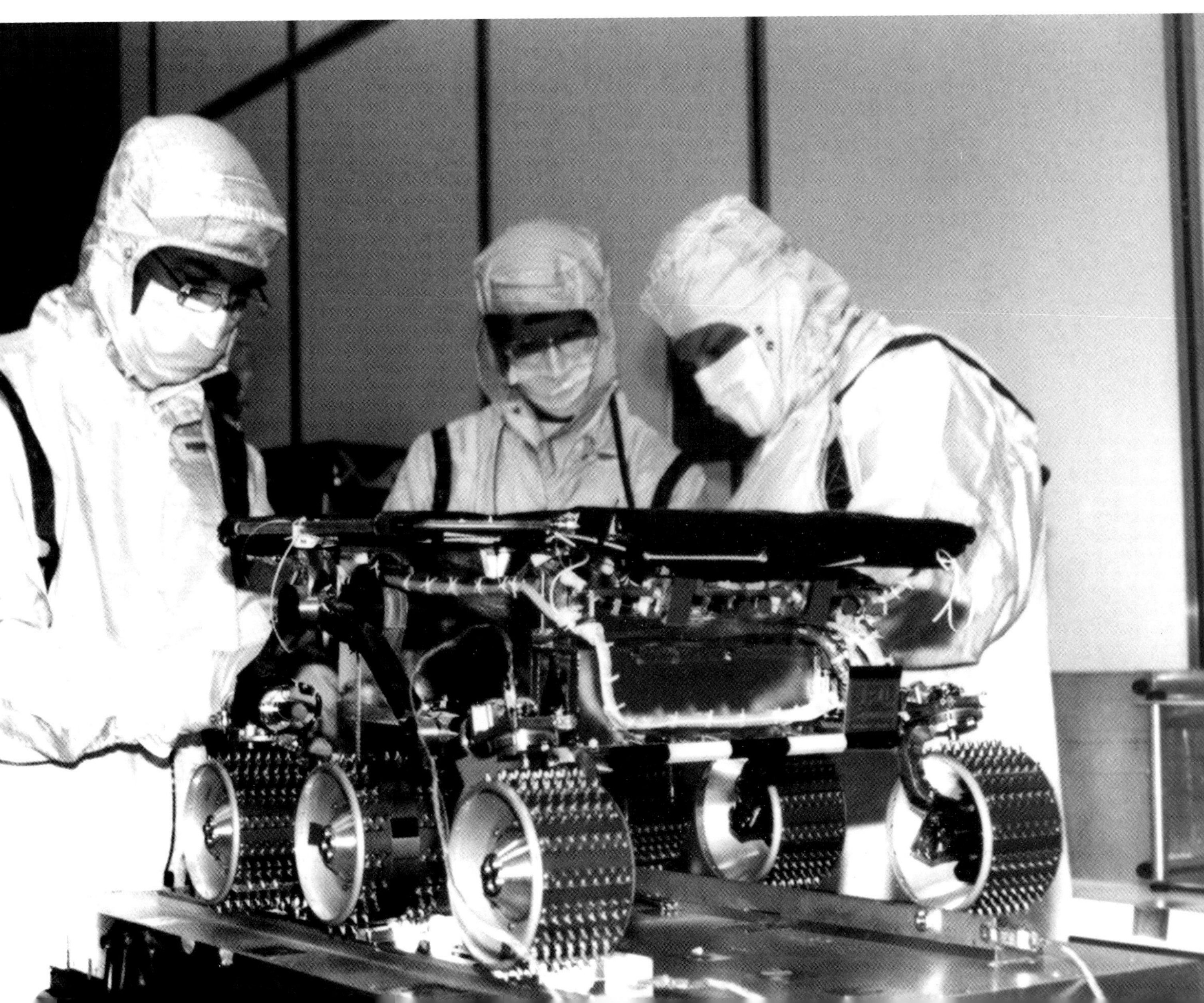

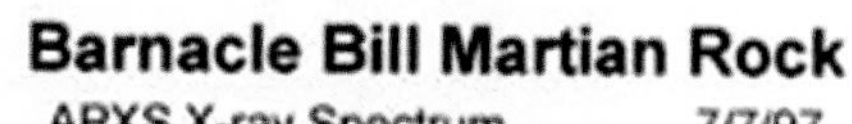

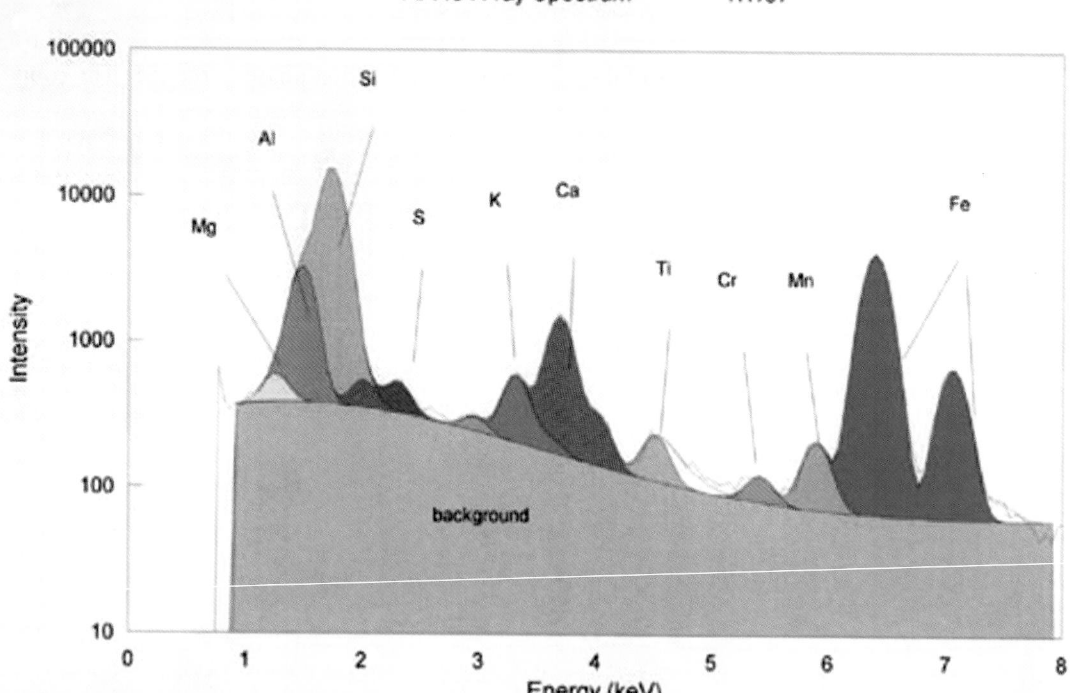

The Alpha Proton X-Ray Spectrometer (APXS) analyzed the Martian rock nicknamed "Barnacle Bill" and sent this report on July 7, 1997. The elements detected are (left to right) magnesium, aluminum, silicon, sulfur, potassium, calcium, titanium, chromium, manganese, and iron. (Courtesy of University of Chicago and Amptek, Inc.)

The package entered the Martian atmosphere and was slowed by parachute. When it neared the surface, retro rockets fired to brake its descent. Airbags beneath the spacecraft cushioned the landing. The *Pathfinder* touched down on Mars and bounced 16 times before coming to rest. It included two components: a stationary lander and a surface rover stowed inside.

Two days after touchdown, the rover emerged from the lander and ventured onto the surface. It began analyzing rocks and soil. Concurrently, the lander performed its own missions in meteorology, atmospheric analysis, and photography, among others.

Besides analyzing multiple soil samples, the rover performed detailed analysis of three rocks nicknamed "Barnacle Bill," "Yogi," and "Scooby-Doo." After further study of the data, JPL scientists concluded that the rocks most closely resemble types found in Iceland and the Galapagos Islands.

The Pathfinder mission generated an unexpectedly large amount of information and transmitted it to Earth. The data included 16,500 images from the lander's camera, 550 images from the rover's camera, 16 chemical analyses of rocks and soil, and 8.5 million measurements of atmospheric pressure, temperature, and wind.

Temperatures on the surface ranged from a low of –107°F to a high of +8°F. Daytime winds were light, at only a few miles per hour. Nighttime winds picked up to about 10 to 20 miles per hour.

Communication between JPL and the *Mars Pathfinder* mission was lost on September 27, 1997. By then, *Pathfinder* had convincingly demonstrated the potential for low-cost landing and exploration of Mars.

97 International Space Station

President Ronald Reagan announced the decision to build a permanently manned space station with international participation as part of his State of the Union address to Congress on January 25, 1984. Other nations had already expressed interest, but it would be another four years before the first multilateral agreements were signed. More planning and negotiating, as well as actual preparations, were required during the next 14 years in order to reach the definitive agreement on the project.

The Intergovernmental Agreement on Space Station Cooperation signed in Washington on January 29, 1998, when Russia was officially added, established the framework for cooperation among the partners for the design, development, operation, and utilization of the Space Station.

Fifteen nations agreed to participate in the International Space Station (ISS) with the United States. They included Brazil, Canada, Japan, Russia, and 11 countries of the European Space Agency. Those nations are Belgium, Denmark, France, Germany, Italy, The Netherlands, Norway, Spain, Sweden, Switzerland, and the United Kingdom.

NASA's participation with Russia in the Shuttle-Mir program from 1994 up through 1998 constituted the first phase of the ISS. The cooperation produced valuable experience and knowledge for building and operating the ISS. Examples included modification to hardware, tools, and procedures inside the station and for spacewalks outside, as well as improving methods for training crews for long-duration missions in space.

Assembly of the ISS in orbit began with launch of the Russian-built control module Zarya from the Baikonur Cosmodrome in Kazakhstan on November 20, 1998. The Space Shuttle *Endeavour* joined Zarya in orbit two weeks later to deliver the Unity connecting module, built in the United States. When *Endeavour*'s crew attached the two modules, the event marked the beginning of construction in orbit. In June 1999, the Space Shuttle *Discovery* delivered two tons of tools and cranes on the third flight to the station.

The crew of Space Shuttle *Atlantis* flew the fourth mission to the station in May 2000. They

Six astronauts and a cosmonaut comprised the crew of Space Shuttle Atlantis *for mission STS-101 to the International Space Station in May 2000. Mission Commander James D. Halsell (right) and Scott J. Horowitz, pilot, are in front. Others (from left) are Mary Ellen Weber and Jeffrey N. Williams, cosmonaut Yury V. Usachev, James S. Voss, and Susan J. Helms, all mission specialists. The crew delivered supplies to the station and prepared it for arrival of the next components. (NASA)*

Space Shuttle Atlantis *astronauts photographed th International Space Station with solar panels spread wide soon after the spacecraft separated over northern Mongolia on May 26, 2000. The crew spent five days servicing the station. The two main components of the station at this time were the control module and connecting module. Solar panels are spread wide. Mongolia's Lake Hovsgol appears in upper right. (NASA)*

delivered supplies and performed maintenance tasks to prepare the station for arrival of the Zvezda service module, the third major component. Zvezda arrived and docked with the station on July 25, 2000.

The first resident crew arrived aboard the station on November 2, 2000. Its members were American astronaut Bill Shepherd and Russian cosmonauts Yuri Gidzenko and Sergei Krikalev. They remained aboard for four months. By mid-2002, three more crews, each comprising three astronauts and cosmonauts, had resided aboard the ISS for periods ranging from four to six months.

Concurrently with those resident expeditions, a succession of NASA and Russian missions flew to the ISS to continue maintenance, construction, and resupply of the station. Looking ahead, NASA plans to fly four Space Shuttle missions per year to the ISS.

When completed, the ISS will be an orbiting laboratory with capabilities for performing long-duration research by its international partners. Working and living spaces will accommodate up to seven astronauts/cosmonauts and scientists at a time.

98

Eileen Collins, First Female Shuttle Mission Commander

U.S. Air Force Colonel Eileen M. Collins became the first woman to command a Space Shuttle Mission when she and her crew flew *Columbia* into orbit on July 22, 1999 for the five-day STS-93 mission.

A native of Elmira, New York, Eileen Collins earned a bachelor of arts degree in mathematics and economics from Syracuse University in 1978; a master of science in operations research from Stanford University in 1986; and a master of arts degree in space systems management from Webster University in 1989. Colonel Collins joined NASA's astronaut program in 1990 after serving as an Air Force C-141 transport commander and T-38 instructor pilot. She graduated from the Air Force Test Pilot School immediately before joining the astronaut program, and became NASA's first female Space Shuttle pilot, flying the shuttle *Discovery* on the February 1995 mission that made the first rendezvous with Russia's Mir space station. Colonel Collins also flew as pilot aboard the shuttle *Atlantis* in May 1997 on the sixth flight to dock with Mir.

Crew of Space Shuttle Columbia *photographed in zero gravity during mission STS-93, July 23–27, 1999. In front are astronauts Eileen M. Collins, mission commander, and Michel Tognini, mission specialist from France's space agency. Behind them are (left to right) mission specialist Steven A. Hawley, pilot Jeffrey S. Ashby, and mission specialist Catherine G. Coleman. (NASA)*

The Gulfstream V is the first ultra-long-range business jet, capable of nonstop flights up to 6,500 nautical miles. City pairs such as New York to Tokyo or San Francisco to Moscow are within its nonstop reach. (Gulfstream)

The primary mission objective for Collins and her crew was to deploy NASA's Chandra X-ray Observatory. Its X-ray detection capabilities allow scientists to study the origin, structure, and evolution of the universe in greater detail than ever before. Chandra complemented two other space observatories in Earth orbit: the Hubble Space Telescope and the Compton Gamma Ray Observatory. The observatory was named for the late Subrahmanyan Chandrasekhar, an Indian-American Nobel Laureate.

99 Business Jet Fleets Expand

Business jets first appeared in the mid-1960s, with the Learjet leading the way. Early models of the Learjet carried four passengers at high subsonic speeds for a distance of about 1,600 nautical miles. As more companies began building business jets and competition intensified, passenger capacity and range both increased. The Gulfstream V business jet, certified in 1997, offered room for up to 19 passengers with a range of 6,500 nautical miles.

From the debut of the Learjet and its competitors, corporate customers recognized the capabilities of business jets, and more of them put the aircraft to use as business tools. The National Business Aircraft Association (NBAA) reported that the worldwide fleet of business jets in 2001 totaled 11,799 aircraft, a figure more than double that of 1980.

Fractional ownership of aircraft such as business jets and turboprop business aircraft is a phenomenon that began in the mid-1980s and expanded sharply into the late 1990s. Under the concept, companies or individuals own a fraction of an aircraft instead of the whole thing. They gain the immediate advantages of accessible business aircraft without having to spend large sums to set up their own flight department.

The NBAA reported that in 1986 there were only three fractional owners. The number grew to 89 in 1993. The concept expanded rapidly late in the decade. The Federal Aviation Administration (FAA) reported current data in its March 2002 publication, *FAA Aerospace Forecasts, Fiscal Years 2002–2013*. The report stated, "According to copyrighted preliminary data from AvDataInc of Wichita, Kansas, at the end of 2001 there were more than 3,500 entities with almost 5,000 shares involved in fractional ownership of more than 650 aircraft. Despite this record growth, it is believed only a small percentage of this market has been developed."

The FAA estimates that business jets will be the fastest-growing category of general aviation aircraft over the years 2002 to 2013. The projected growth is attributable to three major factors. First, the FAA anticipates that the economy will rebound beginning in 2002/2003. Second, demand will increase as more companies seek the freedom offered by business jets. Third, that demand will be reinforced by the popularity of fractional ownership programs.

The National Aeronautic Association awarded the Collier Trophy to business jet teams for two consecutive years. The 1996 award went to Cessna Aircraft Company and the Citation X design team for creating the Citation X, the first U.S. commercial aircraft to cruise at Mach 0.92. The Collier Trophy for 1997 was presented to Gulfstream Aerospace Corporation and the Gulfstream V industry team for the world's first ultra-long range business jet.

Gulfstream V is a registered trademark of Gulfstream Aerospace Corporation.

100 Regional Airlines Take Off

What are regional airlines? The Regional Airline Association (RAA) defines them as airlines that operate "short and medium-haul scheduled airline service connecting smaller communities with larger cities and connecting hubs." As defined by the RAA, regional airliners are turboprop aircraft carrying from 19 to 68 passengers, and regional jets with 30 to 100 seats. Passenger traffic of the regional airlines grew briskly during the decade of the 1990s. The RAA reported 82.8 million passengers enplaned aboard regional airlines in 2001, "more than double the total in 1991."

In its report, *FAA Aerospace Forecasts, Fiscal Years 2002–2013*, the Federal Aviation Administration predicts that passenger traffic for the regional airlines will continue to grow at a higher rate than the larger airlines. From the 2001 level, by the year 2013, the FAA anticipates the regional air-

A 50-seat Embraer ERJ 145 regional jet airliner in flight. The ERJ 145 flew for the first time on August 11, 1995. (Embraer)

lines will carry more than 151 million passengers, nearly tripling the 2001 load.

The FAA credited the advent of regional jet airliners with much of the recent growth and future expansion or air travel. In the 2002–2013 forecast, it mentioned "phenomenal customer acceptance" and the regional jets' range and speed as positive factors. The FAA forecasts the number of regional jet aircraft to grow from 732 in operation in 2001 to 1,698 by 2007 and to 2,930 aircraft by 2013.

Bombardier CRJ200 regional airliner of Atlantic Southeast Airlines (ASA) in flight. The 50-seat CRJ200 comprises a significant percentage of the lift capacity of the U.S. regional airline fleet. ASA is an affiliate of Delta Connection. (Courtesy of Bombardier Aerospace) *Trademark of Bombardier, Inc.*

The Apollo 11 *astronauts left this plaque on the Moon. Its inscription reads, "HERE MEN FROM PLANET EARTH FIRST SET FOOT UPON THE MOON. JULY 1969 A.D. WE CAME IN PEACE FOR ALL MANKIND." (NASA)*

Looking Ahead

The history of flight is a story of progress, innovation, and occasional setbacks. The milestones of the first century of flight presented in these pages are but a small sample of the countless others that deserve recognition.

Looking back over the first century of flight, it is clear that the benefits of aeronautics and space programs have made the miraculous become commonplace and enabled fantasy to become reality. Humans expect the unexpected to happen through progress in flight.

As the aerospace industry celebrates its first centennial, it is recovering from the devastating effects of the terrorist attacks of September 11, 2001. Tomorrow's challenges are as great as ever and will inspire men and women who have the opportunity to be a part of the second centennial of flight to even greater heights and bolder accomplishments.

Looking ahead, what sort of milestones will mark the second century of flight?

A few informed guesses can be presented in the form of questions.

Will 1,000-passenger super-jumbo airliners enter service?

Will a Mach 5.0 hypersonic airliner be built?

When will humans return to the Moon?

When will humans first set foot on Mars?

Will humans depart our solar system for deep-space voyages to other galaxies and return?

Will the human race meet with other intelligence out among the stars?

Will time travel be developed?

Will anti-gravity devices be perfected?

Those questions may not be answered for decades, if ever. However, it is certain that developments in this special realm of flight will be exciting. The combination of flight's eternal appeal and the innate human desire to explore and master the unknown makes anything possible.

Acknowledgments

The concept of AIA's selecting 100 milestones of the first century of flight originated with James P. Linse. I am grateful to him for the spark of creativity, and to the members of the panel who selected the 100 milestones in this book.I thank Alexis Allen and Janet Neale of the Aerospace Industries Association of America, Inc.; Walter J. Boyne, renowned aerospace author and former Director, National Air & Space Museum; Tom D. Crouch, Chairman of the Aeronautics Division, National Air & Space Museum; Al Frascella, Corporate Communications, TRW Aerospace; and David M. North, Editor in Chief, *Aviation Week & Space Technology* magazine. Their enthusiasm struck the initial spark that led to creation of this book.

The book would not have been realized without the willing cooperation and assistance of scores of persons in the aerospace and historical worlds. They responded to questions, checked facts, provided leads to sources of data and photographs, and were always cordial and helpful.

My heartfelt thanks go to every person in the organizations on the list below who helped out. If an organization has been omitted, it is my error and I apologize.

Aerospace Industries Association of America, Inc.
Air Transport Association
Airbus
American Helicopter Society
Amptek, Inc.
BAE SYSTEMS
Bell Helicopter
Berlin Airlift Historical Foundation
The Boeing Company
Bombardier, Inc.
Defense Visual Information Center
Department of Transportation
DoYou Graphics
Embraer
Federal Aviation Administration
Fédération Aeronautique Internationale
Florida State Archives
Goodrich Corporation
Gulfstream
Harriet Quimby Research Conference
Henry Ford Museum & Greenfield Village
Imperial War Museum
International Air Transport Association
Kaman Corporation
Library of Congress
Lockheed Martin Corporation
Martin-Baker Aircraft Co. Ltd.
MITRE Corp.
Musée de l'Air et de l'Espace/Le Bourget
NASA Ames Research Center
NASA Dryden Flight Research Center
NASA Headquarters
NASA Johnson Spaceflight Center
NASA Langley Research Center
National Aeronautic Association
National Air & Space Museum Archives Division, Smithsonian Institution
National Business Aircraft Association
National Park Service Headquarters
National Park Service, Edison National Historical Site
Naval Historical Foundation
Navstar GPS Joint Program Office
Northrop Grumman Corporation
Parker Aerospace, Parker Hannifin Corporation
Pratt & Whitney
Raytheon Company
Regional Airline Association
Rolls-Royce Heritage Trust
Russian Information Agency RIA Novosti
Space Science Technology Institute
St. Petersburg Museum of History (Florida)
U.S. Air Force History Support Office
U.S. Coast Guard History Office
Vought Aircraft Industries, Inc.
Washington Airports Task Force
Wright State University

Warm thanks and appreciation go to my associates Simone Hammarstrand, Lisa DeHart, and Katherine Tynberg for their patience and diligence. I also extend my gratitude to Steven L. Thompson and Roxana Hambleton, whose knowledge and care improved the manuscript in style and accuracy, and to Deborah Patton, who created the excellent index.

Special thanks are reserved for James W. Canan, Carroll V. Glines, and Harry M. Zubkoff. Their knowledge of aviation and space matters is extraordinary, and their counsel was helpful.

Photo Credits

Separate credit is warranted for the organizations that provided photos and permission for their use in this book. They include Airbus; Amptek, Inc. and University of Chicago; Aerospace Industries Association of America, Inc.; BAE SYSTEMS; Bell Helicopter, a Textron Company; Berlin Airlift Historical Foundation; Boeing Management Company; Bombardier, Inc.; Defense Visual Information Center; Department of Transportation; EMBRAER; Federal Aviation Administration; Florida State Archives, Office of Florida Secretary of State; Goodrich Corporation; Gulfstream; the Collection of Henry Ford Museum & Greenfield Village; the Trustees of the Imperial War Museum, London; Kaman Corporation; Library of Congress; Lockheed Martin Corporation; Martin-Baker Aircraft Co. Ltd.; MITRE Corp.; Musee de l'Air et de l'Espace/Le Bourget; NASA Ames Research Center; NASA Dryden Flight Research Center; NASA Headquarters Archives; NASA Johnson Spaceflight Center; NASA Langley Research Center; National Air & Space Museum Archives Division, Smithsonian Institution; National Park Service, Edison National Historical Site; Naval Historical Foundation; Northrop Grumman Corporation; Parker Aerospace, Parker Hannifin Corporation; Pratt & Whitney, a United Technologies Company; Raytheon Company; Rolls-Royce Heritage Trust, Rolls-Royce plc; Russian Information Agency RIA Novosti; St. Petersburg Museum of History (Florida); Space Science Technology Institute; U. S. Air Force History Support Office; U. S. Coast Guard History Office; U. S. Marine Corps/ 2nd Marine Aircraft Wing; U. S. Navy/Naval Air Systems Command V-22 Integrated Test Team; U.S. Postal Service; Visions Photo/Mark Greenberg; and Vought Aircraft Industries, Inc.

Robert J. Collier Trophy

I thank the National Aeronautic Association for providing materials about the award of the Robert J. Collier Trophy mentioned in the book. The Collier Trophy dates back to 1911. Robert J. Collier established the award. He was the first person to buy an airplane for personal use, purchasing it from the Wright Brothers. The National Aeronautic Association (NAA) receives nominations and selects the annual recipient of the Robert J. Collier Trophy. The NAA is the National Aero Club of the United States, and represents the United States to the Fédération Aeronautique International. According to the NAA, the Collier Trophy is "awarded for the greatest achievement in aeronautics or astronautics in the United States during the prior year."

Bibliography

Aerospace Industries Association of America, Inc. *Aerospace Facts and Figures 2001-2002* (and earlier annual editions from 1974–1975 forward). Washington: The Aerospace Research Center, December 2001.

American Heritage editors. *The American Heritage History of Flight.* New York: American Heritage Publishing Co., Inc., 1962.

Beard, Barrett Thomas. *Wonderful Flying Machines: A History of U.S. Coast Guard Helicopters.* Annapolis, Maryland: Naval Institute Press, 1996.

Bergaust, Erik. *Wernher von Braun: The Authoritative and Definitive Biographical Profile of the Father of Modern Space Flight.* Washington: National Space Institute, 1976.

Berriman, Algernon E. *Aviation.* London: Methuen & Co. Ltd., 1913.

Berry, F. Clifton, Jr., *Inventing the Future.* Washington: Brassey's, Inc., 1992.

Boyne, Walter J. *Beyond the Horizons: The Lockheed Story.* New York: St. Martin's Press, 1998.

______. *The Smithsonian Book of Flight.* New York: Orion Books, 1987.

______ , and Donald S. Lopez, editors. *Vertical Flight: The Age of the Helicopter.* Washington: Smithsonian Institution Press, 1984.

Canan, James W. *War in Space.* New York: Harper and Row, 1982.

Cochrane, Dorothy, Von Hardesty, and Russell Lee. *The Aviation Careers of Igor Sikorsky.* Seattle: University of Washington Press, 1989.

Collins, Michael. *Liftoff: The Story of America's Adventure in Space.* New York: Grove Press, 1988.

Crouch, Tom D. *The Bishop's Boys: A Life of Wilbur and Orville Wright.* New York: W. W. Norton and Company, 1989.

Davies, R. E. G. *Airlines of the United States Since 1914*. McLean, Virginia: Paladwr Press, 1998.

_________, and Philip J. Birtles. *Comet; the World's First Jet Airliner*. McLean, Virginia: Paladwr Press, 1999.

Dick, Harold G., with Douglas H. Robinson. *The Golden Age of the Great Passenger Airships: Graf Zeppelin & Hindenburg*. Washington: Smithsonian Institution Press, 1985.

Doolittle, General James H. "Jimmy," with Carroll V. Glines. *I Could Never Be So Lucky Again*. New York: Bantam Books, 1991.

East, Omega G. *Wright Brothers*. National Park Service Handbook Series No. 34. Washington: National Park Service, 1991.

Ellis, Paul. *Aircraft of the USAF: Sixty Years in Pictures*. London: Jane's Publishing Company Limited, 1980.

Federal Aviation Administration. *Pilot's Handbook of Aeronautical Knowledge*. Washington: Federal Aviation Administration, 1997.

_________. *FAA Aerospace Forecasts Fiscal Years 2002–2013*. Washington: Federal Aviation Administration, 2002.

Finne, K. N. *Igor Sikorsky: The Russian Years*. Washington: Smithsonian Institution Press, 1987.

Francis, Devon. *Mr. Piper and his Cubs*. Ames, Iowa: The Iowa State University Press, 1973.

Frebert, George J. *Delaware Aviation History*. Dover, Delaware: Dover Litho Printing Co., 1998.

Geibert, Ronald R., and Patrick B. Nolan. *Kitty Hawk and Beyond: The Wright Brothers and the early years of aviation: a photographic history*. Dayton, Ohio: Wright State University Press, 1990.

General Electric. *Seven Decades of Progress: A Heritage of Aircraft Turbine Technology*. Fallbrook, California: Aero Publishers, Inc., 1979.

Gibbs-Smith, Charles H. *The World's First Aeroplane Flights*. London: Her Majesty's Stationery Office, 1977.

Glines, C. V. *Bernt Balchen: Polar Aviator*. Washington: Smithsonian Institution Press, 1999.

_________, and Stan Cohen. *The First Flight Around the World, April 6–September 28, 1924*. Missoula, Montana: Pictorial Histories Publishing Co., 2000.

_________, Harry M. Zubkoff, and F. Clifton Berry, Jr. *Flights: American Aerospace, Beginning to Future*. Montgomery, Alabama: Community Communications, 1994.

Godden, John. *Harrier: Ski-jump to Victory*. Oxford: Brassey's Defence Publishers, 1983.

Goldberg, Alfred, editor. *A History of the United States Air Force, 1907—1957*. Princeton, New Jersey: Van Nostrand, 1957.

Golley, John, and William Gunston. *Whittle: The True Story*. Washington: Smithsonian Institution Press, 1987.

Grossnick, Roy, et al. *United States Naval Aviation, 1910–1995*. Washington: Naval Historical Center, Department of the Navy, 1997

Jane, Fred T., editor. *Jane's All the World's Aircraft 1913*. New York: Arco Publishing Company, 1969.

Jenkins, Dennis R. *Hypersonics Before the Shuttle: A Concise History of the X-15 Research Airplane. Monographs in Aerospace History #18*. Washington: National Aeronautics and Space Administration, June 2000.

Kaman, Charles H. *Kaman—Our Early Years*. Indianapolis: Curtis Publishing Company, 1985.

Kelly, Fred C. *The Wright Brothers*. New York: Bantam Books Aviators' Bookshelf, 1983.

Kennedy, Gregory P. *Rockets, Missiles, and Spacecraft of the National Air and Space Museum, Smithsonian Institution.* Washington: Smithsonian Institution, Revised Edition, 1983.

Komons, Nick A. *Bonfires to Beacons: Federal Civil Aviation Policy Under the Air Commerce Act, 1926–1938.* Washington: Smithsonian Institution Press, 1989.

Lindbergh, Charles A. *The Spirit of St. Louis.* New York: Ballantine Books, 1974.

Logsdon, John M. *Together in Orbit: The Origins of International Participation in the Space Station. Monographs in Aerospace History #11.* Washington: NASA History Division, November 1998.

Luffsey, Walter S. *Air Traffic Control: How to Become an FAA Air Traffic Controller.* New York: Random House, 1990.

MacDonald, Scot. *Evolution of Aircraft Carriers.* Washington: Chief of Naval Operations, Department of the Navy, 1964.

Mack, Pamela E., editor. *From Engineering Science to Big Science: The NACA and NASA Collier Trophy Research Project Winners.* Washington: National Aeronautics and Space Administration, 1998.

Manufacturers Aircraft Association, Inc. *Aircraft Yearbook.* New York: Manufacturers Aircraft Association, Inc., 1919.

Miller, Roger G. *To Save a City: The Berlin Airlift 1948–1949.* Washington: Air Force History and Museums Program, 1998.

National Aeronautic Association. *World and United States Aviation and Space Records.* Arlington, Virginia: National Aeronautic Association, 2002.

National Aeronautics and Space Administration. *Astronaut Fact Book. Washington: National Aeronautics and Space Administration, 2000.*

Neufeld, Jacob. *Ballistic Missiles in the United States Air Force, 1945–1960.* Washington: Office of Air Force History, 1989.

Nockolds, Harold. *The Magic of a Name: Rolls-Royce.* Henley-on-Thames, Oxfordshire: G. T. Foulis & Co. Ltd., 1972.

Norris, Guy, and Mark Wagner. *Boeing 777.* Osceola, Wisconsin: Motorbooks International, 1996.

Pape, Garry R., John M. Campbell, and Donna Campbell. *The Flying Wings of Jack Northrop: A Photo Chronicle.* Altglen, Pennsylvania: Schiffer Military/Aviation History, 1994.

Portree, David S. F. *NASA's Origins and the Dawn of the Space Age. Monographs in Aerospace History #10.* Washington: NASA History Division, September 1998.

Preston, Edmund, editor. *FAA Historical Chronology: Civil Aviation and the Federal Government 1926–1996.* Department of Transportation, Federal Aviation Administration, 1998.

Rumerman, Judy A. *U.S. Human Spaceflight: A Record of Achievement, 1961–1998. Monographs in Aerospace History #9.* Washington: NASA History Division, July 1998.

Smith, Richard K. F*irst Across! The U.S. Navy's Transatlantic Flight of 1919.* Annapolis, Maryland: Naval Institute Press, 1973.

________. *Seventy-Five Years of Inflight Refueling Highlights, 1923–1998.* Washington: Air Force History and Museums Program, 1998.

Society of British Aerospace Companies, The. *A Lifetime of Aviation 1916–1986.* London: The Society of British Aerospace Companies Ltd. and Ducimus Books Ltd., 1986.

Solberg, Carl. *Conquest of the Skies: A History of Commercial Aviation in America.* Boston: Little, Brown and Company, 1979.

Taylor, John W. R., and Kenneth Munson, editors. *History of Aviation. London: New English Library,* 1972. 1975 reprint by Octopus Books Limited.

__________, editor. *Jane's 100 Significant Aircraft, 1909–1969*. London: Jane's All the World's Aircraft Publishing Co. Ltd. 1969.

__________, Michael J. H. Taylor, and David Monday. *The Guinness Book of Air Facts and Feats*. Guinness Superlatives Limited: Enfield, Middlesex, 1977.

Taylor, Michael. *Brassey's World Aircraft & Systems Directory 1996/1997*. McLean, Virginia: Brassey's, Inc., 1996.

Tomayko, James E. *Computers Take Flight: A History of NASA's Pioneering Digital Fly-By-Wire Project. The NASA History Series NASA SP-2000-4224*. Washington: NASA History Office, 2000.

van der Linden, F. Robert, editor. *Aircraft of the National Air and Space Museum. Fifth Edition*. Washington: Smithsonian Institution Press, 1998.

Villard, Henry S. *Blue Ribbon of the Air: The Gordon Bennett Races*. Washington: Smithsonian Institution Press, 1987.

Wallace, Lane E. *Flights of Discovery, 50 Years at the NASA Dryden Flight Research Center. The NASA History Series NASA SP-4309*. Washington: NASA History Division, 1996.

Waters, Andrew W. *All the U.S. Air Force Airplanes, 1907–1983*. New York: Hippocrene Books, 1983.

Weiss, David A. *The Saga of the Tin Goose: The Story of the Ford Trimotor*. Brooklyn, New York: Cumberland Enterprises, 1996.

Yeager, Jeana, and Dick Rutan, with Phil Patton. *Voyager*. New York: Knopf, 1987.

Index

Italics indicate photographs or illustrations.